NICE GUYS FINISH LAST

Paul Gardner

Nice Guys Finish Last

Sport and American Life

Allen Lane

First published in 1974

Allen Lane
A Division of Penguin Books Ltd
17 Grosvenor Gardens, London, SW1

ISBN 0 7139 0728 2

Printed in Great Britain by
Lowe & Brydone (Printers) Ltd.,
Thetford, Norfolk

For K.

Contents

List of Illustrations and Diagrams

'Nice guys finish last . . .'

attributed to Leo (The Lip) Durocher, former
professional baseball player and manager.

Foreword

Dr Fagan put it this way in *Decline and Fall*: 'I can think of no entertainment that fills me with greater detestation than a display of competitive athletics, none – except possibly folk-dancing.' There are those – I am one of them myself – who have a similar reaction to sports books. So let me start by removing those two obstacles. This is not a book about folk-dancing, and neither is it a sports book – at least not in the sense that the term is usually understood.

This is a book about the United States of America, about an aspect of American life that has been given surprisingly little attention by those who would understand Americans: sport, and in particular, the commercialized, professionalized brand of it.

Newspapers and magazines all over the world regularly devote thousands of words to describing, analysing, interpreting, marvelling at, ridiculing and generally dissecting the American Way of Life. The interest in things American – politics, business, music, theatre, law, showbiz, technology – is apparently endless.

There are two perfectly logical reasons for this. Firstly, a desire to understand these people who make up the most powerful nation the world has ever known. Partly this is mere curiosity, but there is a goodly measure of self-interest in it too. What America thinks and does is of vital concern to the whole world. When an American sneeze can give everyone else pneumonia, it's nice to know the state of Yankee health.

A second reason for wanting to know about America is that they are, in so many things, ahead of the rest of the world. I do not mean that they do things better. They do them differently and that difference can usually be traced to the effects of applied technology. It is applied technology that dominates so much the quality of twentieth century life, and it is the United States that is the first to do the applying. The tendency of Americans to exploit, quickly and mercilessly, the advantages of technology means that they set the pace of what is known as 'modern living'. As the standard of living in other countries begins to resemble that of the United States, the quality of life also begins to resemble that of the United States. The Americanization of the world is, in fact, the spreading of the technological consumer-oriented society. In C. P. Snow's words: 'America sets the fashion for the Western World.' From America the rest of the world learns how to do things and, equally important, how not to do things.

The backbone of the consumer-oriented society is, in one form or another, the machine. And the aim (whatever may be the result) is to free man of many of the burdensome aspects of his existence, to allow him more leisure time. Americans today have more free time and more money than any society has ever had before. What they do with that wealth and spare time, how they do it and why they do it, is what this book is about.

It is one of the riddles of social history that until recently sports have not been given much attention in the serious study of cultures. True, no epoch-making ideas or life-changing discoveries will ever come from sports. But it is not for their effects on future generations that sports are worth studying. It is for their reflection of the current generation that they merit attention.

The idea of sports as a key to the character of a people has particular relevance in the United States. For in America, the nearest example we have to a classless society, sports are more an integral part of life *at all levels* than they are in any other country. This fact alone would render suspect any description of American life that did not include sports, but there is more to it than that. For the sports that have gained the widest popularity in the United States are essentially American sports. Basketball, baseball and American football are all sports that were either invented in America, or foreign sports substantially modified to meet American tastes and attitudes. Their study reveals something of those tastes and attitudes: of attitudes to success, of the competitive society, of the revolt against the competitive society, of racism. It tells something about American colleges, and it tells about the ways of American big business.

There is another reason for looking at the world of American professional sports, or pro sports to use the American term.* Simply this: it is a world of excitement, colour, personalities, success, failure, comedy, tragedy and all the things that everyone knows really matter. A beautiful

---

* Or the world of the jocks, to use another American term. A 'jock' is an athlete, the term being derived from 'jock strap'.

way to explore the massive untidy melting pot that is the United States.

Finally, a semi-apology. I have made only passing references to the sport of ice hockey in this book, partly because of lack of space but mostly because I do not feel that it illuminates any points that are not equally well illustrated by the other sports.

*

As the author whose name appears in solitary splendour on the title page it is a sobering thought for me to recall the favours, time, courtesy and attention granted by so many people during the preparation of this book. My thanks to all of them for cooperating so wholeheartedly on what must have seemed at the time a rather nebulous project. To the following I owe particular gratitude: Oliver Caldecott for his always sympathetic and encouraging attitude; Clifford Makins and Don Wood who fostered and – what is more to the point – published my early efforts at describing the American sports scene; Helen Smith for endless help with library problems; Tom O'Connor for his assistance with Chapter 9; and Don Abarbanel, Jim Benagh, Marian Berger, Lyn Fairhurst, Dave Hirshey, Jack McDonough, Brian O'Malley and Manny Vega.

New York, January, 1974   Paul Gardner

1　The Road to the Astrodome

May 1970. South Vietnamese and American troops have invaded Cambodia, causing violent protests on college campuses throughout the United States. At Kent State University in Ohio four students are shot dead by a volley of rifle fire from the National Guard. In New York construction workers and anti-war demonstrators battle in the streets. On the evening of 8 May a troubled and divided nation awaits President Nixon's televised news conference on the situation. This will be the third time in under three weeks that the President has addressed the nation on television. The first two times he had spoken, as was his custom, at 9 P.M. (New York time). But tonight the telecast is scheduled for an hour later, 10 P.M. No official reason has been given for the late timing, but an unofficial one quickly appears. The *New York Times* says there are two reasons: one is to capture the night-time audience (something the President had apparently overlooked before), and the other is 'to avoid interfering with the telecast of the final game of the National Basketball Association play-offs between the New York Knickerbockers and the Los Angeles Lakers. The game starts at seven-thirty o'clock and should be over by ten'.

The thought of a basketball game being faded out to make way for the President of the United States was too much. Richard Nixon's comments on the crisis would have to wait until Messrs Willis Reed and Wilt Chamberlain and Bill Bradley and Jerry West and others had finished throwing a ball through a hoop.

In 1970, sport was that important in the United States. Signs of its growing influence had been there during another moment of crisis back in 1963. Within hours of the assassination of President Kennedy the National Football League had announced that it would play its regularly scheduled games the following Sunday. There were precious few enterprises that could have got away with that without a storm of public wrath breaking about their heads, but professional football was one of them.*

---

* Throughout this book the word 'football' means the rugby-style game of American football. 'Soccer' is used to denote association football.

An extraordinary state of affairs and a far cry indeed from the way things had begun in colonial days 350 years earlier.

If the first thing the Pilgrim Fathers had done on landing had been to organize a game of bowls, or even of cricket, it would, no doubt, have been terribly English of them, but they did no such thing. It was, after all, December, and if the bitter New England winter was not enough to deter thoughts of recreation, the settlers brought with them an attitude to leisure activities that was even more icy than the weather. In a word, they disapproved.

One of the things they most objected to in England, hence one of the reasons why they had set out for America, was the way that James I allowed, nay, encouraged amusements on the Sabbath. In his *Book of Sports*, published in 1618, the King had set out the 'lawfull sports to be used', including a list of those in which his subjects could indulge on a Sunday – after church of course. They included dancing, the setting up of maypoles, archery and 'leaping, vaulting, or other harmless Recreation'. To the Puritans the very idea of a harmless recreation was deplorable, and was yet another sign that the country was going to Hell. In England, where the King held the reins, there was not much they could do about it. What they did was to transport themselves to the New World and there set up their own church-state without any of this Merrie England on Sundays stuff.

As things turned out, there was not to be much Merrie anything in Puritan New England. Life in the new colony was cruelly hard, a continual struggle against weather, disease, hunger, and Indians. Under these conditions the sombre and serious Puritan way of life had a good deal to recommend it. The colony's very existence was continually threatened and, whether or not leisure activities were sinful as the Puritans insisted, there were clearly more vital things to get on with.

For the first fifty years or so of its existence New England was virtually a theocracy, and the Puritans made the most of their opportunity. They planted their particular obsession, that work is virtuous and idleness sinful, deep into the American consciousness, where it has remained alive and well to this day. The novelist Nathaniel Hawthorne believed that it was the second generation of New Englanders, those born in America, who 'wore the blackest shade of Puritanism, and so darkened the national visage with it that all the subsequent years have not sufficed to clear it up. We have yet to learn again the forgotten art of gayety'.

Without a doubt the sternest – and most frequent – warnings against idleness came from two redoubtable clergymen, Increase Mather and his son Cotton Mather, both of them Massachusetts-born. Cotton, in particular, could hardly put pen to paper without bemoaning his fellow man's laziness: 'Idleness, alas! Idleness increases in the town exceedingly; idleness of which there never came any goodness.'

The fact that a great many laws and ordinances soon became necessary, forbidding almost every sort of amusement, is a clear sign that the citizens were growing restless. In Massachusetts there were laws banning dice, cards, quoits, bowls and 'any other unlawful game', not only in public but in home and garden too. Tobacco-smoking in public was banned, as were singing and dancing. As for the theatre, that was the Puritans' pet hate, and they refused to countenance it in any shape or form; actors were the most ungodly idlers of all.

Eventually, the Puritans overdid it. As the dangers of the early pioneer days began to wane, and as more and more non-Puritan immigrants began to arrive, the atmosphere of unrelieved seriousness became less and less acceptable.

One of the first indications that life was too cheerless was the rising popularity of the tavern. Rum was absurdly cheap, and drunkenness among the labouring classes caused much alarm to the select men who managed the New England towns. By the end of the seventeenth century the most restrictive aspects of Puritanism had been rejected and Cotton Mather, the arch-representative of the old order, was greatly displeased at what he saw: 'Some of our Rising Generation have been given up to the most abominable Impieties of Uncleanness, Drunkenness, and a Lewd, Rude Extravagant sort of Behaviour. There are the Children of Belial among them, and Prodigies of Wickedness.'

While the northern colonies, especially Massachusetts and Connecticut, had been trying to suppress the very idea of leisure, a totally different attitude had arisen in the southern colonies of Virginia, the Carolinas, and Georgia. The difference was in many ways an extension of the Roundhead-Cavalier division in England, with the Puritan Roundheads having settled in the northern colonies and the Cavaliers, many of whom came from the English aristocratic 'leisured' class, in the South.

There seems to have been something about the South, the warm climate perhaps, that encouraged thoughts of recreation. When Sir Thomas Dale arrived at Jamestown in 1611 to take over as Governor, he found the townsfolk playing at bowls. He abruptly put a stop to that, but such restrictions were not destined to last. The way of life that quickly developed in the South, based on large plantations worked by slave labour, gave rise to a leisured aristocracy of plantation owners. These were the people who, searching for something to do with all their spare time and money, took to horse-racing and cock-fighting, and in the process brought the first organized sport to America.

Horsemanship was a mark of the Southern Gentleman, and fox-hunting was one of his favourite pastimes. The large estates had their own stables, and what could be more natural than to organize races between their best horses, occasionally just for the fun of it, more usually so that they could wager on the result. Gambling was in at the birth of American sport and it was to remain a constant and troublesome companion throughout the years.*

It was not the intention of the southern gentlemen to provide entertainment for the masses. They wanted to keep their sports aristocratic and they even passed laws to that end. In 1674 a Virginia tailor was fined for having betted that his horse could beat that of a Mr Mathew Slader; the trouble was that Mr Slader was a gentleman and the tailor was not, and it 'was contrary to law for a labourer to make a race, being a sport for Gentlemen'.

By 1740 English horses were being imported for breeding purposes and some 'professional' jockeys were being used. These were Negro slaves and, while they had little say in the choice of their career and were not paid directly, they were certainly the nearest thing so far to full-time athletes.

When the time came for the colonies to rise against Mother England, the North and the South had to reconcile their sharply differing attitudes in the name of unity. The result, far from being a compromise, looked like total victory for the ascetic northerners. The Continental Congress, meeting in 1774 with all the colonies except Georgia represented, agreed to 'discountenance and discourage every species of extravagance and dissipation, especially all horse racing, and all kinds of gaming, cock-fighting, exhibitions of shews, plays, and other expensive diversions and entertainments'.

Having made that clear, the new nation then went to war under General George Washington, who was the very essence of the southern gentleman and who, by his own admission, liked nothing better than fox-hunting and dancing and was frequently seen at the theatre.

It was the upheavals caused by the War of Independence more than any official pronouncements that did most to discourage sporting

---

* See Chapter 9.

activities. The leisurely plantation life was disrupted for six years, and when the fighting was over there was a nation to build and sport had to take a back seat.

The period between the War of Independence and the Civil War, (from 1781 until 1861) was one of spectacular growth. The nation itself was expanding as the frontier pushed ever further westwards; cities were being built and the railroads were spreading rapidly. It was a time when Americans seemed devoted only to work, a time of fourteen-hour days, a time when repose – even a break for eating – was grudgingly taken. Charles Dickens, visiting America in 1842, found that the American male 'having bolted his food in a gloomy silence bolts himself in the same state'; at the mealtable he found 'no conversation, no laughter, no cheerfulness, no sociality, except in spitting'. The atmosphere sounds like the answer to Cotton Mather's prayers, but that austere gentleman would not have approved. The devotion to work was inspired not by God, but by Mammon.

Out on the frontier, where there were plenty of physically active young men, the story was the same: no time for relaxation. Such games as the frontiersman did enjoy were competitive extensions of his work – rail-splitting or log-cutting contests, shooting matches, plus some wrestling and foot races – and were all activities in which the accent was on physical strength.

Back in the eastern colonies, the popularity of horse-racing had spread to New York, where no attempt was made to limit it to the upper classes, and crowds of 50,000 were recorded at the Union Course on Long Island. But horse-racing had two drawbacks. It was inextricably linked with gambling (something that kept it out of New England, where the Puritan tradition was still strong), and it was a sport primarily for spectators.

For those who wanted to participate, the leading sport at this time was cricket. In 1850 there were nearly 1,000 cricket clubs in America, and interest was strong enough for an All-England team to undertake the first-ever international tour in 1859. One of their games, played at Hoboken, New Jersey, drew 25,000 people, but the calibre of the American team was evidently not of the highest order. They were allowed to send twenty-two men to the wicket in each innings, but they still lost by an innings and sixty-four runs. That was cricket's zenith in America. Another sport – faster and cheaper – was beginning to spread throughout the land.

Baseball. This was a game, claimed its devotees, with an 100 per cent American pedigree (there were one or two dissenting voices, malcontents

1 Cricket flourished in the United States during the 1850s, and was still popular enough in 1872 to draw a large crowd to this game featuring a touring English XI in Hoboken, New Jersey.

obviously), a game that destiny had selected to be America's own. And right from the start it led a charmed life. The Civil War, which might have been expected to cut short its growing popularity, actually helped it by bringing together in the Union Army young men from all over the country (except the South, of course). Baseball was their recreation and at the end of the war they returned home to spread the gospel. The game did go South, too, taken there by returning Confederate soldiers who had learnt it in Union prisoner-of-war camps. By 1876 a professional league was operating, made possible by the newly built railroads linking the major eastern and mid-western cities.*

Whether the 1890s were the Gay Nineties, or whether they were the Naughty Nineties, the names unmistakably indicate an unaccustomed spirit of hedonism in the newly united States. The nation now had a new aristocracy, the *nouveaux riches* Vanderbilts and Goulds and Morgans who had made their money rapidly and who showed no evidence that they had even heard of Puritan ideals. They lived like eastern potentates, spending, gambling, partying, dining, wenching, drinking and playing, all with a maximum of publicity and a minimum of taste. Their antics were followed with detached amusement by an obscure sociologist named Thorstein Veblen, who pilloried them in his classic *The Theory of the Leisure Class*. To Veblen sports were the property of the leisure class, by which he meant the upper class, and which he mocked mercilessly. 'The addiction to sports in a peculiar degree marks an arrested development of the man's moral nature', he wrote, and it was an addiction that the leisure class shared with 'the lower-class delinquents'. He exempted the 'common run of individuals among the industrial classes' from his scorn, because he believed they were resistant to the 'sporting propensity'.

This was a strangely short-sighted judgement. Writing at the end of the nineteenth century, Veblen can perhaps be excused for not fully appreciating that America's wealth was to be almost limitless and that this, plus the progressive shortening of the working week, would allow his leisure class to grow from a privileged few to a majority of the population. What is not so understandable is how he could ignore the

---

* A truly nationwide league, including cities on the West Coast, was impossible because of the immense distances (up to 3,000 miles) involved. In fact, Los Angeles and San Francisco did not join the league until 1958, the year that the jet plane was put into commercial service. In today's coast-to-coast league a team like the New York Yankees travels over 45,000 miles in the course of a season, nearly all of it by plane.

significance of the great bicycling boom that was going on at the very time that he was writing.

The new 'safety' bicycle complete with pneumatic tyres was the sporting rage of the nineties, with estimates of the number of riders going as high as ten million, drawn from all classes and from both town and country. Here was proof that the masses were every bit as sports-susceptible as the leisure class, and here was proof that sports – far from being just idle time-wasting – could have important economic and sociological consequences. Organizations like the League of American Wheelmen soon sprang up that were largely responsible for improvements in the conditions of the roads. Industrial involvement was considerable, with manufacturers turning out over one million machines a year.

Cycling attracted large numbers of women and struck an early blow for Women's Lib by freeing them from the cumbersome costumes that had been hiding their ankles and legs for so long and that were completely impractical for bicycle riding. And cycling did something that was to be of fundamental importance to the development of sport in America. It invaded the Sabbath.

The Sabbatarians wanted no exertion – neither work nor play – on Sunday, and while Americans had gladly thrown out most of the Puritan blue laws, they were less certain about changing the character of their Sundays. Not that they necessarily went along with such as the leader of the Women's Sabbath Alliance, who was certain that 'all criminals start on the downward path by working on Sunday', but there was evidently genuine popular feeling against the 'open' Sunday. During the 1900 Olympic Games in Paris, a number of Americans were required to take part in events on Sundays. Left to make their own decisions, eight of the thirteen involved decided not to compete.

Even baseball, triumphant in almost everything it did, had failed to make much impression here. In 1900 only three cities allowed games to be played on Sundays – Chicago, St Louis, and Cincinnati – all of them in the mid-west where large numbers of recent immigrants, mostly German, had brought the relaxed, carnival-type continental Sunday with them. The East resisted. It needed a pledge in Al Smith's 1918 campaign for the Governorship of New York State to bring Sunday baseball to New York City. Pittsburgh and Philadelphia held out until 1933. The advance was slow, but it would have been a good deal slower without the hordes of cyclists who defied the minister's warning that 'You cannot serve God and skylark on a bicycle' and began the erosion of the Puritan Sabbath in the 1890s.

2 Philadelphia, 1866 – a scene from baseball's early days. The cricket-like atmosphere of social gentility disappeared abruptly with the rise of professionalism in the 1870s.

Despite the tenacity of the Sabbatarians, the Church (i.e. the Protestant Church) was drastically altering its attitude to sports. Unable to beat them, it was about to join them, to take up the cult of muscular christianity that had begun in England in the 1850s. The Young Men's Christian Association had pointed the way, and by the 1890s it was operating 260 gymnasiums throughout the country. Far from being idle, sinful and soul-destroying, sports were now thought of as wholesome and character-building. The educational value of sports had been discovered. It was a theme that was to crop up repeatedly in the subsequent history of American sports, a theme that demonstrates that the old Puritan horror of idleness is as strong as ever. Sport cannot be enjoyed for its own sake – it must have some serious purpose.

What better purpose could there be than the building of righteous citizens? This became the rationale for dozens of sports programmes backed by the churches, or industry, or the police, or government agencies. More often than not it meant nothing more elevated than keeping boys off the streets, but, no matter, that too showed that sports could be useful.

Then there was sport as a democratic, Americanizing force, a catalyst in the melting pot that provided immigrants – or more likely their sons – with a relatively painless entrée into the mainstream of American life. Of course there were other paths such as education or politics or even crime, but as D. W. Brogan observed, sport 'does the job more dramatically . . . and sport is rigorously democratic. The sons of Czechs and Poles can score there, can break through the barriers that stand in the way of children of "Bohunks" and "Polacks"'.

Although baseball was more widely played, the newer sport of football had a special significance as a yardstick against which ethnic groups could measure their progress, because at this time it was exclusively a college game. To star at football, a boy had first to gain entry to a college, and that meant not only sporting success, but academic acceptance too.*

The sociologist David Riesman studied the names on the yearly All-American college football team (a list of the supposedly best players in the country) and found that between 1889 and 1895 they were almost exclusively made up of English names. After 1895 Irish names began appearing regularly, followed by Jewish names and in 1904 by the first obviously Polish name. By the 1920s the 'foreign' names predominated

---

* Then again, perhaps it didn't mean anything of the sort. The academic qualification of college sports stars has always been a subject for controversy. See Chapter 8.

(though the English-type names were to make a comeback in the 1950s as black players made their long-delayed appearance).

The decade of the 1920s marked the Golden Age of the American entertainment industry. From the movies, from jazz, from radio, and from sports came a parade of magic names: Rudolph Valentino, Charlie Chaplin, Mary Pickford, Paul Whiteman, Duke Ellington, Babe Ruth, Red Grange. These were the giants of an age in which the pursuit of happiness began to take on the appearance of a Gadarene stampede. Yet even in this permissive climate, sports could not escape being burdened with Significance. The trend established some sort of a record in April 1928 when Professor William Phelps of Yale University introduced a guest lecturer to his literature class. It was Gene Tunney, professional boxer. Tunney told his audience that 'Shakespeare was a sport', said he had read *A Winter's Tale* ten times before he could understand it, and discoursed upon heroes and combat in *Troilus and Cressida*. The noted newspaper columnist Heywood Broun (who had started his career as a sportswriter) found the incident less than amusing:

Tunney did better against Shakespeare than anyone had a right to expect. My own student days came before the Jazz Age, and I have a residue of resentment against prize-fighters, trained seals and motion-picture stars in the class room. The world has gone beyond the notion of us veteran classical scholars. Go-getters sit in the seats of the mighty. Harvard, I trust, will counter by asking Babe Ruth to tell the boys at Cambridge just what Milton has meant to him.

Wild and uninhibited, the 1920s were the anything-goes Jazz Age that Scott Fitzgerald chronicled, and it was Fitzgerald who put his finger on a crucial aspect of it when he wrote that 'Americans were getting soft'.

The complaint had been heard before. 'I am satisfied', Oliver Wendell Holmes had written in 1858, 'that such a set of black-coated, stiff-jointed, soft-muscled, paste-complexioned youth as we can boast in our Atlantic cities never before sprang from loins of Anglo-Saxon lineage', and the loins were evidently doing no better by 1900 when Theodore Roosevelt was urging his fellow Americans to toughen themselves up by leading 'the strenuous life'. Now America was again under indictment as a nation of spectators, full of people just sitting about and watching others exert themselves. Full of people turning soft.

In this sport was faithfully reflecting the attitude of the times, which said that you did not have to work hard any more, you just invested your money and sat back and watched it multiply. It seemed to work beautifully. President Hoover announced in 1928 that with the help of

God poverty would soon be banished from the nation. But somebody defaulted on the deal and in October 1929 things began to fall apart.

The coming of the Great Depression might have been expected to cripple sporting activities, especially professional sports. Amidst breadlines and bankruptcies and millions of jobless, playing games would surely be the last thing anyone would think of doing. And who would spend precious money on something as frivolous as watching a baseball game? To anyone who bothered to think about it, the outlook must have been relentlessly gloomy. Yet such predictions would have been way off the mark. Sport survived the Depression very nicely, and in some ways emerged from it even stronger.

Baseball attendances did drop of course, but never disastrously. From a record high of 10 million in 1930, the low was 6 million in 1933. By 1937 it was back up to 9½ million. College football, the other mass spectator sport of the period, also recovered quickly after initial losses. Sport was now too deeply woven into the everyday life of America to be cast aside when times got hard. Perhaps it was especially needed in just such times, for the ballpark was a great place to forget about the rotten state of the economy, a great place to escape to. In a world that had changed from Eldorado to Gehenna almost overnight, baseball gave a man something familiar to hold on to, an almost religious assurance that not everything he treasured was being swept away. A home run was still a home run and the umpire was still a lousy bum, and for two hours or so out there in the bleachers* it could seem like nothing had changed.

There was nothing quite like it for an affirmation of American values. 'At the baseball match, we encounter real democracy of spirit,' wrote a New York clergyman, the Rev. Roland D. Sawyer, 'one thing in common absorbs us; we rub shoulders high and low . . . we are swayed by a common impulse; we are all equal; the pressure of the crowd makes us one – the office boy who has stolen away, the businessman from the counting room, the clergyman from his study, the clerk from his desk, the girl from the factory, the wife from the home – all are on equal footing.'

On top of all that, baseball had the stamp of presidential approval. In 1910 President Taft had attended the opening game of the season, and

---

* The cheapest seats – nothing more than rows of wooden benches in that part of the stadium furthest away from the action, with no cover. They have the reputation of being the gathering place of the real die-hard baseball fans. Anyone who has sat through a baseball game under a blazing afternoon sun knows why they are called bleachers.

3 The birth of an American tradition. President Taft opens the 1910
baseball season in Washington by ceremonially throwing out the first ball.

taken it upon himself to indulge in a ceremonial throwing-out of the first ball. It had become a tradition. Woodrow Wilson had done it, and Warren Harding, and even the laconic Calvin Coolidge had a go at it.

But by 1931 the stadium was fulfilling its new role as a sanctuary, and those who sought refuge there were much put out one afternoon to find, taking his seat amongst them, the man who was the very embodiment of the Depression they were trying to forget: President Hoover. The fans responded in a way that was unheard of at the time and gave him a first-hand demonstration of democracy in the ballpark. They booed him.

Prominent among the factors that had helped popularize sports was the Press. The first American newspapers, published around the beginning of the nineteenth century, were meant for the monied, mercantile and presumably literate classes, and sport was not to be found in their pages. The successful launching of the *New York Sun* in 1833 changed all that. The *Sun* cost just 1 cent, compared with 5 or 6 cents for the older newspapers; it was aimed at the common man, and this meant a drastic change in content and style. Politics, business, and foreign news were replaced by short human-interest stories, love-affairs, police court-reports, theatre news – the bulk of it local New York material. It was a set-up made for sports news and the only thing lacking was the sports news itself. The *New York Herald*, founded in 1835 by Scottish-born James Gordon Bennett was always eager to cover a major horse race or a prize fight, but these events were few and far between. It meant that there could be no such person as a sportswriter making a living out of full-time sports coverage. When the *Herald* did have a fight or a race to cover, as often as not they would send Uncle Joe Elliott, the superintendent of their delivery room.

After 1876 professional baseball was being played on a regular league basis, and the first baseball writer appeared in the unlikely shape of a bewhiskered and dignified Englishman named Henry Chadwick. Originally a cricket writer, Chadwick had switched sports to become the baseball man with the *Herald* – though he continued to write endlessly about almost every sport that came to his notice. (There are twenty-six volumes of his 'scrapbooks' in the New York Public Library, and an intriguing *Handbook of Winter Sports*, that includes details of 'baseball and cricket on the ice'.) Chadwick quickly became the recognized authority on the game, writing and editing a stream of guides and hand-books that earned him the title 'Father of Baseball'.*

* He is but one of a number of people who have had that title bestowed upon them. The parentage of baseball is discussed in Chapter 4.

Popular journalism, created by the *Sun* and the *Herald*, was carried a stage further by Joseph Pulitzer when he took control of the *New York World* in 1883. By a combination of sensationalism, scoops, stunts, crusades and brilliant journalism, he rapidly raised its circulation from 20,000 to over 250,000 copies. There was now much more regular sports activity in the United States, and Pulitzer was quick to grasp its potential importance as a means of increasing his circulation. He created a special sports department in the *World*.

His spectacularly successful methods were closely studied by Randoph Hearst, who arrived in New York in 1895, bought the *New York Journal* and set out to show that anything Pulitzer could do, he could do better. The result was a bitter fight for readers between the *World* and the *Journal*, a fight in which both sides used every weapon they could devise. The struggle is notorious for what is, hopefully, the last word in circulation-boosting gimmicks: a genuine, full-fledged, international war. Attempting to outdo each other with atrocity stories about Spanish rule in Cuba, the two newspapers whipped up public feeling to such a pitch that a reluctant President McKinley was virtually railroaded into declaring war on Spain.

With the circulation of both newspapers soaring over the one million mark, there could be no denying that the Spanish-American War was good for business. But it was all over in four months, and it was left to sport to provide a more lasting journalistic memory of the yellow-press rivalry. It was Hearst's idea. He gathered all the bits and pieces of sports news together on one page, gave them banner headlines, and hired champion athletes, paying them considerable sums for the use of their names on stories that were ghost-written by staff members. 'Champions Give *Journal* Readers a Sporting Page' was the paper's boast, and they really had hit on something new. Hearst was considered breathlessly daring, if not downright foolish, when he devoted two-and-a-half pages of one issue of the *Journal* to sport in 1895, but his judgement of what the public wanted had never been more accurate. It was quickly proved that good sports coverage sold newspapers, and the sports page became one of the most important sections of the Press. Four or five pages quickly became the norm, and by the 1920s the assistant managing-editor of the *New York World* regretfully acknowledged the logic of the situation: 'When I consider the amount of space given over to sports my intelligence is offended, but my editorial judgement supports it.' A survey carried out in the late 1940s showed that the large dailies gave sport between 12 and 15 per cent of their space, and that most of the circulation managers thought it wasn't enough. By 1973 the *New York Times* sports section averaged four or five pages daily, while the Sunday section went as high as fourteen pages.

Not only did the sports page reflect the interests of millions of ordinary Americans, but it spoke their language too. In using their colloquialisms, their exaggerations and their slang the sports page conveyed much of the liveliness of everyday American speech. In return, the sports page gave numerous phrases to the American language, and it fathered, in Ring Lardner, a writer of real stature in American literature. Lardner's talent lay in his superb handling of demotic American. His masterpiece was *You Know Me Al*, a series of fictional letters from a professional baseball player to a friend. By listening to baseball players and fans, Lardner was able, in Scott Fitzgerald's phrase, 'to record the voice of a continent'. The book drew praise from someone who it can be safely assumed was no baseball expert – Virginia Woolf. What she noticed was that Lardner, writing in a language that was barely English, had none of the self-conscious 'literary' quality that she detected in other American writers. 'He writes the best prose that has come our way' was her verdict.

This was a genuine American voice. Virginia Woolf knew it instinctively, H. L. Mencken knew it because the study of the American language was his particular love. He marvelled that one small book could be such a perfect compendium of American English, and that it was written not by a scholar, but by a sports journalist.*

A newspaper feature even more typically American than the sports page was the comic strip, and the first of these to appear as a regular daily feature was built around a sports theme: the adventures of A. Mutt, an inveterate horse-player, who appeared on the sports pages of the *San Francisco Chronicle* in 1907. He was later given a partner, and as *Mutt and Jeff* the strip made its creator a millionaire.

That was the way it was by 1930. Sports imagery and sports language and just plain sport had taken root too firmly for the Depression to upset them. Quite the contrary. Exactly because of that popularity, sport was ideally suited for use as a weapon against the rigours of the Depression. Among President Roosevelt's New Deal programmes was the Work Projects Administration (W.P.A.), which put the unemployed to work building roads, bridges, airports and other things that were considered

---

* Lardner was not the only one to gain insights from sportswriting. The authors Damon Runyon and Paul Gallico, the political columnist Westbrook Pegler, the vice president of the *New York Times*, James Reston, the American civil war historian Lloyd Lewis, were all former sports journalists.

4 The New York Giants play the Chicago White Sox at Everton's Goodison
Park during a tour organized in 1924 with the aim – not noticeably
successful – of making baseball a world sport.

to be useful. The W.P.A. was soon constructing playgrounds, swimming
pools, golf courses and suchlike at a prodigious rate, and by 1938 it had
spent $1,500 million on recreational facilities.

This was a precedent-setting state of affairs because, for the first time,
the United States Government was giving direct financial aid to sport.
Cotton Mather and the rest of the Puritans were surely spinning in their
tombs, but probably not too rapidly, for there was still plenty of life left
in the stern morality they had espoused some 300 years earlier. True, the
government was spending money on sport, but it had stoutly Puritan
reasons for doing so. It was a way of giving people work and ultimately
of building better citizens.

It was World War II that finally rescued America from the Depression.
It did so by providing a flood of jobs, so many that by 1943 it had put the
W.P.A. out of business.*

It had a marked effect on professional sport because it whisked away
most of the best players, leaving the major leagues to carry on with a

* The war also contrived to show that Americans were not much, if at all,
healthier than the 'paste-complexioned youths' who had so bothered Oliver
Wendell Holmes nearly a hundred years before. Of the first two million men
called up, 50 per cent were rejected as physically or mentally unfit.

motley collection of those whom the armed services did not want because they were not fit enough or were too old, or even too young. The standard of play slumped badly,* but it seemed there was no way in which sport could be damaged, for even this setback turned out to have its advantages. While professional sport suffered, high-school sport, unaffected by draft calls, prospered. In Canton, Ohio, for instance, the high-school football team drew 130,000 spectators (paying spectators, that is) in both the 1942 and 1943 seasons.

This was a strengthening of something that Helen and Robert Lynd had commented on in *Middletown*, their classic study of a small American town (actually Muncie, Indiana) in the 1920s.† The Lynds looked at the various elements that united the citizens and found that the most important 'agency of group cohesion' was the high-school basketball team. The idea of adults, including civic and business leaders, becoming starry-eyed over the performance of a high-school sports team is not one that readily recommends itself to reason; but there it is. It has been going on for more than fifty years, and what the Lynds saw in Muncie during the 1920s is essentially true for hundreds of American towns today: 'No distinctions divide the crowds which pack the school gymnasium for home games and which, in every kind of machine, crowd the roads for out-of-town games. North Side, South Side, Catholic and Kluxer, banker and machinist – their one shout is "Eat 'em, beat 'em, Bearcats!".'

In the mid-west it has always been basketball, but in the small towns of the South it is high-school football that rules. Valdosta, Georgia, is a town of 35,000 people, a town of no particular eminence, except for this: its high-school football team, the Wildcats, won or tied for the school State Championship seven times during the 1960s. In 1969 the Wildcats drew sell-out 9,000 crowds to every one of their nine home games. The coach was given a new car every year by the fans, 500 of whom assembled each Monday night to hear him talk about the previous weekend's game. The 900 members of the Touchdown Club, the Wildcat supporters' club, even subsidized better school lunches for the players, so that when the rest of the school was making do with fish, the Wildcat team-members were feasting on steak.

Civic pride, even the very honour of the community, is centred on the athletic activities of a handful of teenage boys. How is it that high-school

---

* Asked which team he fancied in one of the war-time baseball World Series, a journalist replied: 'I don't think either can win'.

† Lynd, Robert S. and Lynd, Helen Merrell, *Middletown: Study in Contemporary American Culture*, Constable, 1929.

sport has assumed such importance? For one thing, as the Lynds discovered, there is not much competition. Interest in cultural matters has never been a pronounced feature of the American small-town life, while meetings organized by the Chamber of Commerce or the American Legion are pretty pale rivals for the electrifying excitement of a packed gymnasium.

But enthusiasm of this intensity could not be maintained if high-school sport were followed merely on a Hobson's choice basis. There are much firmer, much more positive roots, the ones that sportswriter John Tunis, writing of basketball in Indiana, described in this way:

For this is *our* team, not just the high-school's team. It's Muncie, Marion, Logansport, Jeffersonville, East Chicago, or Vincennes. We know these boys. That six-foot-four-inch center lives two doors down the street. We remember the cold January day he was born, and that hot summer he was so sick with polio; we recall the first day he went to kindergarten, and when he got well and made his grade-school team. That blond guard with the crew haircut tosses the *Sentinel* up to our front porch each evening. Joe, one of the forwards, carries our groceries out from Kroger's on Fridays. Chester, the other guard, cuts our lawn each summer. We've watched these youngsters all their lives, know them and their parents.*

It would be difficult to imagine anything further in spirit from the world of American professional sport, where teams rarely feature any locally-born players, and the links with the community are so often the artificial creation of a public-relations department. Yet the strength of sports interest at the high-school level is one of professional sport's greatest assets. It is here that the future fans and stars are nurtured and – perhaps even more important – it is here that the association between sport and the carefree days of youth is fixed in the minds of the vast majority of American males. In a country where the concept of youth is worshipped as greatly as it is in America, that is no small thing to have on your side.

Behind the restrictions of World War II the forces on which professional sport was to build its spectacular success of the fifties and sixties had been gaining strength. When peace came in 1945 they exploded into a sports splurge that embraced all segments of the population – rich and poor, black and white, north and south, east and west and that took in

---

* Tunis held basketball responsible for what he believed to be the cultural decline of the midwest. Writing in 1958, he found no successors to writers like Sinclair Lewis, Booth Tarkington and Theodore Dreiser – because, he said, all the region's creativeness, energy and talent was now centred on basketball.

all forms of sports. This was not just a repeat performance of the boom of the 1920s, when the accent had been decidedly on watching, rather than playing, sports. The post-war Americans wanted to watch, certainly, but they also wanted to participate. They were quickly to be found boating and ski-ing and bowling and fishing and golfing in quite astonishing numbers.

Americans wanted to enjoy themselves, and from all the measurable standards they had never been in a better position to do it. The war had banished the effects of the economic depression. The country was prosperous and as the only major power with its industries intact, it looked like getting a lot more prosperous. Money was there for the spending, and the other essential ingredient for recreation – time – was becoming increasingly available. The average working week had shrivelled from seventy hours in 1850, to sixty hours at the beginning of the twentieth century, and now the forty-hour week was in sight.

There was naturally no shortage of suggestions as to just how Mr Average American ought to spend his leisure and, more pointedly, his money. The burgeoning 'leisure dollar' was recognized as a significant new factor of the post-war economy and began to attract the attention of businessmen who saw a splendid new field for vast sales. A closer look at all the sporting activities that Americans were taking up so enthusiastically reveals that nearly all of them call for the use of a good deal of equipment, usually expensive equipment. The American desire for recreational sports plus the American fascination with gadgetry – this was really something that the business world could sink its teeth into. The sales of golf clubs and boats and skis and backyard swimming pools and all forms of sporting goods went soaring up, from $450 million in 1945 to over $1,000 million in 1947.

The spectator sports – at the end of World War II, this meant professional baseball and college football – found the rampant recreation mentality much to their liking, not to mention their profit. Attendances at baseball games reached a record high of nearly 21 million in 1948, while college football gates reached 19 million.

It was not to be expected that everybody would be delighted at the way things were going. E. B. White, the essayist, thought that they had already gone quite far enough by 1947, but feared they had further to go. He wrote apprehensively of things to come:

In the third decade of the supersonic age, sport gripped the nation in an ever-tightening grip. The horse tracks, the ballparks, the fight rings, the gridirons,* all drew crowds in steadily increasing numbers. Every time a game was played, an attendance record was broken . . . Customs and manners changed, and the five-day business week was reduced to four days, then to three, to give everyone a better chance to memorize the scores.

He had a vision of crowds at a stadium watching one event live, another on giant television screens, listening to a third on their portable radios, while sky-writing aeroplanes covered the heavens with assorted details from other contests.

So much for fiction – during the 1960s reality overtook White's vision and eventually dwarfed his sardonic exaggerations. Crowds did get bigger and bigger, and when the stadiums were all filled, new teams were created and new stadiums built to house them. People *were* carrying transistor radios to sports events, and there *was* talk of installing giant television screens in the stadiums. If skywriting did not catch on, no doubt one of the reasons was a visit to Rome made in the 1950s by Judge Roy Hofheinz. Sheer size alone was enough to recommend the Colosseum to Hofheinz (he was, after all, a Texan), but the news that the Romans used to have a way of covering it when the weather turned nasty was what really fired his imagination. He determined to build a covered sports stadium of his own. The Houston Astrodome, which opened in 1965, gave the players and 50,000 fans a rain-and-wind-free stadium with a permanent 72° temperature. And it gave them plastic grass. But no sky. Instead of skywriting there was a $2 million scoreboard (The World's Largest, naturally) with 50,000 light bulbs. It showed not only scores, exhortations to the fans, and rude remarks about the umpires, but could project pictures and elaborate 'light-shows' too.

The Eighth Wonder of the World, as the Astrodome soon started to call itself, had cost around $40 million. Six years later, in 1971, when the city of New Orleans came up with plans for a domed stadium nearly twice the size of the Astrodome, the projected cost was $150 million. In New Jersey a sporting Xanadu that included two stadiums, a thoroughbred race track, a basketball auditorium and a hotel was being planned at a cost of $200 million. And all the time the sales of sporting equipment kept on growing. By 1973 they had reached $10,000 million. Sport, always a heavily commercialized affair in the United States, was in the process of becoming big business.

---

* i.e., Football fields – see page 278.

2 Showsport

The three major professional sports in the United States are baseball, football and basketball. Between them, these three operate seventy-seven teams (twenty-four baseball, twenty-six football and twenty-seven basketball) in thirty-nine cities throughout the country. They are 'major league' sports because large numbers of people turn out regularly to watch them, and are willing to pay prices that vary from reasonable to outrageous for the privilege (others prefer to stay at home and watch on television, which costs them nothing, but more about that anon).

The football fan, for instance, pays on average $7 for his seat, while the basketball enthusiast will hand over between $2.50 and $9 for his. Baseball is less expensive – prices range from $2 to $4.50 – but involves many more games in its season. Football games are frequently sold out, basketball less frequently, baseball rarely so these days.

Millions of dollars are changing hands at the turnstiles and the impression that professional sport is a thriving business is confirmed by a look at some 1973 news items:

The San Diego Padres baseball club, including all of its players, is sold for $12 million.

For the rights to televise the season's games, television pays the National Football League $40 million.

Baseball star Steve Carlton signs new contract at a salary of $165,000 for the year.

New $26 million stadium inaugurated in Kansas City complete with $2.7 million scoreboard.

Basketball star Jerry West's salary for the year: $300,000.

American professional sport has never had any doubts that it is part of the entertainment industry, competing with the likes of the movies, the travel industry and the theatre for a share of the leisure dollar. The people who run it are businessmen and their loyalty is to their bank balance rather than to that abstract ideal 'the good of the sport'. There is nothing to suggest that they are any more or any less interested in profits than businessmen who sell, say, boot-polish or cars, but they are more vulnerable to the charge of rapaciousness because they are operating in an area where other, reputedly higher, values are also circulating.

For baseball is not boot-polish. You can be crassly commercial with boot-polish; it is just another commodity to be marketed. But sport, it has been noted many times and in many countries, is a form of religion. It touches the emotions. Just as it would be unthinkable for a church to announce that its sole *raison d'être* was to show a profit, so there is a wide feeling that sport should not be thought of solely in terms of mere pelf. The men who run it don't have to be saints, but they ought to have a higher sense of public service than the average big businessman. That is not asking very much, admittedly, but the evidence suggests that it is more than can be hoped for. The businessmen themselves are the people who have created professional sport and they have left little room for displays of *pro bono publico* unselfishness. Who are they, these captains of the sports industry, these 'owners' who run showsport? They have one thing in common: money. Some are fabulously rich, some comfortably rich, others just rather ordinarily rich. Some inherited their money, others are self-made millionaires, though in both cases the money usually comes from some business other than sport. There are, for example, chewing-gum king Phil Wrigley (owner of the Chicago Cubs baseball team), William Clay Ford of automobile fame (Detroit Lions football team), pharmaceutical manufacturer Ewing Kauffman (Kansas City Royals baseball team), and Jack Kent Cooke, owner of the Los Angeles Lakers basketball team, who made his millions in Canada buying and selling radio stations in partnership with Roy (now Lord) Thomson. Of recent years the ownership trend in sport, as in big business generally, has been away from wealthy individuals towards syndicates and large corporations. The New York Yankees, for instance, were purchased in 1964 by the Columbia Broadcasting System, a conglomerate that owns C.B.S. television and radio as well as book publishing and recording companies, a guitar-manufacturing firm and other concerns. In 1973 C.B.S. sold the Yankees to a fifteen-man syndicate for $10 million.

Professional baseball, football and basketball operate as leagues, and there has developed over the years an almost standard way of setting up a league. It is a game that almost any millionaire can play, and it goes like this. As soon as a sport shows signs of becoming an attraction for large numbers of spectators the wealthy men move in. Let us imagine there are eight of them. They are from eight different cities, and they form an eight-team league based in those cities. Each will own and operate a team in his own area, an arrangement which the league (i.e., the owners themselves) formalizes by granting a franchise* to each owner.

Each franchise holder agrees to abide by the various rules that he and his colleagues draw up for operating the league, and in return he gets the exclusive rights to operate, and hopefully profit from, a team within his own city and its surrounding area.

Thus the owners are completely in control of their own destiny. They created the league, and they run it. They are responsible to no higher body – they *are* the league. Nonetheless, such absolute authority has a built-in weakness. While the owners must all work together to make sure the league prospers, they are also in competition with each other, for they all want to have the best team. Situations arise where an owner finds that the immediate interests of his team and the longterm interests of the league are not at all the same thing. To help smooth over such moments the owners appoint a full-time official – the Commissioner – who is supposed to keep them all in line and to make decisions that take the interests of the sport into consideration. In placing themselves under a Commissioner, the owners are not really giving up much of their authority because they are the ones who appoint him and who pay his salary. A Commissioner who makes independent decisions and whose actions tread on the toes of too many owners is likely to find himself eased out of office.

Even with a strong Commissioner the problem of competition among the owners for players would probably be enough to scuttle any league, were it not for an ingenious scheme devised back in the nineteenth century during baseball's infancy and since adopted by all American professional sports. In 1879 the owners were much exercised by all the money they were having to spend on salaries for their players, and it did not take them long to see that the trouble was all their own fault. If they would just stop trying to outbid each other for players, then salaries could be forced down. They secretly agreed that at the end of the season each club would be allowed to 'reserve' its five best players, meaning that all the other clubs would refrain from bidding for, or approaching, those players. It worked like a charm and was soon brought

---

* *Webster's New World Dictionary of the American Language* gives five meanings for 'franchise', the last of which is identified as an Americanism: 'the right to own a member team as granted by a league in certain professional sports'.

out into the open, with a clause detailing the arrangement included in each player's contract.

What the reserve clause does is to bind a player *for ever* to the club that he first signs for, unless the club decides to release him or to transfer him to another club. The player himself has no control over his movements. Every contract that he signs – they are usually for one year – contains the reserve clause which compels him to negotiate with the same club for next year's contract.* If he refuses to honour this clause, no other club will have anything to do with him, and he can start looking for a job as a furniture salesman. His professional ball-playing days are over until he relents.

Having got on to a good thing, the owners made the most of it and they expanded it until it covered all of the players on each team. The success of the reserve clause cannot be doubted, and it is an important – some would say an essential part – of all major-league sports today.

The agreement not to poach each other's players still left quite a large area open for eye-scratching (and costly) competition among the owners. There were still all those players who were not under contract to any of the league's clubs, the minor leaguers. Competing for their signatures was also a cause of high salaries, and surely that was not necessary? Assuredly not. The owners put their heads together again and the result – though it took many years to perfect it – was the draft system. The idea was to draw up a list of all the minor-league players, so that the owners, instead of fighting over them, could take their turn, in an orderly fashion, to pick who they wanted from the list. This meant that the rich clubs could not get who they wanted merely by throwing their money around, and the order of choice was designed to further reduce their power. It was based on the previous season's league table turned upside down, giving the club that finished last the first draft choice, the next to last club second choice and so on. In an eight-team league the champion club would be eighth in line, after which the last place club would get a second choice, the cycle repeating itself until either all the players were chosen, or the remaining ones were not wanted. The draft was held once a year, and clubs were not allowed to sign players other than through its mechanism.

When a club chose a player in the draft, it was acquiring the exclusive rights to bargain with that player. Again, the player was left with no choice in the matter. He either came to terms with the club that had

---

* The reserve clause is, in effect, the same as the retain-and-transfer clause of English soccer that was ruled illegal by a High Court decision in 1963.

drafted him, or he did not get into the major leagues. The draft system was eventually extended to cover also those players – mostly high-school and college leavers – who had not yet signed a contract of any sort with any club.

The draft system, along with the reserve clause, are the foundations on which the structure of American professional sport is built. They were designed to eliminate squabbling and wasteful competition among the owners and they have done that very effectively. But while they work beautifully for the owners, they are something of a curse for the players. They take away from the player his right to bargain on the open market, his right to sell his services to the highest bidder. If a boy leaving high-school wanted to go into banking and was told that all the banks had got together and decided that he *had* to work for Lloyds, or he would not get into banking, the uproar would be loud and long. Yet that is exactly what the draft system does to boys who want to play professional sports. And how many businessmen would sign contracts with their employers that deny them the right to quit and go to work for someone else, which is what the reserve clause does?

Professional sport has created a condition known to economists as monopsony; a form of monopoly where competition has been abolished and there is only one buyer. It is obviously interfering with the natural supply-and-demand forces of the marketplace, and there are laws in the United States that prohibit that sort of thing. Specifically, the Sherman Anti-Trust Act of 1890 which declared illegal all contracts in restraint of trade. Baseball lived for years in fear that someone would see fit to take the matter to court, with the very real possibility that the reserve clause and the draft system would be declared illegal. It did not happen until 1922, and while organized baseball held its breath, the case went all the way up to the Supreme Court which ruled that baseball was exempt from the requirements of the Anti-Trust Act.

This was evidently a recognition that there are unique considerations in running a sports team, but it hardly led anyone to believe that professional baseball was not a business. From the owners' point of view though, it was all that was needed. It effectively discouraged further legal action, even though it did still leave the question of the reserve clause hanging, as it had not been a specific ruling on that point. The legal front was to remain reasonably quiet for quite a while after that; it was nearly fifty years before another serious legal challenge to the reserve clause came before Supreme Court.

The threats to the monopolies that professional sports operators create do not have to come from the courts. There is always the danger that another group of wealthy men will come along and set themselves up as a rival league. It is something that has happened repeatedly over the years in all sports – as long ago as 1884 in baseball, as recently as 1967 in basketball.

Whatever the sport or the date, the results have always been highly distasteful for the original league owners, and highly profitable for the players. The new league, in trying to muscle in, automatically breaks all the carefully designed advantages of the monopoly; in particular, it ignores the original league's reserve clause as it tries to steal players by offering them more money. The original league is forced to raise its players' salaries to avoid losing them. And, of course, the new league is likely to place teams in cities where the original league has a franchise, making a mockery of the franchise holder's sole and exclusive rights for that area.

If the new league does not go bankrupt after a season or two (leaving the original league financially battered but back in possession of its monopoly), if it shows signs of surviving, then the two sets of owners start to look at their expense sheets. They decide that players' salaries are too high, and they are hit with the realization that if the two leagues (which would not even speak to each other last season) would get together and work out a common reserve clause and a common draft – why, the players would not be able to play one league off against the other in demanding more money. That is how baseball's National and American Leagues learned to live with each other in 1903. To this day the two retain their separate names but they are, in effect, one league. It is also how the National Football League and the much younger American Football League agreed upon a merger in 1966, though this one was a little tricky. Football unlike baseball has never been declared exempt from the anti-trust laws and it was feared that a merger of the two leagues might be declared illegal if challenged in the courts. But sport has many friends in high places, and to avoid future trouble the football lobby went to work in Washington and got Congress to pass special legislation approving the merger.*

A merger also seemed the most likely way that the National Basketball

---

* The merger bill was passed by the Senate, but was given little chance in the House of Representatives where it needed the approval of the House Judiciary Committee, whose Chairman was known to be extremely hostile to the idea. To overcome this obstacle, the bill was added as a rider to one of President Johnson's anti-inflation bills, a move that its supporters justified by pointing out that the

Association would resolve its war with the upstart American Basketball Association which was launched in 1967. The two groups of owners at one point announced an agreement to merge, but in May 1970 opposition arose in a form that was a clear sign of changing times. The basketball players themselves – from both leagues – got together and filed a suit to block the merger on the grounds that it was in restraint of trade. They had, of course, a considerable interest in retaining the two-league set-up as the competition for their services had resulted in salaries jumping by as much as five times.

The rise of organized, or unionized, activity by professional athletes was to be expected given the sports boom of the 1960s. The players saw all that money being made, and they wanted to be quite certain they were getting their fair share of it. Traditionally, the baseball owners, as befits their status as rugged pioneers of private enterprise, had always resisted any attempt at unionization by the players. But the Major League Baseball Players' Association, formed in 1962, grew rapidly in strength and influence. In 1966 it appointed a full-time director, and in 1969 it had grown up enough to make its first strike threat. The players wanted better pensions, the owners said they could not afford to provide them, and for a while it looked as though the 1969 baseball season was going to be postponed indefinitely. It was not, because the owners, who at one time talked about an 'all-out test of strength' with the players, backed down and granted them most of what they wanted. The previous year football players had organized and forced concessions from the clubs, also on the question of pensions.†

The players had at last got together to look after their own interests. The owners, it will have been noticed, had never had any problems in that area, so that left just the fans, good old John Q. Public, without a voice in matters. In big business it goes without saying that if your interests are not represented, you are going to get trodden on. The public was clearly underfoot in the years 1953–5 when no fewer than three (out of sixteen) baseball teams simply packed up and left all their

---

merger bill did contain certain tax provisions for professional football teams. With Congress due to adjourn within one week, discussion on the anti-inflation bill was not protracted; it was quickly passed and the N.F.L. and the A.F.L. obtained legal permission to merge.

† In baseball, for instance, a player who played for four years and who started drawing his pension at forty-five would receive $250 a month. A ten-year player would receive $500 a month. The maximum pension (for a twenty-year player who started drawing at sixty-five) would be $22,000 a year.

fans behind and transferred to another city. The Boston Braves became the Milwaukee Braves, the Philadelphia Athletics became the Kansas City Athletics, and the St Louis Browns became the Baltimore Orioles.

There were good solid business reasons for the moves. All the clubs were losing money in their original cities, and all those cities were trying to support two baseball teams. So it was not as though the fans were being totally deprived of baseball; they could always go to the remaining team's games. The fact that the fans had grown up hating the other team and would not be caught dead going to their games, well, that was just too bad.

The complete humiliation of baseball fans came in 1958. The New York Giants announced that they were moving 3,000 miles to the West Coast to become the San Francisco Giants. Again, there were compelling financial reasons, for the Giants were not drawing fans in New York. It still left New York with two teams, the Yankees and the Brooklyn Dodgers. Within weeks came the bombshell. The Dodgers were moving too, and would henceforth be the Los Angeles Dodgers. This was a different story, for the Dodgers were making money in New York and had the most loyal fans of any team in the country. It made no difference, nothing made any difference, not even New York City's offer to build the Dodgers a new stadium. The owner of the Dodgers had realized that he could make more money in Los Angeles, and the Brooklyn fans could go fly their kites. Which is how two of the oldest and most hallowed names of baseball history suddenly ceased to exist.

The financial aspects of playing professional sport were such that by the 1970s there was not much talk about underpaid athletes any more. All three sports had established minimum wages and were paying an average wage considerably higher, with the super-stars up in the six-figure bracket:

Sport	Minimum	Average	Top wage
Baseball	$15,000	$30,000	$225,000
Basketball	$20,000	$60,000	$300,000
Football	$13,000	$30,000	$238,000

As salaries rose, the image of the professional ballplayer changed drastically, from gullible rustic to shrewd businessman. Where the old-timer had gone out and blown all his money on wine, women and song, the modern athlete is likely to employ an investment counsellor, a lawyer to negotiate his contracts for him, and a business agent to make sure that his name gets before the public as often as possible (for a price, of course).

When the New York Mets won the baseball championship in 1969, each player received a bonus of over $18,000, and most of them chose to invest their share wisely rather than to spend it conspicuously. Three players bought a computer and rented it out to business firms. 'We expected to take a tax loss for a while,' said one of them, 'but we're making money.' Ring Lardner would never have believed it, but that is the language of the modern ballplayer.

For the superstars, their salary is only part of the story, for they can bring in substantial amounts of money by selling their name. O. J. Simpson was a college football star who, on turning professional in 1969, signed a contract under which Chevrolet, in return for his endorsement of their cars, agreed to endorse his bank balance to the tune of $250,000 over three years. All this at a time when Simpson had not played even one second of professional football. He also signed another contract with a soft-drink company, and yet another with A.B.C. television to appear as a sports-caster. It must have been something of an anticlimax when he came to sign his actual playing contract – all he got was $55,000 for his first year with the Buffalo Bills. He did manage to talk the owner of the club into lending him $150,000, but that was a let-down too, as he had asked for $500,000.

After just one year as a professional Simpson found another way of making money. He wrote a book about his career so far, and in it he proudly related how, before he was about to play his first game on artificial turf, he telephoned the Adidas shoe company and casually hinted that he had been talking to their rivals, Puma.

I knew, of course, that I would shock him with that statement . . . After a minute of nervous silence, the Adidas guy said, 'I'll fly to Houston to bring you our Astroturf shoes. And I'd like to talk to you about endorsing Adidas shoes.'

Simpson should not be censured too harshly for his mercenariness. The marvel would be if he were able to resist all the blandishments. He was made to understand before his professional career began that he could make more money off the field than on it. On graduating from college he was besieged by people seeking his signature. These were not professional clubs trying to sign him as a player (he had been drafted by the Buffalo Bills, so there was no competition there), these were business agents sensing that he was a valuable property and likely to bring them in a lot of money. He was eventually signed by Sports Headliners Inc., one of a growing number of companies devoted to the notion that endorsements are an athlete's best friend.

One can at least make out a case that Simpson was doing some work for his $250,000 from Chevrolet, making commercials and personal appearances. Such was not the case with another football superstar, Joe Namath, who simply sold his name to a group of speculators who planned to start a chain of 'Broadway Joe's' restaurants. Namath and his lawyer received in return 240,000 shares in the company, which opened eleven restaurants and started to sell things like Quarterback Burgers and Football Hero Sandwiches. They did not sell nearly enough of them, and eighteen months later, with business looking not at all good, the roles were reversed. Far from Namath's name aiding the restaurants, their poor showing was now damaging his image. Namath resigned his position as chairman of the board and unloaded all his stock.

Ah well, what you lose on quarterback burgers you gain on Hollywood film contracts. Namath appeared as a motorcyclist in *C. C. Ryder*, and as a cowboy in *The Last Rebel*, neither of which is ever likely to be mistaken for a masterpiece. He also grew a large and sinister Fu-Manchu moustache that drew frowns of disapproval from the President of the American Football League, who said it did not 'conform with the generally accepted idea of an American athlete's appearance'. Namath shaved it off. He did so in a television studio, using a Schick electric razor, and the Schick people paid him $10,000. At the time, Namath was getting $100,000 a year for playing football.

Professional sport is steeped in an atmosphere of overt commercialism, and there seems to be hardly any potentially profitable angle that has been overlooked. Doctors browsing through their medical magazines in 1970 came across a huge two-page picture of basketball star Wilt Chamberlain, all 7 ft 2 ins of him. 'There's only one Wilt the Stilt,' said the blurb, 'Long Duration of Action with Virtually No Rebound Problems', grabbing rebounds being an important part of basketball. 'And,' continued the blurb, 'There's only one Afrin nasal spray, which also has "Long Duration of Action with Virtually No Rebound Problems"' (rebound problems now meaning side-effects).

Even nicknames can be exploited, as the Atlanta Braves baseball club proved by signing an agreement with Warner Brothers Inc., giving one of their players the exclusive rights to be called Road Runner II (after the cartoon character) and making it illegal for any other athlete to use the nickname.

Americans are voracious eaters and drinkers during sports events, and among the most consistent profit-makers are the stadium concession-naires who own the rights to sell refreshments such as the traditional hot dog and beer. At New York's Yankee Stadium they need some 400 vendors and refreshment-stand operators to cope with the demand.

The National Football League has organized subsidiary companies to sell all sorts of objects stamped with the insignias of the various teams – blankets, ashtrays, ear-muffs. Another company films every game each week, edits it all down to an hour show and sells it to television. It also puts out half-hour 'Game of the Week' films that are shown at dinners and sports clubs, at regular weekly meetings for the American residents in foreign capitals and that are used by the major airlines as in-flight movies.

There is not much connected with football that is not sold in one way or another, except possibly the goalposts, which are traditionally torn down by the fans after championship games and broken up into hundreds of free souvenir-pieces. In 1961 a West Virginia house-painter, who said he had been thinking about the matter for some time, had an idea to make even goalposts profitable. How about exploding goalposts stuffed with souvenirs? Companies would pay to have their product names printed on the souvenirs, which would be shot all over the field at the end of the game, the inventor explained. His wife was reported as commenting 'I think it's all screwy', but whether she was right or not, one thing is certain: as a source of income, exploding goalposts will never challenge television.

When you talk about the link between television and sport, you start thinking in terms of millions of dollars, because that is what the link is all about. Millions of dollars.

In simplest terms, the equation goes like this. Television pays money to a sport for the rights to broadcast its games. It then hopes to get that money back, plus profit, by selling advertising spots during the games. The sport concerned takes the money and distributes it equally among its clubs.

It appears straightforward, but it is not, for this arrangement has made, and is continuing to make, radical changes in the way sport is run, and even in the way that it is played.

When television began its triumphant reign in 1948, the baseball owners were among the first to leap on the bandwagon. In their eager-ness to latch on to the television money, they allowed games to be tele-vised willy-nilly, without restrictions or local blackouts. The result was a dramatic drop in attendances at the games. It took the major league nearly ten years, but they eventually reclaimed all those 6 million lost spectators.

On minor-league clubs, however, television acted like a toxin. It killed them off by the score. To be sure the ground had been prepared for the final death blow that television gave. The world of the minor leagues was a world of small towns, of backwoods places, all of them hundreds, maybe thousands, of miles from the nearest major league team. A world of low salaries, of run-down stadiums, of badly kept fields, of feeble yellow floodlights. It survived because for most of its supporters it was all they had – there was nothing else to do, nowhere else to go. But it survived too because it had a heart and a soul and people were proud of their team, and because it was a warm living part of smalltown America.

But what cares technology for things like that? The car, the radio, the airplane arrived, and there were other things to do, other places to go. Television was but the last – albeit the most effective – of the agents of progress that crippled the minor leagues. Why take the trouble to go out to a moth-eaten stadium to see a bunch of stumblebums play second-rate baseball when you could sit at home and see the major-league players – for free?

The number of minor leagues shrank from 59 to 23, the number of clubs from 500 to 155 between 1949 and 1970. It meant maybe 2,000 fewer young players and it meant that one of baseball's greatest strengths, its deep cultural involvement in American life, was being chipped away.

The baseball owners were apparently unconcerned as they allowed their sport to become more and more reliant on television money. They were not alone. Both football and basketball were soon dipping their hands into the TV kitty and football in particular came away loaded.

The amounts of money that the three national television networks were paying into sports in 1973 were:

Sport	TV network	Total	Per club
Basketball (National Basketball Association)	C.B.S.	$9,000,000	$530,000
Football	A.B.C.	$8,600,000	
	C.B.S.	$18,000,000	$1,500,000
	N.B.C.	$12,400,000	
Baseball	N.B.C.	$18,000,000	$700,000

For the clubs, this is the best sort of money there is – guaranteed, before the season even starts, come rain or shine, even come spectators or no.* It is hardly surprising that they have come to rely heavily on it. For many clubs it is the only thing that keeps them in business. In 1963 the National Basketball Association was looking for a new Commissioner. They were at that time without a television contract, and the first question they asked the successful candidate was 'Can you get us back on national TV?'. Six years later the rival American Basketball Association had the same problems: no Commissioner and no TV. For their Commissioner they chose not a basketball man but a television man, the former sports director of C.B.S. television.

The dominant role of television money in the world of professional sport raises a practical question: if television is subsidizing sports (which, to all intents and purposes, it is), is it not entitled to some say in how those sports are operated? The answer to which is yes, it probably is. There have been instances where things have been arranged for the convenience of the television cameras: starting times have been altered, playing dates changed, both in the interests of ensuring better 'viewing times'. On one occasion the rules of football were altered for an ex-hibition game, to make it more exciting. And during the 1967 Super Bowl, the most important football game of the season, the second-half kick-off was taken twice because a commercial had been showing when the first kick was made. The television audience never knew the diff-erence.

There is, too, the persistent intrusion of the commercials. This does not worry too much in baseball, which is a game that always contains seventeen inter-innings pauses, so things can be planned beforehand. Basketball and football are not so easy to deal with; the teams can stop the play by calling time-outs, but they might not call enough of them, or at the right moment. And that is why the television director is allowed to interrupt the game to call time-outs, or to prolong pauses to suit commercial requirements. Perhaps none of these things is totally disas-trous to sport, but they represent a foot in the door, and they lend substance to the charge that sport is selling out to television.

Take what happened at Madison Square Garden in New York one

---

* The figures in the table do not tell the whole story. A.B.C., C.B.S. and N.B.C. select games for national viewing via their networks of affiliated stations across the country. But many clubs have contracts with local television stations to transmit their games locally. Baseball, for instance, nets an additional $24 million from local TV and radio.

afternoon in 1969. C.B.S. was televising an ice-hockey game, and those viewers with sharp ears heard hundreds of fans yelling 'C.B.S. stinks!' as the game started. The protesters had paid $4 for their seats only to find that their view was partially blocked by a wooden platform erected to house the television cameras.

Or take what happened to the good baseball fans of Milwaukee. Their team, the Braves (which, it will be remembered, had once been the Boston Braves), was suddenly whisked away from them at the end of the 1965 season, and television was one of the main causes of their loss. When the Braves first arrived in Milwaukee the fans turned out in record numbers – over 2 million a season for the first six years – and everyone was happy. Then the numbers settled down to a more average sort of figure, just under a million, and television revenue became of greater importance. Sad to say for Milwaukee, it happens to be in the wrong place to be a good television town. It is too close to Chicago and to Minneapolis–St Paul, both places that have major-league baseball teams, and the area over which Milwaukee games can be telecast is therefore severely limited. Now, there never had been, up until 1966, a major-league baseball team any further south than Washington. The whole of the south-east United States was virgin television territory . . . and that is enough to explain why the Milwaukee Braves became the Atlanta Braves that year. Milwaukee had been a good baseball town, but it was a dead loss for television.

The intimate financial embrace between television and sport also has its effects on television. Particularly on the way in which games are presented to the public. A newspaperman covering a baseball game is there to describe as accurately as he can what goes on. If the game is lousy, he says so. If a player makes mistakes, he says that too. Not so with television. With their vast financial investment in sport, the television companies are co-promoters of the events they are telecasting. They have an interest in these events being successful ones – after all, they cannot sell commercial time on bad programmes.

The view of sports events through the cathode tube, then, is never less than euphoric. The game is always *great*, it's got to be *great*, or the sponsors won't buy commericals so it's all *great*, just *great*, folks! The main requirement for a television sportscaster is a master's degree in dissimulation. He must wear the rosiest of spectacles and be positive about everything, and never, never, criticize. That would be like a salesman knocking his own product.

In the days of radio it was possible for a commentator to enthral his listeners with a breath-taking account of a real humdinger of a game that bore no resemblance whatever to the dreary affair that he was watching. But with the camera exposing everything, what's a sportscaster to do? A huge repertoire of excuses, euphemisms and clichés helps for a start. An easy catch dropped while the winning run scores? 'Yeah, well it happens to the best, with the tricky wind currents in this stadium . . .' A player clearly shown on screen throwing a punch? 'I guess he delivered a little more effort than he should have.' A fight among the spectators? 'Just a few of the boys having fun on a Sunday afternoon.' The big fear is that a serious injury will cast a pall over the jollity; the standard way of diverting attention from that is to say, 'He's a little slow getting up', and to bring on a commercial.

The worst offenders among the sportscasters are those employed by the local stations, whose job it is to sing the praises of the local team, regardless of whether it is any good or not. Their loyalties are clear, they are fans of the team, and their enthusiasm is supposed to show in their work.*

In contrast to the banality of the talk is the brilliance of the picture. In addition to the play-by-play cameras there is the isolated camera – or several of them – concentrating on one player only, available for instant close-up if he does anything brilliant. And the split-screen techniques, and the invaluable instant replay. Because of these innovations the tele-viewer often does see more than the fan at the stadium. Indeed, the instant-replay mentality is now so common that the fan watching the game live is likely to feel cheated when he does not get a replay.†

So television is pouring millions into sport. It is keeping a number of clubs out of the red, and it is substantially responsible for the prosperous state of professional athletes. What is it getting in return? Oddly enough, two of the major networks say that they lose money on their sport invest-ment. Their executives speak in harassed tones of the amounts they have to pay to broadcast sports, and point to the high per-minute rate this forces them to charge advertisers. Measured in these terms sport becomes nothing more than a vehicle for commercials, and a considerably

---

* Enthusiasm is certainly considered more important than grammar. Dizzy Dean, an ex-player turned sportscaster in St Louis, so systematically mangled the English language that the Missouri Teachers' Association demanded that he be fired. They particularly objected to his using 'slud' as the past tense of 'slide'. 'Well what do they expect me to say?' asked Dean. 'Slidded?'

† But not at Kansas City's Arrowhead Stadium. There the fans do get action replays on a giant 30 x 60 ft screen that is part of the scoreboard.

overpriced one at that. For one minute of time during a Sunday after-noon football game, an advertiser must pay about $75,000. Yet for a mere $60,000 he can buy a minute of prime evening time, and twice as many viewers as well.

What draws television to sport, and particularly football, is not so much the number of viewers as the type of viewer – the belief that the audience makes up in quality what it lacks in numbers. It is supposed to be mainly male, bristling with executives and other top (and, of course, wealthy) people, decision-makers galore and heads-of-the-family, those who have the final say on whether or not to buy a new car, or a new house. The advertising during sports events tends to be big on virility items: beer, cars, shaving cream, razors, anti-perspirants, and various other tough he-man lines like colognes, hair dressings and insurance policies.

As well as providing a blue-chip audience, sport has another asset that advertisers like. It is non-political. And people discuss the programmes the day after, giving them a persistence that most other programmes lack.

Apparently not enough advertisers think like this. Both C.B.S. and N.B.C. say they lose money on sports. Then why do they continue to pay out ever higher sums for baseball and football? Primarily for prestige – sport is considered good for a network's image. Another major reason is simply the fear of being-gone-one-better-than by a rival net-work. Corporate vanity demands that A.B.C. and C.B.S. and N.B.C. indulge in a three-sided tug-of-war for the rights to major sports events. The sports people are naturally well aware of this and have been known to play one network against another with a 'meet our terms or we'll go elsewhere' approach.

Money and prestige are at stake and things are likely to get a little rough. There are signs that the TV people are not above using industrial espionage techniques to make sure they come out on top. 24 January, 1964 is a famous date in the annals of TV-sport. That was the day that the National Football League was going to award its new contract for tele-vision rights. The old one with C.B.S. had brought the league $4,650,000 a year. The league was expecting to get much more this time, and had arranged a nice theatrical publicity gimmick: they were not negotiating with the networks, they were not naming a price. They were saying to them 'How much do you think we're worth?' The answers from the networks were lying that morning in sealed envelopes on the desk of the Commissioner.

The heart-searching, the cajoling, the pleading, the badgering, all the agony the network executives had gone through trying to work out how much they should offer to be sure of outbidding their rivals, all that was now history. All that counted was those three envelopes. A large contingent of journalists and photographers and TV people had gathered for the occasion. The Commissioner, as luck would have it, opened the envelopes in ascending order. N.B.C.'s offer – $10,300,000 a year (breath drawn in all round, over twice the previous contract). Then A.B.C.: $13,200,000 a year (gasps of astonishment). Finally C.B.S.: $14,100,000 yearly – over three times what they had been paying (choked groans and collapse of N.B.C. and A.B.C.).

Let us now retrace our path a little, back to the hours immediately before the great envelope-opening ceremony. In his book *Super Spectator and the Electric Lilliputians*, William Johnson tells how, during those hours, the C.B.S. bid – already high enough to be considered irresponsible by the board chairman – was suddenly raised even higher.* The story goes that C.B.S. had come to know the size of A.B.C.'s bid; and the rumours have gone around ever since that '$50,000 passed from C.B.S. into the hands of an A.B.C. man that day'. Could it be that an informer was at work, could it be that . . . but a wall of *omerta* worthy of Western Sicily has enveloped the incident. Nobody knows.

Ironically, the C.B.S. triumph in landing the contract was eventually to cost the National Football League quite a lot of money. N.B.C. were considerably miffed by the whole charade. They plotted revenge, and within two years they got it. There was, in 1964, a rival professional football league in existence, the American Football League. It had been going since 1960, but was struggling along on small attendances, apparently doomed by its inability to lure the best players away from the older and very prosperous N.F.L. It could not lure them because it did not have enough money. Enter the Good Fairy N.B.C. with a fat television contract that worked out at $850,000 a year for each club for five years. This time television was not only supporting a league; it was practically creating one. N.B.C. was even willing to lend money to some of the A.F.L. clubs so that they could go out and compete with the N.F.L. in signing players. Which they did very effectively. This led to the usual costly salary war between the A.F.L. and the N.F.L. – at least, that was one way of looking at it. Along New York's Sixth Avenue, where all

---

* Johnson, William O., *Super Spectator and the Electric Lilliputians*, Little, Brown and Co., Boston, 1971.

three television networks have their headquarters, it was seen as an N.B.C. *v.* C.B.S. struggle. The result was a victory of sorts for the A.F.L–N.B.C. camp that led to the merger of 1966.

Is it possible that network-backed leagues will give rise to network-owned leagues? This would appear highly unlikely, as something too clearly flying in the face of the anti-trust laws. Even so, in 1964 baseball made a move that seemed to point in this direction. Whatever the merits of the move, its timing could not have been worse. This ought to have been a triumphant moment for sport. A special bill had been shepherded through all the committee stages of Congress and was about ready for approval, a bill that would put an end to all of baseball's (and other professional sports') uncertainty over the anti-trust laws. The bill was cleverly designed to say one thing and to bring about its opposite. The idea was to place all professional sports under the anti-trust laws, and then to grant them special exemptions – e.g., the reserve clause, and the draft and exclusive territorial rights. It was the answer to an owner's dream, and it was only fitting that it was the baseball owners themselves who upset the apple cart.

At this delicate moment they agreed to allow the sale of the New York Yankees, the most famous club in baseball, to – of all people – C.B.S., who also happened to own one of the country's major television networks. The ingenious dream-bill died right there, as perturbed voices were raised in Congress speculating that, with the increasing involvement of television, 'professional team sports, like wrestling today, may degenerate into exhibitions rather than *bona fide* athletic contests'. But it was not necessary to imagine C.B.S. television producers handing out scenario and choreography instructions to players before a game to see the contradictions involved in their purchase of the Yankees. C.B.S. as a television company was interested in buying the rights to baseball games at the best (i.e., lowest) possible price. C.B.S. as owner of the Yankees was interested in selling those rights at the best (i.e., highest) possible price. Was this not a conflict of interests? No, no, said baseball and C.B.S. in a 'how could you suggest such a thing?' tone. Their position was greatly strengthened when the Justice Department announced that it did not intend to bring an anti-trust suit to bar the transaction.

To look on the bright side, television ownership of the leagues would probably prevent the cataclysmic disaster that the Cassandras feel will be the last stage of the febrile TV-sport romance. To wit, that television will decide one fine morning that sport, after all, is not a sound economic proposition, not a good vehicle, and will banish it from the screens, or, at best, greatly reduce their payments. Television could replace sport with more westerns or soap operas or family comedies or anything from its bottomless bag of inanities. But what would sport use in place of television money? Without it, professional sport could certainly not continue to live in the style to which it has become accustomed, if it could continue to live at all.

Electronic sport, though, does not have to be limited to the TV set in the living room. Should sport find itself out of favour with the television people, it might be able to fall back on closed circuit transmissions, in which home showings are completely blacked out, and the event is shown live on giant screens in places like cinemas and conference halls. The enormous financial success of the Muhammad Ali–Joe Frazier heavyweight fight in March 1971 showed what could be done. That event was blacked out on home television everywhere, but was transmitted by closed circuit to 369 auditoriums across the country. With admission prices between $10 and $15 this produced a gross income of nearly $17 million. For the 1971 Super Bowl game, the championship of professional football, television had paid $2.5 million, which everybody had agreed was a phenomenal sum. Now it began to look rather paltry.

The rapid expansion of professional sport in the 1960s was a direct result of the prosperity that television money brought about. Baseball, which had got along with sixteen clubs for over fifty years, added eight new ones during the decade. This meant new owners coming in with new capital, and the way things were arranged that meant more money for the existing owners. When the National League expanded from ten to twelve clubs in 1968, the two new clubs had to pay $10 million each to the league for the privilege of owning their franchises – a windfall of $2 million for each of the ten existing clubs.

While the expansion money and the television money poured in, the fans did not. Baseball attendances dropped by 2 million between 1966 and 1968, causing clubs to look around for promotion gimmicks that would bring back the fans. The favourite was Bat Day – every kid under fourteen years old was given a free baseball bat – provided he was accompanied by an adult. This invariably packed them in. The New York Yankees had a Bat Day in 1970 that drew 66,000 people, the largest baseball crowd in five years, even if 42,000 of them were under fourteen.

Bat Day was thought up by one Bill Veeck in 1951 when he was the owner of the St Louis Browns. They are remembered as one of baseball's more hopeless teams, and he almost *had* to give things away if he wanted anyone to attend the games.* When a bankrupt manufacturer offered him 6,000 bats for next to nothing, Veeck bought them, and gave them out at the first Bat Day.

Veeck was cast in a very different mould from the majority of the owners. His theory was that going to a baseball game should be fun. He wanted the whole family to come out to the stadium, and he wanted them to enjoy themselves. To this end he put on a stream of gags and gimmicks before, during and after his baseball games. He gave away Cadillacs to get the fans to come out to afternoon games. He flew in 20,000 Princess Aloha orchids from Hawaii, in a temperature-controlled plane, and gave them out to the female fans. People selected at random from the crowd were presented with gifts that might possibly be useful, like the six step-ladders given to one fan, but more probably were just an embarrassment, like the two dozen live lobsters, or the 10,000 cup cakes, or the five tons of nuts and bolts that others received. When his team played an away game at a stadium where he considered the floodlighting inadequate he had his players groping about the field wearing miner's helmets with lamps in the front. In his own stadium he invented an adjustable-height fence that was raised when the opponents were at bat, and lowered when the home team was hitting, giving them a much better chance of hitting a home run. Well, there was nothing in the rules that said you were not allowed to do it – until the day after Veeck first tried it, when suddenly there *was* a new rule barring fences that changed shape during a game.

A life-long fascination with circuses gave Veeck some of his wilder ideas, including 'Millie the Queen of the Air', who used to come sliding down a tightrope from the stands into the infield. When a fan complained that his view was always being blocked by the vendors selling their beer and peanuts in the stands, Veeck went to a theatrical agency, hired a group of midgets and used them as vendors for one game, selling midget-sized hot-dogs and beers. And he eventually managed to find a way of introducing another of his passions – fireworks – into a baseball game. He invented the exploding scoreboard. Whenever a member of his team (he was at this time owner of the Chicago White Sox) hit a home run, the scoreboard became a riot of crackling Roman candles and rockets, fire-bombs, coloured lights blinking and flashing, while the speaker system played the Hallelujah Chorus from Handel's *Messiah*.

---

* The story goes that when a fan phoned and asked, 'What time does the game start?', Veeck replied, 'Well, what time can you get here?'

5 A favourite gimmick: bat day, on which every child under the age of fourteen attending the game accompanied by an adult is presented with a free baseball bat.

Veeck wholeheartedly embraced the view that baseball was part of the entertainment industry, and he carried it to its logical extreme with his use of showbiz promotional methods. The other owners found his behaviour a bit too much. Veeck was repeatedly accused of cheapening the game, and 'making a travesty' of baseball. In 1961 Veeck sold the Chicago White Sox, and has not been able to get back into baseball since. Many of his showsport ideas, though, have apparently ceased to be cheapening. Bat Day is a regular event for most clubs now, as are Ball Day and Helmet Day, and a growing list of other Days and Nights when various groups are admitted free – Boy Scouts' Day, Ladies' Day, even Nuns' Day. The California Angels have had a Dixieland Jazz Night, and a Teen Dance Night, and have presented each mother with a pair of nylons on Mothers' Day.

Basketball was also infected by the giveaway virus and in 1969 the Philadelphia 76ers were trying to lure the fans with Think Mink Night (one mink coat given away), Victor the Rasslin' Bear Night (a 500 lb bear wrestling volunteers from the crowd), and Blind Date Night, on which sixty fans paid to sit in a special dating section (not too successful, the ratio was fifty-six guys to four girls).

Football, the super-success sport of the 1960s had no need for such flim-flammery. The games were playing to sell-out crowds almost everywhere. The Kansas City Chiefs, for instance, have a stadium capacity of 78,000. All 78,000 are sold out for every game – on a season ticket basis.

The Sporting Sixties seemed to offer profits to just about anyone even remotely connected with baseball, football or basketball. The number of major-league teams in these sports had risen from thirty-six to seventy-seven during the decade, and the *value* of the teams had risen even more sharply. When baseball added two new teams at the beginning of the sixties the cost of the franchises was $2 million each; in 1968, when two more teams were added, the cost was $10 million per franchise.

The financial reports of the Rheingold beer company bore succinct testimony to the profitable sports–business coupling. Rheingold were the sponsors for the New York Met baseball games on TV and radio. When the Mets rose from last to next-to-last place in 1966, Rheingold's sales rose with them. When the Mets sank back to last place in 1967, Rheingold sunk too, and lost $200,000 on the year. In 1969 when the Mets became national champions, Rheingold reported record sales with an income jump of 40 per cent.

Then, with 1970 barely two weeks old, the move that had been talked about, and half expected, for nearly fifty years was finally made: the legality of baseball's reserve clause was challenged in the courts.

Curt Flood, a $90,000-a-year outfielder with the St Louis Cardinals, was informed that he had been traded to the Philadelphia Phillies; the agreement was made, as was the custom, between the two clubs, without Flood being consulted. Flood said he had no objection to playing for Philadelphia, but he did have the strongest objection to being shipped around 'like cattle'. He said he would not go to Philadelphia, and asked St Louis to release him so that he could negotiate, as a free agent, with any club that he liked. Allowing players to negotiate as free agents was, as Flood well knew, the very thing that the reserve clause was designed to prevent, and the Commissioner lost no time in rejecting Flood's request. The baseball owners let it be known that the reserve clause was sacrosanct; without it, they said, 'professional baseball would simply cease to exist'.

So Flood, backed by the Players' Association, took the dispute to court. After two years of lower court hearings and appeals the case reached the Supreme Court, which handed down its decision in June 1972. A decision which, in effect, amounted to a careful avoidance of the issue. The court found that baseball was indeed a business, and agreed that its exemption from the anti-trust laws was an anomaly. But, said the court, baseball had operated on the assumption of exemption for so long that things should be left the way they were. Curt Flood's case was dismissed, and the court then passed the buck to Congress, saying that if baseball was to be brought under the anti-trust laws it was up to Congress to pass legislation to that effect.

3   Sport:
The Last
Frontier

Change – sometimes violent, sometimes insidious, sometimes welcomed,
sometimes resisted – has been the key process of the twentieth century.
Nowhere has it done its work more thoroughly than in the United States.
Anything new has been so automatically admired that the very word
itself has come to be almost synonymous with better. This has led to a
widely held view that Americans do not give a fig for tradition, that they
will gleefully trample all over it merely for the sake of doing something
differently.

At a superficial level, sports and games might seem to bear out the
accusation. This is a field that has been especially vulnerable to the cult
of ephemeral newness. From the bicycling craze of the 1880s, through
roller-skating, yo-yos, skateboards, miniature golf, down to the hula-
hoop, there has been one short-lived novelty after another. But through
all this coming and going, baseball has continued virtually unchanged. It
has had its ups and downs in popularity, but its persistence suggests
some lasting quality as appealing to Americans of the 1970s as it was to
those of the 1870s.

'Whoever wants to know the heart and mind of America', said Jacques
Barzun in 1954, 'had better learn baseball, the rules and the realities of
the game . . .' That is still good advice, even though baseball's un-
molested reign as the national sport has come to an end with the rise of
football and the coming challenge from basketball. The two newer sports
are quite different from baseball in form, but there are certain underlying
themes that closely connect all three. These themes reflect some basic –
one might almost say traditional – American attitudes.

But they must be approached with caution. For sport is a man-made,
totally artificial little world, and it would be surprising if man did not
take the opportunity to idealize or exaggerate the role of those values he
treasures most. A dream world, then? To a considerable extent, yes, a
comfortable refuge where things can be made to go the way they ought
to go, but so frequently do not, in real life.

Democracy, for instance. The idea that all men are created equal, or that they should at least be given an equal chance, is still one of the most potent influences in American life. That its everyday practice is somewhat haphazard makes sport – where it clearly does operate – all the more attractive. It may no longer be true, if it ever was, that any boy can grow up to be President, but it *is* true that a steady stream of young athletes from small towns and big-city ghettoes rise to the top on their merits in that most visible of occupations, professional sport.

Well, not exactly 'rise' to the top, they have to struggle, to fight to get there, they have to compete. Competition is the root of all sports and it is also something of an American ethic. To understand why the version of competition that sport presents is so appealing to Americans, it is necessary first to take a look at the place of competition in American society.

Whether the desire to compete comes naturally to all men or whether it is a product of his culture, there is not much doubt that the climate in the United States has proved ideal for its growth. The American Way of Life is, at base, a competition – a mass of competitions, in fact. As the anthropologist, Margaret Mead, says:

From the beginning, the country was held together by the pitting of group against group in competition that was sometimes healthy and sometimes unhealthy as city was pitted against city, city against state, state against state, the states against the Federal government, North against South, East against West, the Congress against the Executive, the House against the Senate, the Army against the Navy, Harvard against Yale.

At the individual level it is called 'Keeping Up with the Joneses'. It is also known as the 'Rat Race'. Where you have a race, you have winners, and where you have winners you have prizes. Ah, the prizes – it is the prizes that glitter and beckon, the prizes that keep everybody running. There is no mystery about the prizes, they are worldly goods and the things that are misguidedly assumed to go with them: power, respect, happiness. One can quite see the attraction, but it is necessary to stress just how deep it goes. For it is the heart of the modern American Dream, the up-to-date version of the idea of America as the Land of Opportunity. The idealism that saw in America freedom and equal opportunity for all has been stifled by a materialism that sees only refrigerators, automobiles, electric dishwashers and wealth for all. Measured in these terms, says the Dream, success is within everybody's reach. All you have to do is compete.

What all this persiflage hides is the awkward fact that where you have winners you also have losers. In fact the free-enterprise system is always likely to produce more losers than winners. For such a way of life to be made acceptable, it is essential that the losers be ignored, that the attention of the competitors be directed only to the rewards awaiting the winner.

Over the years Americans have invented a series of myths designed to deny the existence of losers, or at least to justify ignoring them. All these myths are demonstrably untrue, but they have carried, and continue to carry, enormous weight in fashioning American attitudes. They are believed because they answer the eternal American call for optimism.

The earliest figure in the making of myths to glamourize the competitive society was Horatio Alger, a writer of boys' novels. Although Alger published over one hundred titles between 1867 and 1898, they are all built around the same basic plot. The titles themselves give the game away: *Strive and Succeed*, *Making His Way*, *Bound to Rise*, *Struggling Upward*, *From Farm to Fortune* . . . the theme was rags-to-riches, the heroes were ragged little newsboys and matchboys, and the message was that anyone, no matter how lowly, could succeed in America.

'I hope, my lad,' says Mr Whitney to Ragged Dick, 'you will prosper and rise in the world. You know in this free country poverty in early life is no bar to a man's advancement.' But this is still a long way from the Rat Race. Alger's *gamin* works industriously, certainly, but his entry into the ranks of the wealthy is usually the result of his acquiring a patron, a kindly rich man who sees the lad's basic goodness and honesty and virtually adopts him. Thus there is still a suggestion that success must be based on moral worth; hard work alone is not enough. This is a vital distinction, and the critic who claimed that it was Alger who 'put free and untrammeled competition on the side of the angels' was off the mark. In Alger's world success is measured in financial terms, but it comes as a result of chance meetings between boy and patron. The American Dream is realized without competition. Obviously, Alger's novels bore little resemblance to the way things really were. There could hardly have been many matchboys with the intelligence and honesty of his heroes, and even fewer who found themselves a kindhearted patron. Alger himself must have known this – he lived for years in the Newsboys' Lodging House in New York – yet his pages are unsullied by tales of the boys who did not make it.

If they had been required to stand on their merits as literature, Alger's books would probably never have been published at all. But the simple values that they pictured were evidently a necessary part of American life, and they sold by the thousand, enough to make a fortune for Alger's publisher (though not for Alger, who neither began in rags nor went on to riches).

The term 'Horatio Alger figure' is still in use but it has acquired a meaning that, while less true to Alger's original, is more acceptable to today's Americans. Patrons are out, the self-made man is in. The term now means someone who has risen through his own efforts from humble beginnings to fame and fortune.

There are no losers in Alger's world, because there is no competition. Success simply drops out of the blue on to the morally worthy. Such villains as there are tend to be the snobbish sons of rich parents, hardly types deserving of compassion. At the time Alger was writing, the last third of the nineteenth century, belief in the classical Puritan virtues such as honesty, thrift, piety and industry, was still strong enough to ensure that his heroes appeared real enough for public approval.

Around the end of the century things began to take on a very different hue. This was the heyday of cut-throat capitalism and it was all too obvious that if there was any connection at all between being virtuous and being rich, it was a negative one. It was no longer possible to blithely ignore, as Alger's books had done, the dog-eat-dog viciousness of the competitive society, but there was at hand a mythology that would explain and excuse it. Darwin's *Origin of the Species* had appeared in 1859, and Herbert Spencer had popularized it with a telling phrase: survival of the fittest. If that was a law of nature, then why should it not apply to man's business activities? If a man did not succeed, it was because he was not one of the fittest; that was the way nature had arranged things, and it was pointless – maybe even dangerous – to do anything that would upset the natural order. Virtue no longer had anything to do with it.

The phenomenal growth of the American economy in the first third of the twentieth century swept away whatever idealism remained attached to the American Dream, and redefined it in the image of the get-rich-quick mania that was attracting millions of immigrants to the United States. Perhaps some of them really did believe that the streets were paved with gold, but certainly no one doubted the new myth that America was the land of unlimited wealth, a land where there was enough for everyone. All you had to do was to go there and take your share. Sure, there would be competition, but if you were any sort of a man you would get your share, and maybe more. If a man could not make it under those circumstances, then he just wasn't trying. The loser became a figure of contempt, a lazy, shiftless, good-for-nothing. This concept was given sturdy dramatic shape in the new Western novel born at the turn of the century, and later in the Western film. Here the losers were so methodically blackened (they were usually made to wear black in case anyone missed the point), and made so villainous that their very existence was a danger to society. They could be eliminated without anyone feeling guilty about it.

The Western novelists were simply doing what Alger had done before them, telling Americans what they wanted to hear, explaining to them the essential morality of their competitive society. The simplistic Western notion that the loser deserved everything he got was never even remotely true in everyday life, but it is such a crucial part of the modern American Dream that it is held by large numbers – probably a majority – of Americans today.

The plight of the loser in the competitive society was the theme of Arthur Miller's quintessentially American drama *Death of a Salesman*. Willy Loman was unsuccessful because he could not compete, because he did not have the aggressive ambition needed to be a good salesman. Because he himself believed in the success myth, Loman's sense of shame at his failure eventually shattered his sanity. A loser had been eliminated – but this was no Western badman, this was a worthy human being. 'But he's a human being, and a terrible thing is happening to him. So attention must be paid,' says his wife. But attention cannot be paid. Willy Loman is the underside of the American Dream, the chronic loser, and he *has* to be ignored. If he is not, if he becomes a source of concern, then the Dream itself, the thing that consumed him, may be destroyed by doubts. What if the competitive American Way were all a cruel hoax?

Those assailed by such apostasy can abundantly reaffirm their faith with a look at the world of professional sport. Here is pure competition at work, where everybody plays according to the rules (or nearly so), where the winners are clearly the fittest, where the losers are clearly identified and where they do not represent a threat to the whole structure. For sports are arranged to keep the difference between winner and loser as small as possible. A loser in sport does not give up, is rarely so hopelessly beaten that he knows he has no chance of future success. He keeps coming back and sooner or later he becomes a winner.

The determination to avoid thinking about losers has led, logically enough, to great emphasis being placed on the importance of winning. From General Douglas MacArthur's 'There is no substitute for victory' down to Willy Loman's dream 'to come out number-one-man' the theme of winning haunts American life. Not surprisingly it finds its most free expression in sport. To start with, American sports are so arranged as to make sure that a clear winner emerges from each contest. In baseball and basketball, games are not allowed to end as ties. If the scores are level at the end of regulation time, extra time is played until a result is obtained.* In football, tied games are theoretically possible, but the high-scoring nature of the sport makes them extremely rare.

The ethic of winning in sports has acquired a supporting 'literature' of its own, composed of suitably muscular maxims and slogans:

'Winning isn't the most important thing – it's the only thing.'
  Vince Lombardi, professional football coach.

'How can you be proud of a losing team?'
  Jim Tatum, college football coach.

'If it's under W for Won, nobody asks you how.'
  Leo Durocher, professional baseball manager.

'A team that won't be beaten can't be beaten.'
  Bill Roper, college football coach.

'A winner never quits, a quitter never wins.'
  Anon.

Like the myths already studied, these slogans serve to hide an unpalatable truth. To win you have to beat an opponent, and to beat him you have to *want* to beat him. Consider these words: 'You have to be mean to be a champion. How can you lick someone if you feel friendly toward them?' This is not the advice of a hard-bitten professional football coach, it comes from tennis coach Miss Eleanor Tennant and was addressed to seventeen-year-old Maureen Connolly before the 1952 Wimbledon final. If the killer instinct is desirable in women's amateur tennis, it is essential in a rough contact sport like football where meanness is a quality much in demand. Recalling the great Chicago Bears team of the 1940s an ex-player remarked, 'They were so damn mean, they wouldn't even talk to each other', while a college coach claimed that one of his stars was 'so mean that he got kicked out of the marines for unnecessary roughness'. Both these comments are meant as praise: if you want to be a winner, the meaner the better.

* An insistence that can be troublesome. The average length of a normal nine-innings baseball game is around two and a half hours. In 1968 the New York Mets and the Houston Astros played a game that took twenty-four innings to decide, lasted over six hours, and did not finish until 1.30 a.m.

There are, it seems, sound psychological reasons for this. In 1958 Francis Ryan, who combines the roles of psychologist and athletics coach, published the results of a study he had conducted to find out what made the difference between a good competitor and a poor competitor. Miss Tennant was right. The good competitors, Ryan found, were the ones who could get angry at their opponents. The poor competitors had the apparently fatal flaw of trying to be friendly with their rivals.

What is fatal in sport is no less disastrous in the pursuit of the American Dream, witness poor Willy Loman, who was unable to compete effectively because he wanted people to like him. None of the slogans so dear to American coaches comes right out and says that you have to be a ruthless rat to win, but the suspicion is that it would not hurt your chances.

If you are not able to be that ruthless and still want to be a winner, you do have an alternative. You just have to be so superbly good at whatever you do that you are unbeatable. Not a very likely alternative, but a very attractive one, especially for the myth-makers. Super-athlete, because he is bound to win anyway, does not have to be tarnished by association with the sordid elements of competition. He does not need to cheat or indulge in gamesmanship, he does not need to hate his opponent, and can even be chivalrous towards him.

This is too much to ask of any mortal, but it was just what was needed for the birth of fictional hero Frank Merriwell, the athletic star of a series of weekly Nickel Novels (5-cent boys' comics) that appeared between 1896 and 1914 and were reprinted for many years after that. Merriwell is the sports version of that favourite American fantasy-figure, Superman. Whatever sport he plays, and he has 'fooled a little' with most of them, Merriwell plays superbly and unbeatably. Any that have escaped him, as cricket seems to have done, he could undoubtedly master in a trice. For his school Fardale, and later at Yale University, he is forever winning baseball and football games single-handed with last-minute heroics, often while playing with secret injuries that would have put anyone else in hospital for weeks.

Rowing against arch-rivals Harvard he inspires Yale to a last-gasp victory, faints immediately, then recovers long enough to ask 'Did we win?' and to refuse a proffered flask – 'I never touch liquor'. Poor old Harvard were always running up against Merriwell at his most Merriwellish:

His lips were covered with a bloody foam, and there was a frightful glare in his eyes. He strained and strove to get a little farther and he actually dragged Hollender along the ground till he broke the fellow's hold. Then he reeled across Harvard's line and fell. It was a touchdown in the last seconds of the game.

The Merriwell saga started in 1895 when Gilbert Patten, an author of mediocre dime-novels, received a letter from his publisher asking if he would be interested in writing a series of boys' stories 'something in the line of the Jack Harkaway stories'. These depicted the life of a student at Oxford in the 1880s, and had enjoyed great success in England. Harkaway was something of an athletic figure – he won his Blue for rowing, cricket and soccer, and got a double first to boot – but he pales to insignificance when compared to the sporting Stakhanovite that Merriwell was to become.

Patten's first task after accepting his publisher's offer (which meant turning out 20,000 words a week) was to find the right name for his hero. 'And then suddenly I had it – Frank Merriwell! The name was symbolic of the chief characteristics I desired my hero to have – *Frank* for frankness, *merry* for a happy disposition, *well* for health and abounding vitality.'

He wrote the stories under the pen-name of Burt L. Standish and to say that they were successful is like saying the Rothschilds were competent bankers. The first Merriwell was a sell-out and the number of copies printed increased steadily with each issue. The publishers never released figures (no doubt because Patten's fees were woefully inadequate for such huge sales), but did once admit that 'over 123,500,000 copies' had been sold. Patten believed, with good reason, that the number was nearer 500 million.

In 1914, after some 850 stories and 20 million words, Patten wrote his last Merriwell yarn.* By that time a whole generation had grown up on the stories and the phrase 'to pull a Merriwell', meaning to pull off some spectacular situation-saving feat, was part of the American language (though it does not seem to be so any more). Patten told of a minister who chose one of his stories as the text for a sermon, and of 'thousands of successful and esteemed men' who found in Merriwell an inspiration and a guide. They included Jess Willard, Jack Dempsey, Babe Ruth, Woodrow Wilson and Wendell Willkie. The influence of Merriwell

---

* Patten was certainly one of the world's most prolific writers. In addition to the Merriwell stories, he wrote hundreds of other tales, including many Westerns – so many, under so many different names that he just lost track of them all. In 1927, eighteen years before his death, he estimated that he had already written over 40 million words.

lasted into the twenties, long enough to claim the boyhood devotion of
Spiro Agnew.

Patten published his first Merriwell novel in 1896, just two years before
Horatio Alger wrote the last of his rags-to-riches epics. Americans now
wanted something more robust than virtuous shoe-shine boys, something with more red-blooded physical action in it. The Westerns were
one product of the changing taste, and Merriwell was another, for in
addition to his sporting feats he was forever preventing damsels from
being deflowered or trampled by runaway horses. But Merriwell did not
make a complete break with the virtuous world of Alger; he was drawn
as a chivalrous, sportsmanlike gentleman who always obeyed the laws of
fair play, even though Patten saw that this was not realistic – 'In one
respect he [Merriwell] was a sap – he always let his adversary strike the
first blow. That was sheer stupidity, for often the first blow decided the
battle.'

Anyway, one suspects that it was not Merriwell's sportsmanship that
endeared him to Americans. The real attractions were his physical
prowess and shrewdness. These are the qualities of the man of action
and, according to the historian Frederick Jackson Turner, they are
fundamental to the American character. In his *Significance of the
American Frontier* (1893), Turner was the first to underline the importance of the frontier experience in forming American attitudes. In a
famous passage he listed the qualities that the frontier demanded:

That coarseness and strength combined with acuteness and inquisitive-
ness; that practical, inventive turn of mind, quick to find expedients; that
masterful grasp of material things, lacking in the artistic, but powerful to
effect great ends; that restless, nervous energy; that dominant individualism
working for good and evil . . .

For the frontiersman the possession of these traits was often a matter
of life or death. But by 1870 the frontier was all but exhausted, and
America was changing from an open-air agrarian society to an industrial
one centred in large cities. The frontiersman gave way to the factory
worker, hardly an occupation where much enterprise or individualism or
even shrewdness was required. Maybe not, but the ideal of the man of
action persisted with enormous strength, simmering away beneath the
surface of an American life that was becoming increasingly regimented,
until, in the 1890s, it boiled furiously to the surface with a force that was
to have lasting effects on the American mind. There was, as one historian
put it, 'everywhere an urge to be young, masculine, and adventurous'; in

other words to re-assert the frontier values. There followed a sudden
mania for outdoor activities – bicycling, camping, birdwatching, and an
enormously increased interest in physical fitness and sports. It was a
decade in revolt against softness, a decade that took the survival of the
fittest at its most literal and determined to show that fittest meant
physically fittest.

The spirit of the time was embodied in the person of Theodore
Roosevelt, the sickly youth who took boxing lessons and walked and
swam to add weight and strength to his feeble frame, and who went
West for several years to work as a cattle rancher in North Dakota, living
a life that was the nearest America could then offer to that of the old
frontier. In 1899 T. R. delivered a speech that summed up what the
fitness movement of the 1890s was all about. He titled it 'The Strenuous
Life' and he praised it as a way of countering the lethargy that he feared
wealth would bring in its train. 'It is only through strife, through hard
and dangerous endeavour that we shall ultimately win the goal of true
national greatness,' he declared, and talked of the 'virile qualities'
needed for success. Here was the competitive theme again, bringing with
it yet another excuse-myth: that it was a patriotic duty. Two years later
President McKinley was assassinated and T. R. – 'that damned cowboy'
as one of his opponents called him – was President of the United States.

A vigorous man of action was in charge of America, a man who used
phrases like 'Play the Game' and who promised everyone a 'Square
Deal', something he had learnt during his cowboy days. The language of
the Frontier and of sport had arrived at the White House.

Roosevelt's definition of manly character included 'unselfishness,
devotion to duty and honesty' – it could have been Frank Merriwell
talking. But these were the lip-service virtues, the ones you practised if
you could afford to. What really linked Roosevelt and Merriwell and the
American public was their belief that Turner's 'strength combined with
acuteness' were the keys to life.

To be acute was to be a clever thinker, a person who grasped situations
quickly and who acted quickly. Not a *deep* thinker, though, that would
smack of intellectualism, something that has always been mistrusted by
Americans. For a country devoted to the egalitarian ideal, intellectualism looms as a threatening form of élitism, and has been countered by
a pervasive anti-intellectualism that is 'older than our national identity'.
The words are those of the historian Richard Hofstadter.

In his *Anti-Intellectualism in American Life*, Hofstadter draws attention to the decisive difference that Americans draw between intelligence

(the value of which is never questioned) and intellect (which is viewed with suspicion).* Intellect merely contemplates and theorizes and gets nothing tangible done, while intelligence is a 'manipulative, adjustive, unfailingly practical quality – one of the most eminent and endearing of the animal virtues'. Intelligence is what the man-of-action needs, intellect is for the scholar, a type who, as Dixon Wecter notes in his study *The Hero in America*, 'has never kindled American imagination'.†

What Americans were looking for was a hero who was, to use their own word, smart,‡ and who had a full share of the other qualities mentioned by Wecter as essential for American heroes: 'hard work, tenacity, enterprise, firmness in the face of odds, and manliness, forthright manliness'. The intellectual is judged to be lacking on all those counts and, for good measure, is frequently held to be effeminate, something that Wecter rates as 'fatal' for aspiring American heroes.§

But . . . manliness, what is that? The American answer was given at the beginning of the twentieth century when the man-of-action developed into the he-man. It was but a small step. The hero's masculinity and toughness were heightened, his sense of fairplay and honesty were played down, and the fictional cowboy was born. The novel that set the pattern was Owen Wister's *The Virginian*, published in 1902 and dedicated to Theodore Roosevelt. Wister was out to glamourize the cowboy as 'the last romantic figure' and he gave to the Virginian those traits that he believed Americans most admired. He chose so well that his version of the cowboy has survived with little change to the present day.

In the world of the Virginian, there is no pussyfooting around on the subject of competition. Life is a struggle and a tough one, and the Virginian's faith is 'let the best man win'. You have to be tough, both physically and mentally, to win. The Virginian, naturally, measures up. He steels his mind to take part in the lynching of his friend for cattle stealing; and he stands up to the bad-guy with the immortal line 'When you call me that, *smile*', ignores his 'get out of town before sundown' order, and finally kills him in a duel. 'Grim, lean men of few topics, and

* Hofstadter, Richard, *Anti-Intellectualism in American Life*, Cape, 1964.

† Wecter, Dixon, *The Hero in America*, Ann Arbor Paperbacks, Ann Arbor, 1963.

‡ Shrewd or sharp, as in one's dealings. *Webster's New World Dictionary of the American Language.*

§ So fatal as to have ruled out, up to now, the emergence of a woman as an American Hero. No American woman has yet been able, as did Joan of Arc and Elizabeth I in other parts and other times, to play the male role well enough for national acclaim.

not many words concerning these; comprehending no middle between the poles of brutality and tenderness . . . but disconcerted by a good woman' was the way Wister described the cowpunchers, 'they laughed seldom, and their spirit was in the permanent attitude of war'.

The image fitted in perfectly with the call for the strenuous, masculine life. It cemented the notion that being tough and being masculine were the same thing, and it provided a check-off list of masculinity symbols that have populated Hollywood films and American novels (*vide* Ernest Hemingway and Norman Mailer) ever since: slow drawl, deep voice, few words, tobacco-chewing, spitting, narrowed eyes, jeans, and the cult of the gun.

To this formidable array of virile virtues, the Virginian added that extra quality without which, it often seems, Americans can admire nothing – sheer bigness. He was tall, a 'young giant' in fact, and as strong as the proverbial ox. This was another characteristic taken from the world of the Frontier, where men of huge stature had long been performing heroic deeds. The earliest was Daniel Boone who began his career as a Kentucky backwoodsman in 1769. Even within his own life-time, Boone became a semi-mythical figure and found himself hailed as a prodigious hunter and Indian-killer *extraordinaire*. Most of this was exaggeration, if not outright invention, and Boone's physique had to be suitably magnified to fit the legend. One of his relatives described him as 'slender and no taller than 5 ft 9 ins' which was nowhere near good enough. The great naturalist, John James Audubon, noted for his meticulously accurate drawings of birds, had met Boone and later recalled him as a great muscular type of 'gigantic' size, which may not have been meticulously accurate, but was much more acceptable.

Boone, like Davy Crockett who followed him, was a real live frontiers-man around whose life there grew up a romantic web of larger-than-life exploits. But the Frontier penchant for tall tales* soon found reality too limiting even as a starting point for their heroes, and totally mythical men began to appear. These were *really* tall heroes, like the mighty lumberjack Paul Bunyan, 'tall as the tallest pine-trees' (one of which he used as a brush for his beard), big as 'a city of ordinary men'. His strength was similarly immense and he personally hollowed out the one

* So called because their heroes were invariably giants, tall tales all contain some fantastic feat of physical strength. They have been described as 'one of America's few indigenous art forms'. *The Oxford English Dictionary* gives the word 'tall' in the sense of 'exaggerated or highly coloured' as being of United States colloquial origin in 1846.

hundred-mile-long Puget Sound in the north-western United States, using a glacier as a scoop.*

Oscar Wilde had noticed in 1882 how the American tended to bow down to size: 'Bulk is his canon of beauty and size his standard of excellence.' In the world of popular heroes and particularly in professional sport, it remains a perfectly aimed shaft, because sport has become a substitute frontier, a refuge for the he-man hero, his last chance to be a part of the mainstream of American life. Here he can use his strength and his shrewdness; not, admittedly, in the crucial task of building a nation that occupied the frontiersman, but in a way that – who can say? – may be equally important: that of entertaining a nation. Americans have made it very clear that they find big men much more entertaining than small men. They have even devised two sports that, in their professional form at least, can be played *only* by big men: basketball where height dominates, and football where all-over bigness is demanded.

In these sports, and to a lesser extent in baseball, the fascination with size has received the final American accolade. It has been reduced to a pseudo-science. The key things to know about a performer are his height and his weight. The statistics become an inseparable part of the player's name, and the combination is mouthed almost as one word by the radio and television commentators – ' . . . and this is Maulgood-six-five-two-forty', meaning that Mr Maulgood is 6 ft 5 ins tall, and weighs 240 lb. The extent of the obsession shone forth from television screens one Sunday afternoon in October 1970 when a football player was being interviewed immediately after a tough game. The inevitable question was asked – 'How much do you weigh, Fred?' Came the meticulous answer – 'Well, right now about two hundred and twenty to two hundred and twenty-five. Before the game I was probably two hundred and twenty-five to two hundred and thirty.' Thus Fred Dryer-six-six-two-twenty or maybe two-thirty, depending on when you catch him.

This sort of exchange always has the commentator in a state of jaw-sagging admiration, and there is no reason to suppose that any of the listeners are less awe-inspired. Even a hardened professional coach, Vince Lombardi, saw fit to praise a college player by simply saying

---

* The telling of tall tales was not entirely limited to the frontier. The East-coast sailors had their Captain Stormalong who commanded vessels so huge that when it was Wednesday in the forecastle it was still Monday aft. Another of his boats just managed to squeeze through the English Channel, scraping some of its paint off on the English side, which is why the cliffs of Dover are white.

Are football players the cowboy heros of the (2011?)

'Damn, that McCoy is big. He is big.' There is a long-standing American idea that bigger means better ('The country seems to try to bully one into a belief in its power by its impressive bigness', complained Oscar Wilde) and one of the reasons why football is cherished is because it is one of the few areas of life where the idea actually works.

There remains that most American of individuals – the tough guy. Given the American propensity not to settle for half measures it was probably inevitable that the he-man (but grudgingly chivalrous) Virginian would develop into the type that George Orwell described in his study of American comic books, the tough-guy who specializes in 'the all-in, jump-on-his-testicles style of fighting'. To Orwell this was the American ideal, the tough-guy, 'the gorilla who puts everything right by socking everybody else on the jaw'. One does not have to agree that this is so to see that Americans are attracted by the aura of the tough-guy, regardless of whether he is solving problems or creating them.

The tough-guy is everyone's mean streak writ large, the guy who spits in the face of fairplay. He is the ultimate competitor; not the guy who merely looks for a way to get round the law, but the guy who does not even acknowledge that the law exists. He is the one who openly proclaims himself No. 1, and everybody else had better watch out.

The role is by no means limited to Hollywood gangsters. It crops up throughout American life, in business, in politics, in the police, and naturally in sport. Perversely, it is probably less pronounced, and certainly of less consequence, in sport than in the other areas, but the tough-guy athlete is operating in full public view and is likely to receive a lot of publicity. For most people it is the ugly athlete who sets the pattern for the tough-guy role. It was a sports image that came to the mind of the journalist Richard Rovere as he watched the late Senator Joseph McCarthy conduct his pogrom against communists, pinkos, queers and effeminate intellectuals in the early 1950s:

McCarthy's particular style, I have often thought, owed a great deal to that of a certain kind of American athlete: the kind who earns and revels in such sobriquets as Killer and Slugger; who looks ugly and talks ugly and wants to deceive no one on this score; who attaches enough importance to winning the Goddamned game to throw spitballs and rabbit punches and do a little Indian Charlie work with elbows and knees in the clinches and pileups. It was not, I imagine, without some such image in mind that he acquired his swaggering, shoulder-heaving walk and his ballplayer's slouch; that he cultivated a five-o'clock shadow with almost cosmetic care . . . He liked to be known as a politician who used his thumbs, his teeth, and his knees and I suspect he understood there is a place for a few such men in our moral universe.

Agreed, the parallel is exact, but it would be unfair to saddle athletes with the responsibility for developing the tough-guy image. It has grown from that same competitiveness of which sport forms a nice antiseptic little showcase, and from the hallowed Frontier virtues. So McCarthy liked to use his thumbs and his knees, and the ugly-athlete throws punches and uses his elbows? Well, good old folk hero Paul Bunyan was paving the way for that back at the start of the nineteenth century in his epic tussle with the giant foreman Hels Helsen:

> ... that Herculean, jaw-hammering, chin-mauling, nose-pounding, side-stamping, cheek-tearing, rib-breaking, lip-punching, back-beating, neck-choking, eye-gouging, tooth-jerking, arm-twisting, head-butting, beard-pulling, ear-biting, bottom-thumping, toe-holding, knee-tickling, shin-cracking, heel-bruising, belly-whacking, hair-yanking, hell-roaring, supreme and incomparable knock-down-and-drag-out fight of all history.*

This should not be surprising for sport does not originate society's attitudes, it reflects them, sometimes directly, sometimes distortedly, sometimes ideally, but always dramatically. 'The games of a people reveal a great deal about them,' says Marshall McLuhan. 'Games are a sort of artificial paradise like Disneyland, or some Utopian vision by which we interpret and complete the meaning of our daily lives.'

As far as competition and the he-man image are concerned, then, sport is reflecting not reality but an ideal: straightforward competition where the best man wins and the loser licks his wounds and gamely keeps coming back until he succeeds. This is far from being the rule in life. The Rat Race is no game, but a deadly serious struggle for success in which the loser is pushed aside to the bleak fringes of American life. With the price of failure so high, winning becomes imperative, and it can hardly be wondered at if the tactics used in the struggle do not resemble the Queensberry rules. Morality becomes blurred and all sorts of dubious practices are accepted with a shrug. Major companies rig their prices, small businessmen overcharge, the Congressman accepts gifts, the policeman takes bribes, payola flows freely, conflict of interest is something that nobody has ever heard of, and everybody cheats on his income tax. Yes, there are laws against all these things, but a guy has to look out for himself, and putting one over on somebody else, or better still, on the

---

* The two contestants flattened a mountian during the affray and, surprise, surprise, Paul Bunyan emerged as the winner.

law, is regarded as the smart thing to do. This is what the competitive society is all about. Not keeping up with the Joneses, not even getting ahead of the Joneses, but being prepared to sell them down the river if that proves necessary.

It is a hard-bitten attitude that rules out any moral component in law. To speak of the spirit of the law, as opposed to the letter, becomes meaningless. There is no spirit – the law is what it says it is, and no more (though it might be considerably less, if you can find a smart enough lawyer). If it does not specifically say you cannot do it, then you can. If it *does* say you cannot, then go ahead anyway – either do not get caught, or get that smart lawyer.

In sport the attitude that laws are made to be subverted would mean instant chaos if it were at all widespread.* A sport is, at base, nothing but a set of rules and if they are too flagrantly flouted the sport that is built on them collapses.

But to pretend that sport has somehow escaped the mentality that sees laws as obstacles to be surmounted rather than as guides to correct behaviour would be quite untrue. What sport does show very clearly is the attitude that you can do anything that the rules do not specifically bar. Remember Bill Veeck and his adjustable-height fence?† Or take the events at a college basketball game between Columbia and Davidson universities. Two seconds remain and the score is tied. But Columbia has been awarded a free throw; if they make it they win, if they do not the game will go into overtime. The player taking the throw is young, in-experienced, and understandably nervous. He gets set to throw, and at the crucial moment the Davidson coach calls for a time-out.‡ The game is halted, the teams go to the sidelines for one minute, then return. The youngster goes through the agony of concentration all over again, and again just as he is ready to throw, the Davidson coach yells for a time-out. The player, by now thoroughly rattled, finally gets his chance to throw – and misses. The game goes into overtime, and Davidson wins.

This was not a professional game, but even in college sport the idea that this was unsportsmanlike would be considered ridiculous. There is nothing in the rules that says you cannot call consecutive time-outs in

---

* The existence of a few dirty players can be supported – as long as they remain a minority they are merely a nuisance (or a box-office attraction), not a major threat to the sport's existence.

† See Chapter 2, page 41.

‡ Each team is permitted a certain number of time-outs; these enable the coach, on appeal to the officials, to halt play for 60 seconds.

that situation, and that is all that counts. Even to call it gamesmanship misses the point, because gamesmanship implies something not quite respectable, vaguely caddish. In this case the Davidson coach would have been considered a fool if he had not called the time-outs.

There are football players who insist that their job is to hit their opponents hard enough to injure them and get them removed from the game. There is, after all, nothing in the rules that specifically forbids you to break an opponent's neck. 'The best instinct a ballplayer can have', said one, 'is to work as close as possible to the illegal limit.'

In baseball, players and managers argue so frequently with the officials over questions of rule interpretation that such disputes must be considered part of any properly played game. It is not difficult to understand why cricket, with its supine acceptance of the umpire's decision as final, failed to recommend itself to Americans.

That was not all that was wrong with cricket from the American viewpoint. It had the additional drawback of being time-consuming. If there is one thing that generation after generation of foreign visitors to America are agreed upon, it is that Americans are remarkably, even frantically, restless people. Things must be got on with, and nowhere is this urge more clearly and neatly demonstrated than in professional sport. In the foreign sports of cricket and soccer there is endless opportunity for time-wasting and aimless play. The batsman does not have to attempt any scoring strokes at all if he does not want to. The bowler does not have to aim the ball at the wicket.* There is nothing to stop a soccer team passing the ball safely around in its own half of the field without making any attempt to score. In the American professional sports that sort of inaction has been legislated out of existence. In basketball a team *has* to attempt a shot within 24 seconds of getting the ball, if they do not the ball goes over to their opponents. In football, a team is allowed just four plays in which to advance the ball ten yards, if they do not make it, the ball goes over to their opponents; furthermore they are allowed 30 seconds to get each play started. In baseball, the pitcher is allowed only three inaccurate pitches, the batter is allowed to ignore only two accurate pitches – and when he hits the ball into fair territory he *must* run to first base.

This look at the inter-relationship between the values of American life and sports has touched upon competitiveness, the frontier virtues of

* The introduction of limited-overs cricket during the 1960s seems to suggest that American-style restlessness is spreading.

strength and shrewdness, the cult of bigness, attitudes towards laws, and the dislike of inaction. These are the values that are found in all American sports. Let us now turn to the individual sports – baseball, football and basketball – all of which have unique characteristics that to a large degree are reflections of the different eras in which they attained popularity.

4 The National Pastime

It is only a game, of course. A man throws a ball. Another man sixty feet away hits at it with a stick. If he makes contact . . . but enough. J. B. Priestley settled that sort of nonsense years ago when he wrote that to describe soccer as twenty-two hirelings kicking a ball 'is merely to say that a violin is wood and catgut, that *Hamlet* is so much paper and ink'. No, baseball is not *just* a game. It is a game with a soul, a deeply American soul that Thomas Wolfe, one of the greatest and one of the most American of writers, worshipped:

> . . . one reason I have always loved baseball so much is that it has been not merely 'the great national game', but really a part of the whole weather of our lives, of the thing that is our own, of the whole fabric, the million memories of America. For example, in the memory of almost every one of us, is there anything that can evoke spring – the first fine days of April – better than the sound of the ball smacking into the pocket of the big mitt, the sound of the bat as it hits the horsehide: for me, at any rate, and I am being literal and not rhetorical – almost everything I know about spring is in it – the first leaf, the jonquil, the maple tree, the smell of grass upon your hands and knees, the coming into flower of April. And is there anything that can tell more about an American summer than, say, the smell of the wooden bleachers in a small town baseball park, that resinous, sultry and exciting smell of old dry wood.[*]

It has been played in America for over one hundred years now, this sport of baseball, and every American living today has felt its impress in one way or another.[†] It is the best of sports, it is the worst of sports, it is the most exciting, it is the dullest, it is forever gaining popularity, it is forever losing popularity, it is a challenge to the intellect, it is an insult to the intelligence, it is the most skilful of sports, it is the crudest of sports.

[*] Wolfe, Thomas, *The Letters of Thomas Wolfe*, (ed. Nowell, E.) Scribner, New York, 1956.

[†] A short description of the rules and action of baseball is given in the Appendices, page 261ff.

Baseball lives at the centre of a never-flagging whirl of irreconcilable opinions. It is a delight for the disputatious, and in nothing is it more American than that.* Because it *is* American, it is 'part of the thing that is our own' and that is one of the few assertions about baseball that will not lead to an argument. But there was a time when a bitter dispute raged over that very point . . . The scene is Delmonico's Restaurant, New York, and the year is 1889. Some 300 guests are gathered, important people; they include railroad magnate Chauncey Depew and writer Mark Twain. The occasion is the return to the United States of a squad of professional baseball players from a world tour. They have played in Honolulu, and in Australia, and before the Prince of Wales in England. Now they are back home, and a rather patriotic flavour is in the air to welcome these ambassadors who carried the great American game of baseball around the world. One of the speakers, a Mr Abraham Mills, makes quite a point of stressing that it has been established, 'by patriotism and research,' that baseball is a game of American origin. His audience cheers him and shouts joyously 'No rounders!'.

For the key to this enthusiasm we must go back thirty years or so before the gathering at Delmonico's. Since about 1860 baseball had been rapidly gaining in popularity throughout the United States. Most of this popularity was gained at the expense of cricket, which was seen as a foreign English sport. Baseball, on the other hand, was an American sport, a home-grown affair that reflected all that was good about America in a way that no imported game could. The famous literary gent sitting in that Delmonico's audience had said it: 'Baseball is the very symbol, the outward and visible expression of the drive and push and rush and struggle of the raging, tearing, booming nineteenth century.' Thus Mark Twain.

It was a tough manly game, made in tough manly America, and it had supplanted the effete lazy cricket that had been thought up in effete lazy England. Yet . . . there was always this annoying habit English visitors had of saying that baseball was really nothing but a somewhat more

---

* The author once sat in a New York park and watched as five young boys arrived with bat, ball and gloves to play baseball. They argued about who was on whose side, which side should bat first, in what order the players should bat, where home plate should be placed, where the other bases ought to be, which fielder should wear which glove, and where the foul lines were. It was nearly ten minutes before the first pitch was thrown. The batter hit it, and the ball bounced off a tree, causing another lengthy dispute over whether the tree was in fair or foul territory.

elaborate (and uncouth) version of rounders, which was played, they said, all over England and even by *girls*, if you can imagine. Just the sort of talk guaranteed to get any red-blooded American's back well up. And that was the reason for the wild scenes that greeted Abraham Mills's pronouncement on the origins of baseball. 'No rounders!'

It was decidedly unfortunate for the supporters of the 'no-rounders' theory that Henry Chadwick, the most respected baseball authority of the day, was an Englishman who knew all about rounders. In 1903 he put his views on record in *Baseball Guide*. He had, he said, played rounders back home as a schoolboy, and it was quite clear to him that baseball was derived from that sport.

This sort of treason was not to be put up with, and the matter had to be settled once and for all. Albert Spalding, an ex-player, the man who led that world tour in 1889, and who was now the owner of a large sporting-goods firm, was the loudest of the no-rounders crowd. He called for the appointment of a committee of trustworthy souls who would 'search anywhere that is possible and thus learn the real facts concerning the origin and development of the game'.

The committee of seven men included two United States Senators and its chairman was Abraham Mills, of Delmonico's fame. The workings of the committee were a classic example of something that has become much more familiar since that time: the 'fact-finding' group that conveniently ignores any facts that do not coincide with a previously decided conclusion. Mr Mills, who seems to have done all the work, collected evidence for three years, and issued his report in 1907. Baseball, said the report, had originated in the United States. To be specific, in 1839, when it was devised by one General Abner Doubleday at Cooperstown in New York State – on a cow pasture.

This was news to everyone, but as it was more or less what everyone wanted to hear, not many questions were asked. The source of this new and somewhat surprising history was a man already advanced into his dotage, Abner Graves, who had been an old army buddy of General Doubleday's. Graves was claiming to remember, in some detail, events that had taken place sixty-eight years earlier. And Chairman Mills was believing him. Yes, said Graves, the boys at school in Cooperstown had played a chaotic sort of ballgame called Town Ball, which was really an awful mess with dozens of players on each side and everyone bumping into each other and injuring themselves all the time. Then came Doubleday. Chairman Mills fell into the spirit of the thing, saying that he quite understood how, faced with all this disorder, 'the orderly mind of the embryo West Pointer would devise a scheme for limiting the contestants on each side and allotting them to field positions each with a certain amount of territory'. Graves conjured up a stirring picture of the future General Doubleday striding about the cow pasture, deciding exactly where the bases should be, and the distance between them.*

Nobody, apparently, felt obliged to point out that Doubleday also happened to have been a friend of Mr Mills, or to ask why, that being so, this story had not been mentioned before.

The natives were not in an inquisitive mood, and the saga of Abner Doubleday and his cow pasture went into the history books. There was really only one thing wrong with it, and that was that not one single word of it was true. Not one single word. It was not for over thirty years that the light of truth poked its way into the dark depths of the Doubleday legend, and it all happened at a most inconvenient moment. For if baseball had been invented in 1839, then it was one hundred years old in 1939, and that definitely called for a celebration of some sort. The plan evolved to build a baseball 'Hall of Fame' (at Cooperstown of course) and to dedicate it before an assembly of all the famous names in the sport.

Now Cooperstown was not exactly the sort of place that anybody would be likely to visit without a reason, or even to pass through. It was well off the beaten track, a small pretty little village with one minor claim to fame as the birthplace of James Fenimore Cooper, author of the Leatherstocking tales (they included *The Last of the Mohicans*) and perhaps the first truly American novelist. Here was a fine chance to add another piece of Americana to the local scene – and what village would not welcome the chance to become the officially recognized birthplace of something so essentially American as baseball?

So the good Cooperstownians discovered where Doubleday's original cow pasture had been, leased it, and called it Doubleday Field. In 1935 it was reported that a descendant of Abner Graves had been rummaging about in an attic and had discovered an ancient ball that had certainly

---

* In as much as many have claimed that baseball has become a religion, one may wonder whether there is not something in the air in upstate New York that encourages religious visions. Modern spiritualism started at Hydesville, forty miles east of Cooperstown, with the discoveries of the Fox sisters. Forty miles to the north-west is Oneida where the Oneida Community, a religious society of perfectionists, was established in 1848. And it was at Palmyra, a mere 120 miles away, that the Mormon religion was born when Joseph Smith had his vision in 1827.

belonged to old Abner himself. From this came the questionable proposition that it had therefore almost certainly been touched by Abner
Doubleday. The first relic of the religion of baseball had been unearthed,
and as it looked likely that others would follow, what was needed was a
shrine where the faithful could come and view the sacred objects. The
Baseball Museum was born – in Cooperstown, naturally – and the relics
began to flow in. By 1937 Cooperstown was already well established as
the centre of baseball history, and the New York State legislature saw
nothing wrong in appropriating $10,000 for the 1939 centennial cele-
bration. The United States Government gave the idea federal support
by authorizing the issue of a special commemorative stamp.

It was into the middle of these preparations that Robert Henderson
interjected his scholarly voice. A librarian at the New York Public
Library, he had been for years delving into the background of baseball.
He had found all sorts of evidence proving that baseball had existed well
before the arrival of Abner Doubleday and his cow pasture. In *Northanger Abbey*, for instance, we have Jane Austen describing her heroine
in these terms:

> ... and it was not very wonderful that Catherine, who had by nature
> nothing heroic about her, should prefer cricket, baseball, riding on horse-
> back, and running about the country at the age of fourteen, to books ...

That was written in 1798. Fifty years earlier, in the *Letters* of Mary
Lepell, Lady Hervey, there is this:

> The prince's family is an example of cheerful and innocent amusement
> ... they divert themselves at baseball, a play all who have, or have been,
> schoolboys, are well acquainted with.

Well, that was a little better, at least it suggested that baseball was for
boys, not fourteen-year-old girls. The earliest reference of all turned up
in something called *A Little Pretty Pocket Book*, published in London in
1744. This was a sports alphabet, and letter 'B' was represented by
Base-ball. The book was published in several American cities later in the
eighteenth century. One can, admittedly, see why the promoters of baseball as the Great American Sport would not wish to know about something called *A Little Pretty Pocket Book*.

The demolition of the Mills committee was complete. Clearly, baseball
was descended from an English game that seemed to vary slightly in
name and form according to which part of England it was played in.
Henderson pointed out that the rules for rounders had been published

in England in 1829 in *The Boys' Own Book*. In 1834 *The Book of Sports* was published in Boston, and the publisher copied the rounders rules, but changed the heading to 'Base, or Goal Ball', saying that these were the names under which rounders was played in the United States.

It should be emphasized that General Abner Doubleday really suffered no loss of prestige in all this. He had died quite unaware of what he was supposed to have done. There is actually no evidence that he ever did go to school in Cooperstown. If he did, and if he was there in 1839, as the legend requires, he must have been absent without leave from West Point Military Academy where he had matriculated the previous autumn.

By 1939 though the legend was too firmly entrenched to be totally erased from the public mind. This was particularly true of the Cooperstown associations. There was Doubleday Field, and the Baseball Museum, and now, coming up any moment, the grand centennial celebration of an event that never happened. To be scrupulously honest about it would require that the Museum be moved somewhere else, that Doubleday Field, now a splendidly turfed arena complete with covered stands, should be returned to the lowly and totally unimportant meadow that it used to be, and that the centennial spree and the plans for building the Hall of Fame be called off. But this was too much to ask. Had not Franklin Roosevelt himself put his blessing on the celebrations, saying: 'We should all be grateful to Abner Doubleday. Little did he or the group that was with him at Cooperstown, N.Y., in 1839 realize the boon they were giving the nation in devising baseball.' The only thing to do was to go ahead regardless and to keep as quiet as possible about the legend.

So the baseball Hall of Fame was built in Cooperstown, and the celebrations went on as planned. A man, an event and a site were solemnly honoured when it was known that not one of them had any right to such honour. But then again, there would have been a Hall of Fame somewhere, so why not Cooperstown?

The invention of Abner Doubleday as the inventor of baseball had quite naturally meant obscurity for the true originator, but Henderson's research and the probings of journalists unearthed him and have pretty well settled matters.* The responsibility for baseball belongs to

* But not completely. In 1952 the Americans were once again informed that baseball was of foreign origin – this time by, of all people, the Russians. 'It is well known', said the Russian magazine *Smena*, 'that in Russian villages they played *lapta*, of which beizbol is an imitation. It was played in Russian villages

Alexander Joy Cartwright Jr, a bank teller of New York City. In 1845 he and some friends formed the first baseball club, though what they were playing was a still rather inchoate sport called townball. Cartwright applied his bank-teller's mind to all the random movement and organized it into a meaningful pattern. He turned up at the grounds one morning with a diagram to explain his innovations and, hey presto – baseball. Only nine men to a side, said Cartwright, instead of any old number, they must bat in a set order, and when three of them were out the whole side was out. The bases were arranged in a diamond pattern (actually a square set on one corner) and the distance between each base was to be ninety feet. This was the stroke of genius that stamps the great inventors. The bases still are today ninety feet apart – because that distance has proved to be almost clinically perfect. If it were any shorter, it would be too easy for the batter to reach base, if it were any longer it would be too easy for the fielding side to stop him reaching base.

Cartwright's club was called the New York Knickerbockers* and while it was ostensibly centred around baseball, the tone was set by the elaborate social occasions that followed the games – the dinners and dances and banquets.

The sport was American baseball, but the atmosphere was decidedly English cricket. The idea was to reserve the sport for the right people, to keep out the lower classes. Membership was limited to forty people, mostly professional men. The way they played baseball would make them the laughing-stock of any modern team – but English village-green cricketers would feel at home in their company. The Knickerbockers had strict rules about swearing and arguing with the umpire (you were fined if you did), and they wore straw hats. When the game was over, both teams went to some nearby hall where they toasted and made speeches and sang songs about what jolly good sports they all were.

The success of the Knickerbockers led to the formation of more clubs, all similarly organized, and all playing according to Cartwright's rules – the New York Game, as it was now called. They played each other and entertained each other, but their little Bastille of gentlemanly

---

when the United States was not even marked on the maps.' The Americans had taken *lapta* and turned it into baseball, which was a 'beastly battle, a bloody fight with mayhem and murder'.

* Which has nothing to do with their dress. When Washington Irving wrote his *History of New York* in 1809, he published it under the fictitious name of Diedrich Knickerbocker; the word came to mean, simply, a New Yorker. The present New York professional basketball team is the New York Knickerbockers.

conviviality was about to be stormed. Increasingly, the dreaded lower orders were attending the games, enjoying them no doubt, but apparently getting most of their pleasure by betting on the result, and making a good deal of uncouth noise about it.

Obviously, this had to be stopped. The Barbarians were at the gates – and that provided a clue for the solution. For there were no gates at the time. The thing to do was to enclose the baseball grounds and charge for admission. And so the amateurs unwittingly pulled the rug out from under themselves. For the admission charge did not reduce the crowds, but merely proved that large numbers of people, including the undesirable working men, would pay to see a baseball game. There was money to be made. The businessmen and the promoters and the hustlers moved in and baseball, barely twenty years old, surrendered without a fight to the invasion of professionalism.

In his book *The Emergence of Modern America 1865-1878*, the historian Allan Nevins has a frontispiece containing illustrations of seven key events of the era – things like steel converters, transcontinental railroads, the negro vote – and the Cincinnati Red Stockings.* Formed in 1869, the Reds were baseball's first avowedly professional team. Until they came along, professionalism had been conducted *sub rosa*, often by giving players absurdly large salaries for absurdly menial jobs, which they never performed anyway.† The team was put together by Harry Wright, an Englishman who had gone to Cincinnati to coach cricket in 1865, and it included his younger brother George Wright, another ex-cricketer. They went off on an extensive tour of the northeastern United States, beating everyone by lopsided scores, but always attracting large crowds, sometimes as many as 10,000.

Although they are remembered as baseball's first professional team, the Red Stockings bore little resemblance to the many professional teams that were quickly formed to ape their success. Harry Wright was a member of the old school, an ex-Knickerbocker in fact, and in signing his players he was careful to make sure that they were 'gentlemanly and temperate at all times'. The Red Stockings even continued the old amateur tradition of ballad singing:

> We are a band of baseball players
> From Cincinnati City,

---

* Nevins, Allan, *The Emergence of Modern America 1865–1878*, Macmillan, New York, 1959.
† A practice not unknown in modern tennis.

> We come to toss the ball around
>   And sing to you our ditty;
> And if you listen to the song
>   We are about to sing,
> We'll tell you all about baseball
>   And make the welkin ring.

The Red Stockings broke up in 1870 and the image of a professional baseball player as a temperate, ballad-singing gentleman vanished forever. The new professional was quite different, and he confirmed all the fears of the amateurs: he drunk like a fish, swore like a trooper, and his manners were anything but gentlemanly. In addition, he was likely to be a gambler. That was the players; and the owners of the clubs were not much better.

But men like that do not arise from a society devoted to honesty and fairplay. The professional baseball player was merely a tiny reflection of America at the end of the nineteenth century, during what Mark Twain called the Gilded Age. The golden surface was being devoutly chronicled by Horatio Alger – but underneath it there was something rotten. In the White House was the civil war hero Ulysses Grant, surrounded by knaves and crooks, refusing to believe that anything was wrong. Below him swirled a mirky maelstrom of corruption, embezzlement, fraud, bribery, swindles and other staples of nineteenth-century capitalism. The scandals even reached up to involve Vice-President Colfax, putting an end to his political life. A high point of sorts was the fight that Jay Gould and Jim Fisk had with Cornelius Vanderbilt over control of the Erie Rail Road, an unseemly gutter brawl that involved specious stock issues and bribed politicians and judges. Out west, in Missouri and Kansas and Kentucky, Jesse James and dozens of others were playing their own version of the get-rich-quick game.

In New York City, the infamous Boss Tweed was building his organization that was destined to milk some $100 million from the citizens. And it was Tweed who controlled one of the most important teams of the age, the New York Mutuals. In upstate New York the Troy Haymakers were owned by John Morrissey, a notorious gambler who used the team 'like loaded dice', instructing them to lose whenever he had money on the opposition.

The ballplayers were of a kind with the times, and the order of the day was that you had to peculate to accumulate. Who cared about laws and regulations and rules when a few dollars (or a few hundred, or even a few thousand) placed in the right hands cleared the path for almost any sort of chicanery? Yet, there was a difference between playing baseball and manipulating the stock market: baseball had to be played out there, in front of everybody, where the people paying their money could see what was going on. The patrons took a look and did not have much difficulty deciding that most of the games were fixed. Tales from the West Coast told of groups of gamblers shooting off their revolvers just as fielders were about to make catches. The open drunkenness of many players was a little difficult to hide, too, though *Baseball Magazine* did not think that that had much effect on the results: 'As every team was composed of drunks, they were evenly matched in this regard.'

The first professional league, the Players' League, was formed in 1871, and appropriately enough it was born at a meeting of owners in a drinking saloon. It lasted only four seasons, collapsing in 1875, undermined by its own corruption. A new league, the National League, was quickly formed, with the object of saving the sport, or at least of proving that it could be made profitable. The new owners knew that they were not going to get anywhere unless they cleaned things up, and they tried to present an image, if not of purity, then certainly of respectability. They ruled out playing on Sundays, banned drinking at the games, and clamped down on gambling. There was to be no shouting of odds and betting at the games – something that had been an intrinsic part of professional baseball up until that time – and any player known to be a gambler would be given the old heave-ho. It happened to four Louisville players who were observed to be wearing diamond stickpins and rings that looked somewhat above their station; they admitted they had been taking bribes to throw games, and out they went, never to return.

The National League is alive and well today, nearly one hundred years on, but its infancy was a sorely troubled one. The fans found that this respectability thing was all right for a while, but it sure was dull. By 1882 the N.L. was beginning to show signs of being fossilized in its own righteousness, and when a group of businessmen got together (in a saloon in Pittsburgh) and announced they were about to form a rival league, the N.L. pooh-poohed such upstart nonsense as a silly dream.

The new league called itself the American Association and had six clubs. It also had quite a few players that it had lured away from the N.L., and it had the idea that fans should be entertained as well as given baseball to look at. As it happened, three of the A.A. club owners were in the liquor business, so there was never any question of banning drinking at their games. The admission price was set at 25 cents, half what the N.L. was asking.

The owner of the A.A.'s St Louis Browns was the leader in the drive to make baseball more entertaining. His name was Chris von der Ahe, and he became interested in baseball when he found that baseball fans were among the best customers at his saloon. With his loud clothes, top hat, red nose and thick German accent, von der Ahe appeared to have stepped straight out of a Bavarian beer hall, but his promotional flair was American all the way, pure P. T. Barnum. In his ballpark he had girls playing trumpets, musical shows, a race track, and a beer garden. The money he took at the gate was ceremoniously wheeled to the bank in a wheelbarrow, with von der Ahe marching proudly behind it. He was rather big on marching, and when his team played away from home, he would lead them in a parade through the streets from the station to the stadium. He called himself 'der Poss Bresident' of the Browns, and proclaimed that 'Nothing is too goot for my poys!'. His ignorance of baseball was legendary,* but he built the Browns into the strongest team in the country. Poor von der Ahe eventually got himself into all sorts of financial trouble, and was arrested – no doubt as he would have wished it – right in the middle of one of his parades.

But by then von der Ahe and his fellow owners of the 'beer and whisky circuit' (as the N.L. contemptuously dubbed it) had made their point. They had not been forced out of business, the standard of their play was at least as good as the N.L.'s, and they often drew more people. The N.L. was forced to acknowledge that its monopoly had been broken. As a broken monopoly is no monopoly at all, the answer was to let the A.A. in on the act. The two leagues signed an agreement in 1883, the main point of which was to spread the N.L.'s reserve clause to the A.A.

That was the way things were done at the end of the nineteenth century. The employers held all the tricks, and the workers had to put up with it. It was seen as part of the gospel of the freedom of the individual. But, as Theodore Roosevelt observed, that freedom had come to mean 'perfect freedom for the strong to wrong the weak', and a revolt was brewing. During the 1880s labour unions began to sprout as the weak found their voice, and the baseball players formed a union, of sorts. The Brotherhood of Professional Base Ball Players compromised its own existence right from the start. Not content with working for the abolition

---

* His non-baseball ignorance was quite formidable, too. He once stood up at a meeting of the A.A. owners and complained that, as a result of last season's foolish scheduling, his team had had twenty-four games rained out, and would they see to it that in future other teams got their fair share of rainy days.

of the reserve clause and for better wages, it decided to go into business and to operate its own league.

At a time when any sort of union organization was apt to be regarded as unpatriotic, the idea of baseball players complaining about their lot caused widespread elevation of blood pressures. The National League, finding that most of its best players were joining the new league, declared war on the Brotherhood which, it said, 'had no moral foundation and must perish'. The Press was generally hostile, ridiculing the players' contention that they were underpaid; one newspaper published an account of a meeting attended by delegates in fur-lined overcoats, silk hats, gold-topped canes and diamond rings, commenting slyly: 'Nor is it a meeting of the Vanderbilts, Goulds, etc. It is but a gathering of the Brotherhood.'

But the Brotherhood had the upper hand – they had filched all the best players, both from the National League and the American Association. When the 1890 season started, there were thus three major leagues operating, and it became spectacularly clear in next to no time that this was at least one too many. Everybody lost money. At the end of the season all three leagues were on the verge of financial collapse. When it came to armistice talks, the Brotherhood were no match for the wily men of the N.L. Both sides were on their last legs, but the N.L. managed to hide their plight. The Brotherhood surrendered without a struggle after only one season of play; the reserve clause, it seemed, had triumphed. But not immediately. The collapse of the Brotherhood league meant that all their players – very much the cream of the crop – were suddenly released. At the sight of all this talent, the N.L. and the A.A. quite forgot about their reserve clause agreement as they fell over each other trying to sign up the stars. Naturally it meant increased salaries, and it produced another disastrous season in 1891 which proved that even two leagues was too many. The N.L. and the A.A. decided on a merger. That was what they called it, though when the details were published it was seen that the N.L. had increased from eight to twelve clubs, and the A.A. had disappeared altogether. It was 1892 and things were back where they had been in 1875, with the National League in sole charge of professional baseball.

By this time the game truly merited the title of 'National Pastime'. 'Every city, every town, and every village, almost every crossroads has its one or more baseball teams,' said a magazine of the time. It was played everywhere, by all ages and all classes, and had, despite its tainted beginnings and the indecorous squabbles between the owners, gained enormously in prestige. That blue-ribbon gathering at Delmonico's proved the point.

But baseball itself should not take all the credit. There were other forces at work, the aspirations of a brash young nation, encouraged and astonished at its own sudden emergence as the No. 1 industrial power, determined to show the world that anything it could do, the United States could do better. Usually they could, but the nagging fear was that this was *all* the U.S.A. was good for, doing better what somebody else had already done. Where were the signs of true, native, American genius?

Enter baseball, complete with forged birth certificate, A. Doubleday, father, bundled unceremoniously to the centre of the stage, and hailed as the very heart and mind of America.

'I see great things in baseball. It's our game, the American game. It will take our people out-of-doors, fill them with oxygen, give them a larger physical stoicism. Tend to relieve us from being a nervous dyspeptic set. Repair these losses and be a blessing to us'. These are not the words of a club owner trying to sell tickets, they are those of a man who was himself one of the earliest examples of true, native, American genius – Walt Whitman. Even if he did make baseball sound like a patent medicine, Whitman sensed that America needed an American game, a showcase that reflected something of the bursting energy that had conquered a continent and built a nation.

The furore over the haughty way in which the English dismissed baseball as rounders (making it yet another something that somebody else had done before) becomes understandable. When Abraham Mills had declared that the American heredity of baseball had been established 'by patriotism and research', he was understating it. Patriotism *demanded* American ancestry for the sport. Mills went on to call baseball 'our national, manly sport'. So it was American, and it was manly, and the implication of that was that if you did not like it you were a traitorous milksop.*

But high-flown talk of patriotism and virility was not necessary to prove that the atmosphere of baseball – whatever its ancestry may have been – was by now pure Yankee. The early gentility of the Knickerbockers had vanished forever. In the 1890s you could find the new atmosphere at any game involving the Baltimore Orioles, a team that

---

* Some 150 years earlier, in 1744, the English poet James Love had written: '*Hail, cricket! Glorious, manly, British Game!*' As the Americans regarded cricket as a namby-pamby pastime played by Little Lord Fauntleroys, this conclusively proved that they were more manly than the British.

played baseball as though it was a form of guerilla warfare. Their specialities were intimidation and cheating. An umpire who gave decisions against the Orioles found the entire team surrounding him, shouting, cursing, and probably manhandling him. Opposing teams were subjected to a constant stream of invective, and if any of them should get on base, they were likely to be bumped or tripped – always when the umpire was not looking, of course. If they survived and made it as far as third base, there was the roughest character of the lot, John McGraw, waiting to grab them by the belt and delay their departure for home plate by a crucial second or two. The trick was exposed by a runner who loosened his belt and took off, leaving it hanging in McGraw's hand. When the Orioles themselves got on base, they ran like madmen, using their spiked shoes freely on opposing feet and shins; and they were experts at taking the short way round the bases, cutting the corners and not touching second or third base – illegal, of course, but then you only did it when the umpires could not see what was going on. The Orioles, said one writer, 'filled the atmosphere with tobacco juice, oaths, and flying fists', while an umpire claimed that they 'breakfasted on gunpowder and warm blood'. But that was only half the story, for they also played brilliant baseball. Their aggressiveness was matched by their intelligence, and they produced an almost scientific approach to the game. One of the key men in this thinking-man's baseball was Wee Willie Keeler, who had the knack of hitting the ball just exactly where the fielders could not get to it. He achieved baseball immortality with his explanation of how he did it: 'Keep your eye clear, and hit 'em where they ain't.' The scientific style was also practised by the Boston team – the Beaneaters they were called – and between them these two clubs dominated the National League throughout the 1890s.

Baseball entered the twentieth century with the National League holding uneasily on to its monopoly. In 1890 Congress had passed the Sherman Anti-Trust Act, aimed specifically at 'restraint of trade' by business monopolies, and the N.L. had reason to worry, for it had been acting as monopolies will. One of the first things it did after swallowing the American Association was to cut players' salaries by as much as 40 per cent, and to reduce the number of players on each club. It was also permitting some extremely dubious practices by the owners, such as allowing the Robison brothers to own both the Cleveland and the St Louis clubs, and letting Ned Hanlon be the manager of the Brooklyn team while he was also President of the Baltimore Orioles.

But the N.L. was in a bind over enforcing discipline. An aggrieved owner or player had only to threaten to take the matter to court, and the league would back down. In 1890 the number of clubs had been cut from twelve to eight and it seemed pretty clear that the N.L. was in trouble.

Help of a sort arrived in 1901. A rival calling itself the American League was launched. It meant unwelcome competition (the cycle of player-poaching and increased salaries was about to break out all over again), but it did put an end to the monopoly problem.

The origin of the A.L. at least indicated that baseball was beginning to acquire some class. Unlike the original league of 1871 and the American Association of 1882, it was not born in a common saloon, but rather a private drinking club in Cincinnati. Its chief mover was Byron Bancroft Johnson, an ex-sportswriter, and the son of a college professor.

The reaction of the N.L. to the new league was all according to the script: they opposed it, called it names, fought it, and tried to undermine it. This time it was not so easy, for the N.L. owners were without a strong leader, continually at odds with each other, and in the middle of another bid by the players to form a union. The American League had no trouble signing up large numbers of the N.L.'s discontented players, and by 1902 it was drawing over 2 million spectators to its games, compared to the National's 1·7 million.

One thing that the fans found to their liking in the American League was the increased discipline on the field. Johnson made it clear that his umpires were to have the last word in every dispute, and that he would uphold their decisions. This sort of power was something quite new for umpires who, until that time, had been universally regarded by fans, players and owners alike as incorrigible rogues to be cursed, abused or set upon, as the occasion demanded. Right from its beginnings, arguing with the umpire had been a hallmark of professional baseball. As crowds grew larger and games became more important, the sheer weight of abuse that the umpires had to put up with made it quite remarkable that anyone at all could be found to do the job. In fact, most of the applicants were old ball-players for whom umpiring was the only thing left to do. They were not men of notable probity and the verdict of the *Chicago Tribune* – 'The average league umpire is a worthless loafer' – was not an unduly harsh one. Another paper thought they ranged from 'indifferent to rotten', but admitted that they were probably 'impartially rotten'. No one could have been really surprised at the low calibre, because the job, as all could see, was a perilous one, and the pay was derisory. The spectacle of the game official being driven off in a police van pursued by angry fans is not an innovation of twentieth-century soccer – it happened in nineteenth-century baseball first.*

Johnson put an end to the umpiring dark ages, but he had to fight to do it and it cost him one of his best managers. The American League's Baltimore club was managed by John McGraw (he who used to hold on to belts at third base) who, as one of the original Orioles, believed that the main function of an umpire was to be vilified. He did not see anything particularly wrong when one of his pitchers spat in an umpire's face, but Johnson did, and he suspended the player. McGraw got tired of Johnson's concern for umpires after a couple of years, and switched to the rival National League.

After the 1902 season, the National League had had enough, and they sought peace. They had in mind the sort of merger that had allowed them to swallow the old American Association. But Ban Johnson would have none of that. He insisted that the A.L. be left to operate as a separate league; but the leagues decided to live in peace. They worked out which should have teams in which cities and, most important, they agreed on a common reserve clause.

Baseball started the 1903 season with two eight-team leagues, taking in the following cities:

National League	American League
Boston	Boston
Brooklyn	Chicago
Chicago	Cleveland
Cincinnati	Detroit
New York	New York
Philadelphia	Philadelphia
Pittsburgh	St Louis
St Louis	Washington

Professional baseball was still, as it had always been, very much a northeastern affair, and it was to remain that way for the next fifty years. St Louis was as far south and also as far west as it went.

The 'two league' arrangement (which was, in effect, one league with two branches) proved to be the stable one that baseball had been looking

---

* A ditty of 1886 began:

      Mother, may I slug the umpire,
      May I slug him right away?
      So he cannot be here, mother,
      When the clubs begin to play?

for. It survives today, with an increased number of teams (twelve in each league) that now stretch all the way out to San Diego and down to Houston and Atlanta.

One of the reasons for the success of this arrangement was that it gave birth to the greatest of American sports events, the annual World Series. The 1903 season had left the nation with two champions, Boston of the A.L. and Pittsburgh of the N.L., and nobody found that a very satisfactory state of affairs. One of them had to be more champion than the other, and the way to find out was to have them play each other. A series of nine games was arranged for the Baseball Championship of the World, extravagant wording but who could deny that the winner was the best baseball team in the world? The Boston Pilgrims (also known as the Puritans, or the Somersets) won the first World Series, beating Pittsburgh by five games to three.

In 1904, an example of self-destructive bloody-mindedness of the sort that was by now almost traditional in baseball threatened to kill at birth the most popular event the sport had yet discovered. The N.L. was won by the New York Giants who let it be known that they would not be found dead on the same field as any of those Johnny-come-latelys from the A.L. One of the men behind this move was the abrasive John McGraw, now manager of the Giants, and an implacable enemy of Ban Johnson. The decision, however, was one of the few McGraw ever made that the New York fans did not agree with. They wanted the World Series to be played, so in 1905, when the Giants repeated as N.L. champions, they met the A.L.'s Philadelphia Athletics, and beat them four games to one. The World Series has been played at the end of every season since then, never missing a year, not even during two World Wars.

The opposing managers of that 1904 Series were the two men who were to dominate baseball in the following years, two men who could hardly have been less alike: the rumbustious McGraw of the Giants, and the quiet, thoughtful Connie Mack of the Philadelphia Athletics. Nicknamed 'Little Napoleon', McGraw ran his club like a tyrant, making all the decisions himself, treating his players like children, cowing them into instant obedience. There was even supposed to be a young player who, when asked by a reporter if he was married, replied apprehensively: 'You'd better ask Mr McGraw.' He behaved as though he hated everyone, and seemed to get a great kick out of the fact that in turn he was roundly loathed throughout baseballdom – except by the New York Giant fans, for he knew how to produce a winning team. Between 1904 and 1924 the Giants won the National League ten times under the driving McGraw who, when he was not throwing baseballs at the umpire, was usually threatening to take on everyone in the ballpark. It was all part of his idea to keep his players as mean and aggressive as possible, like the way he yelled 'Wipe those damned smiles off your faces!' at them during games. McGraw was the prototype of the 'winning is everything' coach, a man to whom the sport had ceased to mean anything unless it could be measured in victories: 'In playing or managing, the game of ball is only fun for me when I'm out in front and winning. I don't care a bag of peanuts for the rest of the game.'

McGraw was a manager for thirty years, which was nearly a record. The man who managed longer was Connie Mack, who took over the Philadelphia Athletics in 1901 and did not retire until 1950. His real name was Cornelius McGillicuddy, but the story was that during his playing days they never could fit it into the scorebooks, so he became Connie Mack. He always called his players 'Mr', rarely shouted at an umpire, and never went out on to the field. While every other manager wore the same uniform as the players, Mack dressed in civvies – suit, high white collar, and a straw hat. He treated his players with great patience, and tried to sign men with a college education. Ironically, one of his greatest stars was a player who had had almost no schooling at all, and whose wild antics on and off the field eventually snapped even Mack's patience. Rube Waddell was one of the fastest and the greatest left-handed pitchers in the history of baseball. He loved the game, but he also loved fire-engines (and once rushed off the field during a game to follow one in full flight), bar-tending (missing from another game he was found, fully aproned, behind a bar), and marching in parades dressed as a drum major. He toured with a melodrama called *The Stain of Guilt*, in which his part called for him to rough up the villain, something he did so successfully that they had to keep hiring new villains. He married several times, went to jail for non-support, wrestled alligators, climbed into a lion's cage and got bitten, and never had enough money. Mack eventually had to hire a fulltime keeper for him.

Waddell was only one of a whole group of superb pitchers during the first decade of the twentieth century. It was an era when pitching dominated the game yet, perversely, the greatest star of the period was a man who did just about everything on a baseball field except pitch. Ty Cobb, who many rate the greatest baseball player ever, hit the major leagues like a one-man cyclone in 1905. His style was perfected McGrawism, there was virtually nothing he would not do if it meant winning, being first. He hit safely more often than any other player ever had, which meant that he got on base more often. Once there, he was a nightmare to the fielding side, stealing bases with truculent ease, mercilessly spiking anyone foolhardy enough to get in his way. Cobb came from the South and they called him 'The Georgia Peach', but he left everyone wondering whatever happened to the image of gentlemanliness and chivalry that Southerners were supposed to project. He nearly throttled his room-mate who had, for once, occupied the bathroom before him. The room-mate could not understand what all the fuss was about, but Cobb thought that his credo, 'I just have to be first', amply justified physically assaulting a friend.

He was not a popular man, but nobody ever doubted his enormous talent, or his monastic devotion to the sport. His career records – for the number of hits, stolen bases, lifetime batting average – still stand. He was one of the best paid players of his time, and his investment in Coca-Cola, before anyone had ever heard of it, eventually made him a millionaire. Cobb ought to have been the perfect example of the American success story, but he was never a happy man. After his retirement, he stated that if he had to do it all over again, he would rather be a doctor.

Baseball prospered mightily before World War I. In 1902 the total paid attendance had been 3·5 million, and by 1911 it had risen to 6·5 million. There were some small areas that the owners were not happy with – something that had always bothered them, for instance, was the reluctance of fans to throw back balls that landed in the stands* – but by and large these were blissful times, and money was being made.

That was the cue for a lot of rich and envious heads to be turned in baseball's direction. A group of wealthy men, mostly industrialists, decided to form yet another new league, the Federal League, and another of baseball's recurrent trade wars was under way. The new men had plenty of cash, especially New Jersey oil-magnate Harry Sinclair,† and Robert Ward, who ran a chain of bakeries in Brooklyn that made Tip-

---

* Some clubs sent the police into the stands to reclaim the balls, but it was neither a popular nor a successful move. A club lost, perhaps, 500 balls in a season in this way. Today, it may be as many as fifty in a single game.

† The same Harry Sinclair who was involved in the Teapot Dome scandal, perhaps the most juicy of Warren Harding's scandal-ridden Presidency. Sinclair's company received drilling rights in what should have been a protected area, as a result of what looked suspiciously like the bribing of a government official. Sinclair was tried and acquitted, but went to jail anyway as he had hired detectives to tail members of the jury.

Top bread (and who therefore decided that the name of his team should be the Brooklyn Tip-Tops). What they lacked was a sense of timing.

Nineteen fifteen was just about the worst possible year to try and find out whether America was ready for another baseball league. There was talk that America would soon have to involve itself in the war raging in Europe, relations with Mexico were deteriorating, and new forms of entertainment like the automobile and the cinema were beginning to draw money away from baseball. The result was a season when only seven of the twenty-two clubs made a profit, and not a very good profit at that. The Federal League disappeared from the scene, though some of its leading operators, notably Mr Sinclair, got quite a handsome settlement from the N.L. and the A.L. for agreeing to go quietly. The fear of legal action was still haunting organized baseball.

When the war came in 1917, baseball was singularly ill-prepared to resist the army's demand for healthy young men. No lobbying had been done in Washington, so that while other entertainment-world people, like movie stars and opera singers, had been declared essential for the war effort and hence exempt from drafting, baseball players were classed as 'non-essential'.

It was a decided shock. The National Pastime, that always had American flags flying at the stadiums, that always started with the playing of the national anthem, that was more American than chewing-gum – how could this be non-essential? But there was now a higher form of patriotism than baseball in the air, and nobody paid any attention to the complaints of the owners. Baseball players were told to do essential work or be drafted. Luckily for the sport, World War I ended in 1918 and at a nice convenient time of the year giving time to get things back to normal for the 1919 season.

Whatever else it was, 1919 will not go down as a normal season. It looked normal enough at the time – the Cincinnati Reds won the National League and went on to beat the American League's Chicago White Sox in the World Series. The wave of post-war euphoria brought out huge crowds, and baseball was back as a profitable business. There was, though, a faint whiff of corruption discernible by those with sensitive noses. A newspaperman named Hugh Fullerton got a sniff of it, and by the time he'd finished investigating the stench was overwhelming. The 1919 World Series had been fixed by gamblers, who had bribed eight of the Chicago White Sox players to lose.*

* For a full discussion of the mechanics of the fix, see Chapter 9, page 189.

Baseball, which the owners liked to present to the public as a lady of undefiled virtue wrapped in the American flag, was suddenly naked, and she looked like a cheap whore. That was bad enough, but the tergiversations of the owners, as they tried to decide whether to expose the full extent of the scandal or to hush it up, made matters quite a bit worse than they need have been.

The *New York Times* said flatly that 'the men financially interested in the game are incompetent to run their own business' and it was a view that was widely shared. The owners faced a dilemma: either to continue business as usual, hoping that all would blow over, but facing probable catastrophe if it did not, or to appoint an independent 'strong man' to clean up the sport, hoping that public approval of such a move would, in the long run, outweigh any scandals he might uncover. While they argued, the pressure mounted to the point where there was no alternative: it would have to be a strong man.

The man they chose was a Federal Judge with a topographical name – Kenesaw Mountain Landis (the first part of his name came from a site in Georgia where his father had been wounded during the Civil War). Appointed a Federal Judge by Theodore Roosevelt, Landis had a reputation of being very much his own man, unafraid of big names and powerful people. In 1907 he had made John Rockefeller travel to Chicago to testify in a case involving his Standard Oil Company, and had then fined the company $29 million. Eleven years later he had before him the Socialist leader Victor Berger, guilty of sedition for impeding the war effort. Landis sentenced him to twenty years' imprisonment.*

Neither of these forthright decisions stood for very long. They were both overturned on appeal to superior courts, and here was an aspect of the new job that must have appealed to Landis. As Baseball Commissioner his decisions would be final, there would be no higher authority to go to. There was also the matter of salary. As a Federal Judge he was getting $7,500 a year. The baseball people were offering him $50,000. Judge Landis became the Commissioner of Baseball, the sport's strong man.

Landis is generally credited with having 'saved the national pastime', ruling with a firm hand until 1946. It is said that his tough decisions – he promptly banished the eight dishonest White Sox players (the Black Sox, as they came to be called) from baseball for life – and the aura of personal

---

* He also ordered the Kaiser to come to his court to answer for the sinking of the British ship *Lusitania* in 1915 which resulted in the deaths of 128 Americans. The Kaiser did not put in an appearance.

incorruptibility that he emitted rekindled public confidence in the sport.

Yet there is not really much evidence that the Black Sox scandal, however much it may have put the wind up the owners, caused fans to cover their eyes and stagger backwards from the stadiums. In fact attendance went up so sharply that in 1920 the American League alone drew five million people. Of course, this deluge could have been thanks to Landis and the new odour of sanctity. But there was something else in baseball in 1920. That something else was Babe Ruth, and he really *was* something else.

Back in 1909 President Taft had complained that the bunt* was being used too much in baseball. 'I believe they should hit it out,' he said, 'I love the game when there is plenty of slugging.' Babe Ruth was a man after Taft's own heart. No bunting for him – when he swung, he swung with everything he had. When he connected, which he did with exhilarating frequency, the ball travelled unheard-of distances. He revolutionized baseball with his prodigious slugging, and in the process he became the most lionized star in the history of American sport.

During World War II Japanese soldiers were genuinely shocked to hear of the crude profanities that the Americans heaped on Emperor Hirohito. The Emperor was a divine figure, not too far removed from God, his name to be mentioned only in subdued reverential tones. In retaliation, the Japanese picked out a suitably God-like American on whom to shower abuse: 'The Hell with Babe Ruth!' they shouted.†

This was 1942, and the Babe had been retired for seven years, yet to the Japanese – and probably to the rest of the world – he was still the most famous and the most loved of Americans. To insult Ruth was to pierce the heart of America.

Admittedly, it did not help the Japanese very much, but it was, for its time, quite a shrewd piece of psychological warfare. For Ruth was the embodiment of many of the values and dreams that Americans cherished. He had come up the hard way. He had reached the top without special training, without a college education; he was a graduate of 'the school of hard knocks'. He was a big man, with big appetites. He was irreverent

---

* To bunt the ball is to push it gently out in front of home plate – the bat is hardly swung at all. A fast runner can often beat out a bunt, i.e., get safely to first base before a fielder can get to the ball, pick it up and throw it to the first baseman.

† So it is said. One suspects that, like some other famous battle cries, the phrase has been bowdlerized for civilian consumption.

and scornful of authority. He liked kids. And he made a lot of money.

Of German descent, Ruth was born in Baltimore in 1895. His father worked as a barman and Ruth, like baseball itself, spent much of his infancy in an atmosphere of boozing, gambling and swearing. At the age of seven his parents put him into St Mary's Industrial School for Boys where he stayed, on and off, for the next twelve years. On and off, because his parents could never quite make up their minds whether they wanted him or not. Five times they took him out of St Mary's and five times they sent him back. When he left for the last time, in 1912, it was to join a professional baseball team. As he was under twenty-one, the team's manager had to become his legal guardian before he could leave. But it was not Ruth's hitting that was attracting attention, it was his pitching. That same year, Ruth went straight into the major leagues with the Boston Red Sox – as a left-handed pitcher, and a very good one. Every so often he would come to bat and hit the ball further than anyone remembered seeing it hit before. A revolution was under way, but it took a little while for the meaning of Ruth's tremendous drives to sink in. By 1919 it was clear to the Boston manager that, even though Ruth was one of the best pitchers in baseball, he was even more valuable as a hitter. Babe's pitching days were over. He was turned into an outfielder, and as such he could play in every game (a pitcher needs to rest his pitching arm and can play only about one game in four).

In 1919 Babe hit twenty-nine home runs, a new record for a season; the old one had been twenty-seven, set back in 1884. As his fame spread, Ruth became very much aware of his own value. He hired a business manager, and demanded a $20,000 salary for the 1920 season. This was more than the Boston club could pay, and Ruth was transferred to the New York Yankees for $100,000. The Yankees were not the slightest bit interested in Ruth's pitching. They wanted him to hit the ball out of sight as often as possible, and he obliged. In his first season he nearly doubled his old record; fifty-four homers he hit, and everywhere the talk was about the Babe, the Sultan of Swat, the Bambino. The crowds flocked to see him, to see him swing exuberantly into the ball – even when he missed, the sheer power of his swing had the crowd gasping. The New York Yankees grew richer and richer, rich enough to build a massive new stadium. It cost them over $2 million and they called it Yankee Stadium, but to the journalists it was The House that Ruth Built.

Throughout the twenties and on into the thirties Ruth went on hitting home runs, and America rejoiced to have such a swashbuckling hero.

6 Babe Ruth: the man whose mighty left-handed hitting and irreverent
life-style buoyed Americans during the Depression years of the 1920s.

The man was irrepressible. He drove his huge car like a maniac and he gave talks on road safety. He drank and ate enough for two men, ignored training rules and curfews, yet he played baseball better than anyone else around. The all-American hero's favourite foods were the all-American hot-dogs and soda-pop, and they went down in heroic amounts. One veteran player watched with horrified fascination as, just before a game, Ruth rapidly consumed six hot dogs and six bottles of pop, belched loudly and yelled 'Let's go!'.

In his prime as a player, Ruth looked anything but the part. He could have been Humpty Dumpty in a Christmas pantomime, with legs incongruously insufficient for his huge pop-bellied body. After each massive clout for a home run, he would make his way around the bases with delicate little tippy-toe steps, almost as though his knees were strapped together (and, said Ty Cobb, complaining of gas pains and bellyache all the way).

With a fat cigar sticking out of his squashed, almost two-dimensional face, Ruth greeted all and sundry with 'Hiya Kid!', or maybe 'Hiya Pop!'. He never could remember names anyway, and even the President's escaped him – 'Hiya Prez!' was the best he could do when they introduced him to Coolidge. The Supreme Allied Commander in World War I, Marshall Foch, was greeted with, 'Hey, Gen, they tell me you were in the war?'. Ruth, it seemed, could get away with anything, while Americans chuckled and muttered in envious admiration, 'That Babe...'

In 1925 Humpty Dumpty had his great fall. Ruth's long-suffering stomach struck back, and he was rushed to hospital with a 'big belly-ache' and operated on for an intestinal abscess. The Yankees, who were paying Ruth a staggering $52,000 that year, were not amused. Ruth missed the first two months of the season, and when he did return, continued to flout all the club's training regulations. When the manager fined him $5,000 (a record fine, of course) and suspended him, Ruth could hardly believe his ears. He took the matter to the club owner, and threatened to go to Commissioner Landis. This time he was on his own. Nobody supported him, and he was going to have to toe the line like... well, like an ordinary baseball player. The big-hearted Babe turned contrite. He paid the fine, and they lifted the suspension after only nine days.

But Babe was not an ordinary baseball player, not by a country mile he wasn't. Oh, they could put him on a special diet for a while, and they could pay him his enormous salary in specially arranged instalments so that he would not go straight out and blow the lot, they could do things like that. But they were not going to tame the Babe. The Babe would

succeed, not because of the discipline, but despite it. His baseball talent
was raw and natural. Like Don Bradman he came untaught and un-
coached and he was as good as the best right from the start. The top of
the ladder was reached in 1927. That was the year the Babe hit sixty
home runs. *Six-tee*. In 1876 the sum total of homers for all eight clubs
had been forty. Ruth had set baseball on its ear. The crowds were larger
than ever and now a whole crop of muscular hitters was swinging from
the heels. The delicate science of 'hitting 'em where they ain't' was out –
unless it meant hitting 'em out of the park.

As the records fell, the legend grew. Babe the folk hero could do no
wrong. So what if he called Commissioner Landis 'a long-haired goat',
and his manager 'a miserable shrimp' and fought with umpires? Didn't
he also love children, wasn't he forever signing autographs and visiting
boys in orphanages? And as his salary climbed up and up the dreams of
America soared with it. There *was* limitless prosperity and everyone
could live happily everafter. Babe Ruth proved it. When he demanded a
salary of $80,000 he was told, why, that was more than President Hoover
was making. 'So what?' said Ruth, 'I had a better year than he did.'

Putting Ruth live on the radio was asking for trouble. They did, and
they got it. Carefully rehearsed to refer to 'The Duke of Wellington's
historic remark that the Battle of Waterloo was won on the playing fields
of Eton', Ruth spouted: 'As Duke Ellington once said, the Battle of
Waterloo was won on the playing fields of Elkton.' He later explained:
'About that Wellington guy I wouldn't know. Ellington, yes. As for that
Eton business – well, I married my first wife in Elkton, and I always
hated the goddam place. It musta stuck.'

Ruth retired in 1935. He wanted desperately to stay in baseball, as a
manager or, for a start, as a coach. But baseball did not want him. He
had stopped hitting homers, so there was no longer any reason to put up
with his indiscipline and his excesses. For thirteen years Ruth wandered
around the outskirts of baseball, trying to get back to the bigtime of the
sport that owed him so much. It ought to have been an unbearable weight
on baseball's conscience, but by now the sport, thanks largely to Ruth,
was flourishing nicely, and it did not want to hear about things like that.

Babe Ruth died in 1948 of throat cancer. Baseball may have spurned
him, but the kids he had always loved did not. Groups of boys gathered
outside the hospital. Some of them even brought roses, a risky gesture
in the tough world of boyhood, but for the Babe they did it.

Riding along on Ruth's home runs, the New York Yankees had become
the most powerful club in baseball, and they kept right on winning after

his retirement. It was a case of The King is Dead, Long Live the King, for Ruth had barely departed when the Yankees came up with another superstar. In 1936 they signed young Joe Di Maggio who, though he might not hit the ball as far as Ruth, hit it nearly as often, and did everything with a style and grace not usually associated with baseball.*

While Ruth was working his one-man revolution on baseball, there were other factors bringing about changes in the game. Radio broadcasting had begun in the 1920s (one of the very first regular programmes had been a reading of baseball scores over a Pittsburgh station in 1920) and by 1923 the baseball owners had discovered it as a new source of income. They were selling broadcasting rights to their games, despite vehement protests from newspaper writers who said the practice would kill the circulation of the afternoon papers. The money from radio rights was the first trickle that turned into full flood in the 1960s when television began paying millions of dollars for broadcasting rights.

Radio also began the job, again efficiently completed by television, of killing off the network of minor leagues. The plight in which the minor leagues found themselves led them in 1930 to experiment with games played, under artificial lights, at night when, presumably, more spectators would be able to attend. The major league owners, less financially pressed, saw little merit in floodlighting. They seem to have regarded it as a short-lived gimmick, and as something foreign to the very nature of baseball, which was meant to be played in the sunlight. Their opposition lasted until 1935, by which time the exigencies of the Depression were causing all manner of people to revise their thinking on all sorts of issues, and many of those owners who had cried 'Never!' to night baseball now found that it might not be such a bad thing after all. The mind-changer was falling attendances, particularly in Cincinnati which had had a disastrous 1934 season. The first night major-league game came in 1935 when President Roosevelt pressed a button in Washington and the Cincinnati stadium, 300 miles to the west, sprang to artificially-lit life. The heresy spread as it became clear that night games did not upset the players' digestion or cause them to go blind. Today, a stadium without floodlighting is unthinkable,† and over half the season's games are played at night.

* In 1954 his name became a household word among people all over the world when he married Marilyn Monroe.

† Well, almost unthinkable. The chewing-gum millionnaire Phil Wrigley, who owns the Chicago Cubs, will not have floodlights in his stadium, making Chicago one of the few places where midweek games are played in the afternoon.

Then there was the ball itself, which had undergone several changes in its composition since Cartwright's time. The idea behind the tinkering was to make sure baseball provided what the fans wanted to see. If the hitters were getting too many hits, then the ball was deadened, and if the pitchers got on top, then the ball was made bouncier again. Babe Ruth was responsible for such a change, and no doubt profited from it. In 1924 Ty Cobb, whose short-hitting, aggressive base-running style was about to be eclipsed by Ruth's slugging, said: 'Just watch the ball next year, they'll start juicing it up like a tennis ball because Ruth has made the home-run fashionable.' And so they did. In 1961, when almost everyone seemed to be hitting home runs, it was widely believed that the ball had again been pepped up, despite official denials. The *New York Times* set a firm of consulting engineers to work on new and old balls with tests that included battering by an explosive-driven ram, vernier caliper measurements, surgical dissection, and study by a rubber technologist. After all that, they still could not tell. There were those who took the matter into their own hands. For years one of baseball's craftier managers is alleged to have stored his club's supply of baseballs in a cool, damp place, and to have wiped off the mildew before handing them to the umpire for use in a game. He had a weak-hitting team, and his reasoning was that the soggy, dead baseballs would hinder power-hitting opponents more than his own players, none of whom was likely to hit one out of the park anyway.

When the Japanese attacked Pearl Harbor in 1941 and America found itself caught up in another World War, Commissioner Landis wrote to President Roosevelt to find out whether, this time, baseball would be considered essential. The answer said that it was, and at the same time, it was not. Roosevelt said he considered baseball 'a definite recreational asset' and that it would be 'best for the country to keep baseball going'. But there would be no special deferments for baseball players. The Leagues had to make do with what they could get, and that included a one-armed outfielder, a pitcher with an artificial leg, and a fifteen-year-old boy.

In 1945 the war went away, but as wars will it left behind deep changes in society. One of them was to have an immense effect on baseball: the increasingly insistent demands of America's black population that their traditional role as second-class citizens cease. Ever since its first few years, professional baseball had systematically excluded Negroes and it was not until 1947 that the colour bar was breached. Within twelve years there were black players on every major-league team, showing quite

7 A bird's-eye view of a baseball stadium. The batting team has
runners leading off both 1st and 3rd bases.

conclusively that they could play the game every bit as well as whites. At least as well.*

The man responsible for bringing the Negro into baseball was Branch Rickey, an innovative manager who had also been responsible for the idea of 'farm systems' back in the 1920s. As manager of St Louis, he built up a network of minor-league teams all owned or partially owned by the St Louis club. It meant a large expenditure on scouting and evaluating hordes of youngsters, but it meant that a player, once signed by one of those clubs, was destined to become a St Louis player if his original promise held up. In 1942 the St Louis system included twenty-three farm teams at various levels of the baseball ladder.

Inevitably what worked for the poorer clubs worked even better for the rich ones. The New York Yankees built up their farm system to the point where their top minor-league team of the 1950s, Newark, was probably better than some of the major-league sides. The Yankees in fact continued to sweep all before them in post-war baseball, and the rest of the owners became increasingly fed up with it. They began to make rules designed to 'break up the Yankees', to ensure that all clubs got an equal shot at signing young players, and to stop the Yankees waxing ever fatter. With the introduction of the free-agent draft in 1964, they managed it. From then on not only minor-league players, but high school and college leavers as well, were subject to the draft. It did not matter how much money you had, there was no way you could sign players other than by waiting your turn in the draft. And the weakest teams got first choice.

The funny thing was that by 1964 it really did not matter all that much. The Yankees were already on the verge of total collapse, and in 1965 they sank to last place and have not won anything since. What the free-agent draft did do was to ensure that no other team replaced them as a self-sustaining dynasty. From then on the league titles changed hands nearly every season.

Commissioner Landis had died during the war, and the owners had thought twice about appointing another man of his hardy independence. The supposed danger that the public would lose confidence in the sport had passed long ago, so who needed a knight in shining armour any more? Between 1944 and 1968 they got through three Commissioners all of them rather pliant men who had the happy knack of agreeing with the owners on what constituted the interests of baseball. The most

* The role of the black athlete in American sports is the subject of Chapter 7, page 134.

astonishing appointment came in 1966 with the announcement from the owners that they had selected General William D. Eckert, late of the United States Air Force, as the new commissioner. No one in baseball had ever heard of General Eckert, and it turned out that very few people outside of baseball had ever heard of him either. 'My God!' exclaimed one baffled sportswriter, 'They've appointed the Unknown Soldier.'

Eckert did his best for a couple of years, but it would have been better for all concerned if he had stayed at home. After a while it became embarrassing. His remark to a baseball writer, 'You had an excellent story today. You've really been writing fine stuff lately', was typical. The writer was out of work, having formerly been on the *New York World-Journal-Tribune* that had ceased publication three months before.

It was under this sort of non-leadership that the franchise shifting went on and a public-be-damned attitude became unmistakable. The paying fans, anyway, had lost some of their importance, because now there was always the money from television.

In the sixties came the Great Sports Boom, and with it came expansion. Both the American and the National Leagues added four new teams each. One of these new teams was the New York Mets, who brought a new dimension to baseball – or at any rate, one that had been hidden for quite some time. They showed that there *was* more to the sport than balance sheets and tax write-offs, that baseball could be human and that, above all, it could be fun. In the process they became something of great rarity in American sport, a popular losing team.*

Baseball expanded yet, paradoxically, it was clearly losing popularity. Even its position as the National Pastime was challenged, threatened as it was by football, a very different type of sport with a very different type of image. Next to this brash assertive newcomer baseball began to take on the air of a mildly old-fashioned diversion, out of step with the contemporary scene, while football – both on and off the field, in play and in business – gave off a muscular glow of fast-moving efficiency, of purposeful drive.

* The phenomenon of the New York Mets is investigated in Chapter 11, **page** 249ff.

5   The
Body-Contact
Game

The attempt, during baseball's early days, to limit it to the 'right' people failed quickly and completely. Quite rightly so, in a country that prides itself on its lack of class barriers. Baseball was promptly established as the property of the American people, all of them, a sport for the masses. But this was not the way it was with football. For the first fifty years of its existence football was almost exclusively a university affair.*

It developed from the same sort of wild-kicking mêlées that in England led to the birth of soccer and rugby. Early colonists brought the idea with them and it caused just as much annoyance to the authorities in New England as it had done to those in Olde England. King Edward II had taken a pretty sour view of the whole business back in 1314, and had issued a celebrated warning to Londoners:

For as much as there is great noise in the city caused by hustling over large balls . . . from which many evils might arise, which God forbid, we command and forbid on behalf of the King, on pain of imprisonment, such game to be used in the city in the future.

A mere 300 or so years later and 3,000 miles further west, the people of Boston brought a strikingly similar warning down on themselves, the Town authorities proclaiming in 1657:

Forasmuch as sundry complaints are made that several persons have received hurt by boyes and young men playing at foot-ball in the streets; these are therefore to Injoyne that none be found at that game in any of the Streets, Lanes and Inclosures of this Town, under the penalty of twenty shillings for every such offense.

Neither of these elegantly worded proclamations produced the desired effect. In both countries the sport, if it could be called that, gained in

---

* A short description of the rules and action of football is given in the Appendices, page 274 ff.

popularity and by the beginning of the nineteenth century had been taken up by high schools and universities in both England and America. There is no evidence that either country was aware of the other's problems even though they were almost identical, and consisted of the fact that each school and university had its own version of football. In England the situation was further complicated by the emergence, around 1820, of rugby football. Cambridge University came to the rescue in 1848 with the first written set of rules. The game they outlined is quite close to modern soccer, even though some handling of the ball was permitted (a player could catch, or stop, the ball with his hands, but must immediately kick it and not run with it). In 1871 the Rugby Union held its first meeting, and the separation of the two sports was complete.

Across the Atlantic, the Americans found the English rules and their variations difficult to follow and anyway had ideas of their own. By 1860 schools were playing each other on Boston Common with sixteen-member teams that included such positions as infielders, rushers-in, and a tender-out. Whether the game they played was rugby, or soccer, or – more likely – a bit of each, is not known. The rules drawn up by Princeton University in 1867, however, were clearly related to those that the London Football Association had published in 1863. When Princeton met nearby Rutgers University in 1869 the game would have been clearly recognizable to any Englishman of the day as soccer. There was no running while holding the ball, which had to be kicked or headed, the goalposts were 25 ft apart, and the ball was round. The game was not considered a big deal by the students and only 200 of them turned out, unaware that this was a historic occasion they were watching.

Years later, when the historians got to work, they decided that it was this game that marked the birth of the sport of football. That made 1969 the Centennial Year, and called for celebrations. The Post Office issued a special stamp, Rutgers and Princeton staged a replay of the original game, using the old rules, and colleges all over the United States arranged Centennial programmes to honour the occasion. There was, of course, a Centennial Queen who was blonde and cute and came from Texas.

And once again they had picked the wrong date. In 1939 baseball had commemorated an event that never happened, and in 1969 football did almost the same thing by celebrating an event that was not what it was made out to be. The sport that Princeton and Rutgers played in 1869 was clearly not football. It was rudimentary soccer, played with a round ball, and very similar to the soccer that was being played in England at the time.

That may be, say the historians, but this was the game that developed into American football. Wrong again. The game that was to become American football was started up in Boston by Harvard University in 1871. They *did* allow a player to pick the ball up and run with it, a rule so different from any that the other colleges used, that Harvard found itself without opponents. When a challenge arrived from McGill University in Montreal, it was gratefully accepted even though McGill was known to play a game called rugby, which nobody at Harvard knew very much about.

It is the game between these two universities, in 1874, that ought to be regarded as the birth of American football. Once they had seen McGill in action, Harvard abandoned their hybrid rugby-soccer play, and wholeheartedly turned to rugby proper. Or nearly proper – the Canadian game was already different from the English parent version, and Harvard was soon to start the series of changes that led to American football.

Other universities – Columbia, Yale and Princeton – took a look at Harvard's rugby and liked what they saw. Despite considerable opposition from those who wanted to stick to the original soccer-oriented rules, it was agreed at a meeting of the four in 1876 that in future their game would be rugby style. The English Rugby Union rules were adopted, with certain modifications. It was a close thing, but soccer lost out to rugby, and the autumn pastime of American colleges was destined to consist of carrying an egg-shaped ball, rather than kicking a round one.

One of the first rule changes that the Americans introduced made it pretty obvious that they expected cheating to be a part of the game. They insisted that the referee be augmented by two judges, one appointed by each team. This was an early manifestation of one of football's most persistent traits: that the rules were not regarded with any special awe. They have been altered, substantially or slightly, in almost every year of football's one hundred-year history.*

Under its new and continually evolving American rules, football spread rapidly across the country, infecting university after university and college after college with its urgent appeal to the manliness of young Americans. These were the 1890s, that very moment in American history when the demand for manly activities was reaching a crescendo, and the lively, rough, *tough* game of football was ideally suited to the

* In sharp contrast to soccer rules, which are called 'laws' and carry an almost Mosaic mystique of authority and immunity to change.

climate. Tough it certainly was, for Americans do not do things by halves. If the game allowed you to tackle an opponent, which it did, then that tackling was predictably going to be violent. There was also nothing in the rules that said you could not punch opponents, so punching, or slugging, became an accepted feature of the sport. When Harvard objected, the other colleges outvoted them. Slugging was red-blooded, and it would stay.

Slugging, just possibly, might be excused as an individual's reaction to the heat of the moment. But no such excuse could be offered for the methodically thought-out mass plays that led to a crop of serious injuries. The 'flying-wedge' was the aristocrat of these, and it owed its existence to the American rule that permitted 'blocking', i.e., players running ahead of the ball-carrier to push would-be tacklers out of the way. It was the invention of a chess expert, one Lorin Deland, who had never played football. He had observed plays in which a number of players linked arms to run in front of the ball carrier, and it occurred to him that if all ten other players could link up in front of the ball carrier, and better still if they could all be in rapid motion before the kick-off, an irresistible force might be created. One lone player stood with the ball at his feet on the kick-off spot, while his team-mates were some twenty yards behind him, five to the right of him, five to the left. At his signal they all started running pell mell towards him; as they reached him he tapped the ball and passed it off to another player. By now, the two lines of players, each one hanging on to the one in front, had joined to form a V travelling at full speed, with the ball-carrier concealed somewhere in the middle of it. Like a huge twenty-two-legged pantomime horse the flying-wedge descended upon the foe, who were supposed to bounce off when they tried to stop its progress. It was the rise of irresponsibly dangerous plays like this, thought up by grown men for young men to put into practice, that gave football a bad name – even at the prestigious Ivy League universities. The *New York Post* commented that 'no father or mother worthy of the name would permit a son to associate with the set of Yale brutes' who made up the college's football team.

'Mostly they stood bolt upright and fought it out hammer and tongs, tooth and nail, fist and feet,' said one of the players, adding that 'arguments followed almost every decision that the referee made.' Calls mounted for the banning of the game, and those very colleges that had so recently embraced it, turned against it. Rules were changed, but coaches found new and ingenious ways to continue the mayhem. It took a command from the White House to produce real action, and it was the new marvel of action photography that triggered the command. President Theodore Roosevelt picked up his newspaper one morning in 1905 and saw a picture of a college football player, his face battered and bloody, staggering off the field. The same season was to see the death of eighteen players and serious injuries to 159 others. This was taking the strenuous life a little too far, and Roosevelt called together representatives from Yale, Princeton and Harvard (for it was still the upper-class eastern colleges that ran the sport) and told them to clean it up, admonishing them that 'Brutality and foul play should receive the same summary punishment given to the man who cheats at cards'.

The rule makers went to it again, and they produced a change that revolutionized the game. They made it legal to pass the ball forward so that it could be caught by players speeding downfield towards the enemy goal-line. A move that at once opened out the game and eliminated the ponderous bulldozing of the mass plays.

A second approach to the injury problem was to provide the players with protective equipment. Starting with shin guards and flimsy helmets like rugby scrum-caps, football has slowly added a whole arsenal of safety devices to the footballer's uniform, until today he takes the field hung about with so many pads and guards that his very shape is ludicrously distorted. Plastic helmet; face guard; gum shields; shoulder pads; arm, elbow, hand, hip and thigh pads; and yards and yards of tape, all to a total cost of around $200 per player.

At the turn of the century most of this paraphernalia was but a gleam in some equipment manufacturer's eye, but one thing was becoming perfectly plain to the colleges: there was money to be made from football. In 1903, a 57,000 capacity stadium – the largest reinforced steel structure in the world at the time – was opened. Not by a professional sports club, but by good old Harvard University, America's oldest and most revered seat of learning. The Groves of Academe were about to enter the fields of sports promotion.* College football was prospering, and, just as they had done in the early days of baseball, the professionals moved in. Baseball's amateur opposition had quickly melted away, but in football the story was to be a very different one. There were two factors that militated against the professionals. In the first place the exclusively college background of the sport gave it a quality that the English had tried to build into their sports, the concept of players (who were professionals) and gentlemen (who were amateurs). In other words:

* Of this topic, more later – see Chapter 8, page 168.

snobbism. The people who followed football were mostly university types, and they regarded the early pros with distaste as men who were cheapening the college spirit of the sport, who were putting it in the same category as professional baseball which everybody knew was played by drunken, gambling, ne'er-do-wells. The second obstacle to professional football was that it simply was not as good as the college version. It was to be many years before it reached that level.

Just as it was the industrial cities of northern England that bred the first soccer professionals in the 1870s, so it was the coal and steel cities of western Pennsylvania that saw the birth of professional football in the 1890s. The money was not exactly on the grand scale – one of the pioneer pros received $10 a game for his efforts.

Professional football spread slowly, hampered by its unsavoury reputation and its inability to entice the college stars to turn professional once their college days were over. It was not until 1919 that there were enough reasonably stable teams to form a league; this was the American Football Association, and its president was Jim Thorpe, the only nationally famous name that professional football had yet attracted – and even then his fame came mostly from non-footballing feats. Thorpe is still referred to as the greatest all-round athlete that America has ever seen. He was an American Indian (plus a smidgen of Irish and a trace of French blood), and he was built along satisfyingly heroic lines (6 ft tall, 180 lb in weight). He went to Stockholm with the 1912 United States Olympic team and walked off with the gold medals for both the pentathlon (in which he won all five events) and the decathlon. But the Red Indian never did get a fair deal from the paleface, and when it was discovered that Thorpe had played one or two semi-professional baseball games before going to the Olympics, he was ordered to return his medals, and his name was erased from the record books.* He turned to professional football where, it is recorded, 'he was absolutely fearless, smashing through a line or ripping into a rival runner or making a savage block with cruel recklessness', after which he might look down compassionately at his almost dismembered opponent and remark: 'A fellow could get hurt playing this game – if he don't take care'. Thorpe was a classic example of the triple-threat† – he could run with the ball, he could pass

---

* In October 1973, twenty years after his death, the Amateur Athletic Union restored Thorpe's amateur status, thus opening the way for the return of his Olympic medals.

† The phrase is commonly used by Americans to describe someone who is expert in three skills, e.g.; an actor who can also sing and dance.

it, and he was an expert kicker. His reign as league president lasted only a year – he was far more interested in playing* than in administration – but the league was there to stay. In 1921, with thirteen teams, it became the National Football League and as such it exists in considerable affluence today. In 1921 it was a struggle, with 4,000 considered a good gate. Players were now getting between $75 and $150 a game, but the playing and travelling conditions left much to be desired.

The big break for professional football came in 1925 with the arrival of Red Grange. At last the professionals had been able to lure one of the top college stars (some would have said *the* top college player of all time). Grange had starred with the University of Illinois team for three years, where he had acquired almost legendary fame for his evasive running that left opponent after opponent clutching thin air. It was a fame that spread across the country in a flash, carried by the newsreel that enabled millions, not just a few thousands, to see the Galloping Ghost in action. Grange meant that the professionals now had a box-office attraction, but he meant much more than just that. He meant respectability. And he made it clear that there was now money to be made from a career in professional football. His contract with the Chicago Bears was negotiated by his agent, the theatrical promoter C.C. (Cash and Carry) Pyle, and it guaranteed him $3,000 a game. For his first game as a professional there were 36,000 fans on hand, and the Bears could not be faulted when it came to cashing in on their star. They lit off on a barnstorming tour that involved seven games in eleven days, that drew 73,000 people to the New York game, but that left Grange – always the main target for the opposing players – battered and exhausted. Balm for his wounds was to be found in Grange's financial state, which had a very healthy glow about it. For a movie, not yet started, he had received $300,000, and endorsements of all sorts of things from sweat shirts to cars and dolls and ginger-ale were bringing in thousands more. And for eighteen games in under three months, Grange had earned $100,000.†

The professionals may have been making money, but there were still plenty of people who insisted that the college game was better and, of course, tougher. 'I don't *look* for tackles,' said one college coach, when

---

* In 1923 Thorpe assembled an 'invincible' team of Indians whose roster included Wrinkle Meat, Running Deer, Red Fang, Arrowhead, Gray Horse, Little Twig, Tomahawk, Eagle Feather, and Xavier Downwind. The team was less menacing than the names, and it dissolved after one indifferent season.

† Grange never made any bones about why he turned professional: 'I don't like football well enough to play it for nothing,' he said.

asked if he had seen one particularly vicious tackle, 'I *listen* for them.' Knute Rockne, the coach at Notre Dame University,* was certain that a good college team could lick any of the pros. He got his chance to prove it in 1930 when they arranged a game for charity between a side of Notre Dame stars, coached by Rockne, and the professional New York Giants. It was a great afternoon for the Unemployment Relief Fund (45,000 fans in the stands), but a complete débâcle for Rockne's All Stars. Beaten 22–0, they never once managed to move the ball into their opponents' half of the field.

By the end of the thirties professional football could point to several indicators of solid, if not spectacular, success. The franchise cost, a trifling $25 per team when the N.F.L. was formed in 1920, had risen to $50,000 by 1940. College stars were entering the sport, and salaries of over $10,000 were not uncommon. The league had stabilized at ten teams, split into an East and a West Division, an arrangement that provided a climactic game between the two division leaders to decide the championship. But the wide variations in attendances at these championship games (from a low of 15,000 to a high of 48,000) showed that professional football was not yet an automatic crowd-puller.

The league was playing its regular schedule of Sunday afternoon games on 7 December 1941, when the first news flashed in that the Japanese had bombed Pearl Harbor. Crowds at the games heard the urgent announcement over the public address system that all servicemen were to report immediately to their units. By evening, football no longer seemed very important.

The war years meant the same for football as for baseball – makeshift teams of youngsters and players dragged out of retirement, poor playing

---

* Rockne is revered as the greatest of all college coaches, and as such has the dubious honour of having had a Hollywood film devoted to his life. *Knute Rockne, All American*, starred Pat O'Brien as Rockne, and included the famous locker-room pep-talk: 'Win one for the Gipper.' George Gipp, a legendary player at Notre Dame, died at the height of his fame, aged twenty-three. According to Rockne, who was present at his death, he had asked the coach, 'Sometime, Rock, when the team's up against it, when things are wrong and the breaks are beating the boys, tell them to go in there with all they've got and win just one for the Gipper . . . ' Rockne, a real Svengali when it came to inspiring his team, used the incident at half-time during a 1928 game that his team was losing to the Army. The fired-up Notre Dame rushed out and won the game. Pat O'Brien's melodramatic rendition of the speech became his party piece, which was requested wherever he performed and 'Win one for the Gipper' became a phrase of encouragement for anyone struggling against the odds.

standards and falling attendances. In the immediate post-war years both baseball and football flourished as sports-starved fans flocked to the stadiums. But once this entertainment splurge had passed, the two sports went in opposite directions. While baseball entered a period of falling attendances (much of it caused by the sport's own policy of televising every game in sight), football went from strength to strength. The N.F.L. withstood the challenge of a second league, the All America Conference, that lasted from 1946 to 1949 and that meant increased salaries and larger signing-on bonuses for the players. For the owners this was a painful necessity, but it was really just what football needed, for the extra money attracted many college players who would otherwise have chosen another career. All the publicity that surrounded the war between the leagues did not hurt either.

In 1950 the N.F.L., in sole command again and stronger than ever, made a rule-change that had a profound effect on the way the game was played. It allowed unlimited substitution – which meant that any player could enter or leave or re-enter the game as many times as the coach wished. This was the go-ahead for the intense development of specialist skills: a player could be sent onto the field just for one special play and taken off again immediately afterward. Every team, in effect, became two teams; one for offence, that operated as long as it retained possession of the ball, and one for defence that took over when the ball was in the opponents' possession. The day of the player who stayed on the field for all sixty minutes of a football game was over. All-rounders were not wanted, and the age of the assembly line, with each player doing his own specialized thing, had caught up with football.

One of the most specialized roles turned out to be that of field-goal kicking, i.e., kicking the ball, from a set position, between the uprights and over the bar of the H-shaped goalposts. The kicker might be called into action only two or three times during the game, but his efforts could mean the difference between winning and losing. The hunt was on for prodigious kickers. According to Margaret Mead, Americans, histori-cally, have never bothered to learn skilled crafts. They have preferred to import craftsmen from Europe, study how they do the work, and then build a machine to do it more efficiently. The goal-kicking machine has not yet arrived, but the importation of kickers has. Prompted by the thought that Europe must be full of spectacular soccer-style kickers, the Kansas City Chiefs sent a party to England to conduct try-outs. That most of the kickers had not the remotest notion what American football was all about was neither here nor there. All they would have to do was to run on the field and kick a ball. Either they scored a field goal or they did not, but in any case at that point the game stopped, and they ran, or even walked, off the field again. In the United States, boys who had emigrated from soccer-playing countries suddenly found a new career opportunity. For Pete Gogolak, who left Hungary at the time of the 1956 revolution, and who was quite a competent soccer player, football proved a veritable crock of gold. With the New York Giants he earned $33,000 for the 1969 season, which worked out at around $11,000 for every minute of his actual playing time.

The 1950 championship game had drawn 30,000 people, and the winning players had taken home a bonus of $1,100 each. By the end of the decade, the crowd was 57,000 and the winning bonus was $4,700 per player. Signs of affluence; and inevitably they drew covetous attention from wealthy men who wanted in. Among them was Lamar Hunt, son of oil-magnate and possibly richest-man-in-the-world, H. L. Hunt. When Lamar found that the N.F.L. was not going to let him in, he did the only thing that any self-respecting millionaire could do under the circumstances: he went off and formed his own league. Thus sired by wealth out of pique, the American Football League started up in 1960, and the customary round of bidding wars, increased salaries and bonuses followed. The A.F.L. did not do at all well* in its first years and was treated with haughty contempt by the N.F.L., which refused to even consider the idea of the two champion teams meeting. But then came the celebrated N.B.C. television contract of 1964, and the A.F.L. was able to sally forth, *nouveau riche*, looking for top college-talent to snatch away from the N.F.L. The change in the A.F.L.'s fortunes was nowhere more dramatic than in New York, where its team, the Titans, did their utmost to confirm the N.F.L.'s view that the new league was nothing but a joke.

The Titans were owned by Harry Wismer, a former broadcaster whose numerous eccentricities included the conviction that he was forever being followed, a habit of greeting everyone with 'Congratulations!' and a further habit of never having any money. It was this last that caused the Titan players so much anguish. Aside from the likelihood that their own pay-cheques – assuming they got them – were likely to bounce, they had to put up with things like having no laundry service, or the driver of the team bus refusing to start the engine until he was paid, in cash, because of the rubbery reputation that Titan cheques had acquired.

* The story is told that H.L. Hunt was informed that his son must be mad to try and float a new league, and that he would lose $1 million a year. 'At that rate', said H.L., 'he'll be broke in 150 years.'

Their presence in New York aroused a city-wide yawn, and their games were played before intimate gatherings of a few thousand, augmented at the very last moment before the kick-off, when the stadium gates were opened and all the neighbourhood kids let in for nothing. Absurdly inflated attendance figures were announced, prompting one journalist's comment that, of the 20,000 fans claimed one afternoon, 15,000 had come disguised as empty seats. By the end of the 1962 season the Titan players were being paid by the League, not the club. The bankrupt team was taken over in 1963 by Sonny Werblin, who had been spectacularly successful as a theatrical agent; he renamed them the Jets, and when all the television money became available in 1964, he set about finding a star attraction. It cost him a $400,000 bonus, but the following year he signed a brilliant young quarterback named Joe Namath, straight out of college. This was the move that forced the N.F.L. to realize that the A.F.L. was now a serious threat. Any club that wanted to sign even a half-way decent player had now to start thinking in terms of a $250,000 bonus (the record was $600,000). It was, as one of the N.F.L. owners said 'economic suicide'. Within a year, the merger of the two leagues had been worked out and approved by Congress, and the convenience of monopoly replaced the bothersome uncertainties of competition.

The agreement meant that at last the champion teams of the two Leagues could meet. Here was the long-awaited matchup, an occasion absolutely made for the publicity boys to exploit. The first meeting was in 1967 and, obviously, it just *had* to be the greatest football game ever played. The Super Bowl they called it,* and it was publicized and advertized and eulogized until the actual playing of the game was bound to be an anti-climax – which it was. The N.F.L. had been right all along, it seemed, for their champion Green Bay Packers toyed with the A.F.L.'s Kansas City Chiefs while beating them 35–10, and while the television cameras had a tiresome afternoon trying to avoid shots with empty seats in the background. The Packers won again, almost as easily, over the Oakland Raiders in 1968, confirming what everybody already knew, that they were the top team of the sixties.

They owed their success, this small town in the big city league, to the drive and verve of their coach, Vince Lombardi. Lombardi, the man whose credo was 'Winning isn't the most important thing, it's the only thing' epitomized the values that football's supporters found so attractive (and that its detractors found so repellent). He was tough, he was

---

* Bowl games – e.g., the Orange Bowl, the Rose Bowl – are a feature of college football, the word coming from the bowl-like shape of the stadiums.

hard, he was a disciplinarian, he was religious (and very fond of locker-room recitals of the Lord's Prayer before and after games) and, something without which all the other qualities might not have appeared quite so impressive, he was successful. The Packers were N.F.L. runners-up in 1960, and champions in 1961, 1962, 1965, 1966 and 1967.

Green Bay, just one of thousands of small inconsequential towns all over the United States, became a household word because it supported the best football team in the land. Every home game saw the Packers' stadium jammed with 50,000 people, leaving things pretty quiet elsewhere in town, for the population of Green Bay is only 64,000. For the 1967 title game the Green Bay fans were at their most fanatic. When the game began the temperature was 13 degrees (Fahrenheit) below zero (45 degrees below freezing point); low even by the frosty Green Bay standards. After a helicopter had hovered over the stadium, blowing the snow off the seats, the 50,000 faithful took their places, with their blankets and their face masks and their whisky flasks, the whole crowd letting off a misty rising cloud of water vapour with each exhalation, each frantic yell. They stayed right to the end too, as the Packers left it until the final 13 seconds before getting the winning touchdown.

Playing football at all in that sort of weather had to be insanity, but then again, was not this the ideal showcase, the ultimate test, for the rigorous *machismo* that was football? Especially the football that Vince Lombardi preached, Lombardi who, said one of his players, 'seemed to enjoy watching every fresh collision', who, said another, treated all his players the same – 'like dogs', Lombardi who refused to believe in injuries (hurt is in your mind, he said) and who deliberately sent injured players back into the game, Lombardi who said, 'Football is not a nice game, we've got to get a little meaner', and who once flew into a rage because a player's wife ordered ice-cream, shouting at her that when she travelled with the team, she ate what the team ate, and that meant no ice-cream.

It was the sort of attention to detail, the knack of not overlooking anything, that made Lombardi, and football, such an inspiration to the worshippers of efficiency, of whom there has never been a shortage in America. Football also contrived to give off an air of technical, almost scientific, proficiency. Baseball, for instance, had the umpire calling out which pitches were strikes and which were not, and if it was a close thing, it all depended on his human, and regrettably fallible, judgement. Now, in football there is this crucial matter of deciding whether the ball has been advanced 10 yards, or maybe only 9 yards 2 ft 6 ins. Such a decision cannot be left to the referee's guess, it has to be measured scientifically. And so it is done by two men dressed in Harlequin-type costumes who run up and down the sideline carrying a chain exactly 10 yards long. When a close measurement is required, they trot onto the field and stretch out their chain, and no one dares to argue with that.* It may not be a micrometer, but it is surely better than a referee's guess.

Even in the notoriously tricky business of estimating a young player's talent, of deciding whether he has what it takes to become a star, football has managed to work out a scheme based on scientific measurements. Player-scouting has been lifted from the hit-and-miss judgements of one man to the carefully controlled assessments of the computer. This is another of those operations where the clubs have found that cooperation is more efficient and decidedly more economical than competition. Partly, this cooperation was the result of the introduction of the college draft. As a club is allowed to sign only those players it is able to choose in the draft, the extensive – and expensive – scouting of players all over the country has become a practice of dubious value. Clubs have joined together in scouting cooperatives, firms that do all the basic talent-spotting and submit identical reports on the players to each club. This still leaves each club free to employ a limited number of its own scouts to follow up players they are particularly interested in.

The Dallas Cowboys work this way. They belong to a cooperative, have five of their own scouts, and run the most sophisticated information-evaluation system in football. The idea is to give each facet of a player's skill a numerical value. That is no trouble with the two cardinal dimensions of American sport, height and weight, they come in numbers† anyway, and to them can be added a third, speed over a distance of 40 yards. But the Cowboys' system also gives numbers, ranging from one (poor) to nine (exceptional) for more elusive abilities like catching passes, or shaking off tacklers, or performing under pressure. Every player scouted is rated in this way over a whole range of skills. The scout no longer has to write a personal report; rather, he makes a series of ticks on a standard card, rating the player one to nine on the abilities listed.

* The fact that the position of the ball (which is the crucial point of the measurement) has to be marked by the referee, who often has to dig it out from underneath a pile of bodies, is apt to make a mockery of the chain-gang's elaborate rigmarole.

† Though the figures may not be as solidly exact as they appear to be. There are those who claim that a player measured just after getting up in the morning can be as much as an inch taller than he is later in the day, after gravity has got to him.

These include, in addition to physical skills, things like character, mental alertness, and competitiveness. The computerized way of calling a player dumb is to give him a nine rating opposite the statement: 'He finally catches on after much repetition.'

The cards containing all this homogenized information are devoured by computers (a process that costs the Cowboys $200,000) which perform all the subtle 'weighting' adjustments necessary to allow for the fact that a seven score on one skill may be more significant than a nine on another, or that one scout may be a harsher judge than another. When the computer is through, each player has an overall score that, by simple direct comparison with other players' scores, tells the Cowboys which one is better. As new information on the players becomes available, the computers revise the ratings until, on the day that the college draft is held, the Cowboys have a neat list of all the likely college players, graded in order of ability.

The staging of the annual draft is another of football's smooth technological triumphs. Representatives of each club – there are twenty-six of them – gather in the conference room of a large New York hotel. Each has a cloth-draped table on which is a sign bearing the club's name and colours, some papers, an ashtray, and the inevitable American gadget, around which the whole operation revolves, a telephone. From each table a line is kept open to the club's home-city office – in Dallas or Los Angeles or Pittsburgh or wherever – throughout the two-day session. As the clubs take their turn to announce their choice of players, the representatives telephone the names back to their offices. In this way each club continually adjusts its list, so that when its turn comes, it can select the best (best for its own needs, that is) of the so-far unpicked players. After twenty-six choices, with each club having selected one player, the first round is over. There follow a second and a third round and so on until seventeen rounds have been completed and 442 promising young college players have been drafted by the nationwide system of open telephone lines.* For the sake of science it would be encouraging to report that all this technology results in the best players being chosen first. But there is a certain cussedness about human behaviour that baffles even the wiliest computer. Top draft choices have been known to

---

* The conduct of the draft has something of the procedure and tension of a long-range chess game. The contestants sit facing a large screen on which each new move by the opponents – i.e., their choice of player – is recorded. The next team to choose must make its move within a specified time limit – 15 minutes in the early rounds, 5 minutes for the later rounds.

flop in the professional ranks, and it is not all that uncommon for late round choices to go on to fame and fortune.

Functioning as the lifeline for the draft is not the end of the telephone's contributions to football. It is also a crucial instrument during the actual playing of the game, when it is to be seen, right there down on the field, alongside the coach and all those substitutes on the bench. In almost constant use throughout the game, it is the link between the coach and his spotters, who are sitting way up in the stands where they can get a bird's eye view of the various formations and patterns that the opposition is using.

In many ways, football is a dream sport for gadgeteers. Computers, telephones, mounds of player equipment – and films. Heaven knows how many miles of film are used by the professional football world each season, but it must be of globe-encircling proportions. Every game is recorded by several cameras, and even practice sessions are religiously filmed – not to mention the movies of college games that are essential for scouting. All to be pored over and played back in slow motion and studied almost frame by frame, by coaches and players alike, for hour after hour. Films of a team's own games are used for post-mortems, while films of opponents in action are used to prepare tactics for up-coming games. Once again, the teams cooperate. They do not all have to employ several crews of cameramen to travel all over the country filming future opponents. They merely film their own games and, in accordance with a League rule, make copies available to all the other clubs. Not just one film, but two: one of the defence in action, one of the offence.

The upshot of all this diligent movie-watching is the game-plan, a guide to the strategy and the tactics to be used against the next opponent; what sort of plays the opposing offence can be expected to run, what sort of plays are likely to succeed against their defence.* It is just another example of football's disciplined approach to everything, of its mania for regimented organization.

The game-plan is actually only one of many, for the sport fairly bristles with plans. The crucial item of a football player's possessions is not his shoes, or his helmet, or some other piece of protective equipment, but his play book. In this he has recorded all the precisely planned plays that he and his team-mates have assiduously practised, written them down and captured them on paper with diagrams that look like Heath

---

* The term 'game-plan' appeared frequently in the political news in the 1970s as President Nixon used it to describe his plans for the nation's economy.

Robinson nightmares, arrows and straight lines and wiggly lines for movement, squares and circles and triangles for players. Each play is identified by its code name. There may be as many as one hundred of them in the playbook, and the player must know them all – or at least, he must know his own role in each of them. That is football, a series of one-act dramas, each lasting about 4 or 5 seconds, pitting one team's well-rehearsed offensive plans against another's defensive plans, inevitably less well-rehearsed, for they are reacting to their opponents' moves, not initiating their own.

Rehearsing things and writing them down on paper, as any spy worth his salt will avow, are procedures fraught with risk. The enemy may be watching or, even more dastardly, he may filch the secret plans. The football player is pledged to guard his playbook with his life. If he loses it, his club may fine him as much as $500. Ideally, practice sessions would be held at dead of night behind locked and guarded doors. Reality, usually in the form of an open field in broad daylight, falls far short of this, and is a recurring source of alarm to the more suspicious coaches. Cleveland coach Paul Brown, who was particularly paranoiac about spies, used to search his team's locker-room for bugging devices. He regularly halted practice sessions if a helicopter appeared overhead, and once stopped a session because he was convinced someone was watching it through binoculars from a nearby building, from which, he said, he had caught the glint of lenses. In 1967 Vince Lombardi took his Green Bay Packers to the West Coast to play a key game against Los Angeles, and they practised on a field belonging to the University of California. Lombardi presented the University with $3,000 and had them encircle the field with a huge wall of canvas screening. You cannot be too careful, as the 1970 College All Stars found out, after they had devised and practised (in secret indoor sessions) a surprise play. When the game got under way, it did not take long for them to realize that their surprise play was no surprise at all to their opponents – and then they remembered the guy who had been, apparently, fixing lights or something way up in the roof of the field house during one of their practice sessions.

But secrecy, along with gadgetry and planning and technology are satellites busily circling around what is at the centre of the football world – Violence. This is football's *leitmotif*, recurring again and again – as in the title of a television documentary about a player, 'The Violent World of Sam Huff'; in the title of a football book, *Violence Every Sunday*; in quote after quote, 'That's why people love it, it's a violent

sport', 'the most violent sport man has invented'; the newspaper headlines: 'Violence: The Fury and the Art'.

The particular form of violence that football has to offer consists of
collisions between players, or body contact, as it is called. This brings up
again the matter of size, for bigger players mean bigger (and *ipso facto*
better) collisions. A look at the Miami Dolphins team that won the 1973
Super Bowl reveals just how big these men are. The players had an
average height of 6 ft 2 ins (shortest 5 ft 8 ins, tallest 6 ft 6 ins), and an
average weight of 220 lbs (lightest 175 lbs, heaviest 277 lbs). Professional football players shorter than 6 ft, or lighter than 190 lb will soon,
no doubt, join the Dodo and the dinosaurs.

The biggest of the breed are the linemen, those who spend the game
in man-to-man struggle with their opposite number, more wrestlers than
ballplayers, for they rarely even touch the ball. Several of them have
topped the 300 lb mark, including a huge lumbering giant with an
exquisitely descriptive name: Sherman Plunkett. In 1968 Plunkett was
asked to report to the New York Jets' training camp weighing 'not more
than 300 lb'. He rolled in at 336 lb and said he could not understand it
as he had not eaten anything. His wife confirmed that he had been on a
diet, but thought he might have been cheating away from home.
Astonishingly, Plunkett set no records that year. Down in Miami, Sam
McDowell – who was supposed to weigh-in at 295, buckled the scales at
371, and he could not understand it either, as he said he had only weighed
316 back home.

For those who treasure the grace and beauty of athletics, watching
players like Plunkett in action is a traumatic experience. Waddling rather
than running, their gross bodies grotesquely out of shape, they resemble
the flabby, pop-bellied heavyweights who populate the provincial boxing
and wrestling rings. When they hit the ground, they look like nothing so
much as beached whales.

Well, so what? – demands the football fan. Nobody ever said this
was a sport for ballerinas. The Plunketts get their job done. For 4 or 5
seconds they wrestle off an opponent trying to get at the quarterback,
and you do not have to look pretty to do that. The small part of the field
where all this wrestling goes on, where the two lines clash, is known to
the players as The Pit. It is the apex of football violence, where, according
to one of the participants, 'we're like a bunch of animals kicking and
clawing and scratching at each other'.

Language like that crops up all the time when talk turns to football.
Try to find a newspaper report of a game in which the blocking is not

8 During the 1960s football, a violent sport played by large men (made
even larger by copious padding), replaced baseball as America's No 1
spectator sport. Its rapid rise owed much to television.

savage or brutal, or the tackling not bone-jarring or crunching, or the ball-carriers are not battering or slashing or bruising or bulldozing or blasting or searing their way through their opponents. To some extent this is journalistic dramatization, but when one turns to the undramatized, matter-of-fact language of the players themselves, the sense of violence is even more real:

> . . . I came into him, elbows and knees flying. Now I could have jumped over him, touching him just enough to down the ball. But I didn't. And the result was that I broke three of his ribs. (Johnny Sample, ex-New York Jets, who called his autobiography *Confessions of a Dirty Ballplayer*)

> You get in a good lick around the head area, it rattles the man. You can beat a dazed man easier than an alert one. It's that simple. (Chris Hanburger, Washington Redskins)

> If I can hit a man hard enough so he has to be carried off the field, I'll be glad to help him off. (Deacon Jones, Los Angeles Rams)

> I've got to knock him on his ass. That's the way to impress a guy in this game. (Jerry Kramer, Green Bay Packers)

And so on. The litany goes on, a string of unemotional assessments on the best way to damage an opposing player, because, as one coach put it: 'I have never known a professional football player who did not want to hit you with everything he had. Hitting is the nature of the animal and the game.'

Predictably enough, this approach leads to plenty of injuries, so they too have to be accepted as an everyday occurrence, as something it is not necessary to be squeamish about: 'He threw that shoulder of his into Geri so hard that he popped Joe's eyeball clean out of the socket! I mean it was hanging right out there.' By the time Jerry Kramer retired from football, he had had twenty-two operations, 'most of them major, many of them the direct result of football injuries'. Kramer recovered, more or less, from all of them, but there is a disturbingly long list of others who have suffered permanent injury while playing football. During the 1970 season, fifty-three professional football players (out of just over 1,000) suffered major injuries, i.e., injuries that required surgery or that finished the player for the rest of the season. Five per cent of the players out of action, crippled. The same proportion emerged from a study of forty-four college teams: 160 players out of 3,090 who needed hospital treatment, though a direct comparison is misleading as injuries in college games are likely to be more serious. The players are not as well trained, nor as evenly matched, nor as experienced as the pros. This is even more true in high-school football, and every year a number of boys are killed playing the sport.*

The carnage explains why all that padding is considered necessary, but here football is trapped in a vicious circle of escalating violence, because there is no doubt that the more heavily the players are padded, the more brutal is the game. The equipment, particularly the hard plastic helmet, becomes a weapon – a weapon that is frequently a treacherous one for its user. A battering-ram technique of blocking by butting the opponent in the chest with the helmet – 'spearing' – is the cause of many of the neck and spine injuries, and it is those that do the butting that get hurt. There are even players who complain that years of spearing make them a few inches shorter by the end of their careers.†

Injuries are likely to occur in any vigorously played sport, but the problem is particularly vexing to football which is in the Pecksniffian position of deploring injuries while at the same time promoting the very thing that leads to them: the image of football as a he-man sport full of violence. That was an image tailor-made for the 1960s, a period when American life exhibited even more than its usual share of violence, and a period in which football swept irresistibly forward. But it was also an image that was bound to come under fire as the reaction against violence began to make itself felt.

* In 1972 there were sixteen deaths among high-school players directly due to football injuries, plus another ten 'indirect' deaths caused by factors such as heat stroke and heart failure. The 1971 figures were fifteen and seven.

† Continually banging the head into solidly built opponents slowly pushes it down into the shoulders, or so the theory goes, until the player's neck virtually disappears. It seems unlikely, but there is no doubt that the massively muscled no-neck type is to be found on every team, the type the other players joke about – 'he has to unbutton his shirt to blow his nose'.

6 Sport, Politics, Crumbums and Commies

One of the consequences of the American idealization of the he-man is a markedly equivocal attitude towards violence. Even for obviously criminal acts there is invariably an undertone of barely hidden admiration that on occasion brims over into outright adulation. When three bandits shot up the Kansas City Fair in 1872, injuring a small girl and making off with $1,000, the *Kansas City Times* was so impressed by the daring of the robbery that it proclaimed 'we are bound to admire and revere its perpetrators' and expressed pride that it was Kansas that had been the scene of such fearlessness.

True, those were the far-off frontier days, but as we have seen, the frontier attitudes have remained deeply embedded in American life. It is not at all clear whether Americans think of their Al Capones and Dutch Schultz's as villains or heroes. Witness what happened in 1971 when Lieutenant William Calley was found guilty of killing unarmed women and children in Vietnam. Immediately there was a massive outpouring of support for Calley, motivated not so much by a desire to excuse his crimes, as to promote him as a genuine American hero.

Violence, in short, is not viewed as something to be avoided, or used only as a last resort when things get desperate. Rather, it is merely another way of getting things done. As such, it does have certain attractions for the efficiency minded, because it is frequently successful and it is likely to work with dramatic rapidity.

This acceptance of violence, or, at best, the lack of a clear condemnatory attitude, was bound, sooner or later, to produce a glut of the rough stuff. And this is what happened in the 1960s, as America found itself swept along in an accelerating rush of violence. Political leaders were gunned down, cities exploded into bloody riots, the incidence of violent crime moved unstoppably upwards, even the traditionally docile university campuses were in an uproar. While all this was going on at home, the United States Government was busy teaching the South-East Asians how to run their affairs with the aid of bombs, gas, defoliants and napalm.

President Johnson appointed a National Commission on the Causes and Prevention of Violence, learned books on the subject began to appear, and at Brandeis University a Center for the Study of Violence was founded. Like Mark Twain's weather, violence was much talked about, but not much was done about it – perhaps for the reason that black militant Rap Brown so tellingly stated: 'Violence is as American as cherry pie.'

In such an atmosphere, football became America's most popular sport, nosing aside baseball which had once been hailed as the very essence of things American. But enormous changes had occurred in American life during the twentieth century. The country had been transformed from the comparative simplicity of a predominantly rural society to the technological complexity of a nation of large-city dwellers. The changes in American attitudes that accompanied this shift have been described by Charles Reich in his book *The Greening of America*.* Using the word 'consciousness' to denote the 'total configuration in any given individual, making up his whole perception of reality', Reich depicts the original American Consciousness I as that 'appropriate to the nineteenth-century society of small town face-to-face relationships and individual economic enterprises'. This was the society that bred baseball, a sport that required the large open spaces of small towns and rural areas, a sport in which the action centred on the face-to-face struggle between pitcher and batter, and in which – especially in its early form – there was little co-ordinated team play but a good deal of individual enterprise.

With the twentieth century came science and what Justice Brandeis called 'the curse of bigness'. The two combined to form the technological and corporate society that gave rise to Reich's Consciousness II, the way of thinking that represents 'the values of an organizational society'. One of the key characteristics of this new Consciousness II, says Reich, was that it 'believed primarily in domination and the necessity for living under domination'. The cult of the individual, which had been the basis of Consciousness I, had led to the economic collapse of 1929 and the Depression. It was superseded by a desire to organize and co-ordinate the activities of society, to arrange things 'in a rational hierarchy of authority and responsibility'. It was now the huge impersonal structures – business corporations, labour unions, government agencies – that made the wheels go round, while the individual became less and less

* Reich, Charles, *The Greening of America*, Allen Lane The Penguin Press, 1971.

important. He was increasingly an instrument controlled by the organization he worked for, while at the same time the advances of technology ensured that his work grew progressively more mechanical.

In *The Technological Society* Jacques Ellul put forward the view that: 'In sport the citizen of the technical society finds the same spirit, criteria, morality, actions and objectives – in short all the technical laws and customs – which he encounters in office or factory.'* Ellul did not mention football, but he could hardly have wished for a better example. The favourite sport of the world's most technologically advanced society, it is a veritable showcase of Consciousness II values. The football player must certainly have a belief in the 'necessity for living under domination' for football coaches are a strongly authoritarian group devoted to the idea of discipline. Each player must perform according to his assigned role in each play, while individual enterprise, which could be fatal to the team's carefully planned action, is at a minimum. Even the player's individual appearance is erased by his padding and helmet. Actually, the uniforms do more than just depersonalize. They dehumanize, giving the players the appearance of artificial, laboratory-manufactured beings. These mechanical creatures are the working parts of a team that, computer-like, has to be reprogrammed with a new play fed into it every few seconds.

Significantly, football drew its most solid support from the people who had most to do with the running of the technological society – the business executives. Its appeal to this group of decision-makers led in turn to its popularity with television advertisers.

Ironically, baseball, which had once been exalted because it was so much faster than dull old cricket, now found itself losing ground because it was 'too slow' when compared with football. Another factor in baseball's original appeal had been the assertion (false, as it turned out) that the game was 100 per cent American. Once it became, as it quickly did, a successful business as well as a cultural institution (the capital-letter National Pastime) the rather shrill appeals to patriotism died down. They were heard only when the owners felt their business monopoly threatened and found that wrapping themselves in the American flag was a more acceptable defensive manoeuvre than talking about loss of income.

When patriotism returned to sports after World War II, it attached itself to football rather than baseball, and the mood was anything but

---

* Ellul, Jacques, *The Technological Society*, Knopf, 1954.

defensive. The Cold War demanded that America be a jump ahead of the Russians all the time, and chief cold-warrior John Foster Dulles had opined that it was immoral to be neutral in the struggle. Appeals to rally round the flag became a regular part of American post-war life. The ideal response was an aggressive, straightforward our-side-is-better-than-their-side, we'll-beat-the-hell-out-of-'em approach. Which was the football mentality to a tee, exactly the sort of thing that coaches – professional, college, and high-school – could be heard imparting to their players any day of the week. Football became a symbol for all that was good in American life, for all the values that the communists were threatening to destroy. There were times when it began to look less like a sport than a political movement, as when the assistant athletic director of the United States Naval Academy announced: 'This great sport of ours has gone so far and fast those pinkos can't touch it.'

In the marriage of football and cold-war patriotism, the advantages were not all on one side. Football had always suffered from the carping of the uninitiated who were shocked by the violence and who were forever asking embarrassing questions about the enormous amount of time and money that the colleges spent on promoting the sport. Now it had a surely unassailable answer. It was creating the sort of Americans who were needed to win the Cold War. The Americans were going to beat the Russians because in addition to God (well known as a perennial fan of American causes) they now had football on their side.

Much was made of the fact that President Eisenhower had been a football player during his days as an army cadet at West Point (though not quite so much was said about the fact that he was not good enough to make the first team), and Ike recalled how so many of his best World War II generals had been ex-footballers: 'Personally I think this was more than coincidental. I believe that football, almost more than any other sport, tends to instil into men the feeling that victory comes through hard – almost slavish – work, team play, self-confidence and an enthusiasm that amounts to dedication.'

The progression from football player to soldier is logical enough, for the particular quality of football that most stirs the patriot's heart is its avowedly Spartan, quasi-military discipline. The coach at a football practice session yelling at his players and making them run until they drop loses nothing when compared to the drill sergeant belabouring recruits. In fact, the coach is likely to be tougher, because he is dealing with willing volunteers. Witness the coach at Syracuse University who refused to end the practice-session until he saw some blood, or the coach at Arizona University who made slackers run up the side of a mountain under a blazing sun. The American Football Coaches Association invited the assistant commandant of the U.S. Marine Corps, General Lewis W. Walt, to their meeting and he told them: 'There are in fact a lot of similarities between the training that makes a marine and the training that makes a football player.' Even down to using the same language. Football's vocabulary is full of military terms like blitz (an all-out attack on the opposing quarterback), bomb (a long forward pass), offence, defence, platoon, squad. In South-East Asia American commanders were using the football term 'end run' to describe outflanking operations; jungle-clearing bombs flattened an area 'about the size of a football field', and Commander-in-Chief President Nixon explained a military action thus: 'It's like football. You run a play and it fails. Then you turn around and call the same play again because they aren't expecting it.'

By enlisting sport as an aid to national policy, the Americans were not breaking any new ground. The Spartans had certainly known all about it, but it was the English who had set the pattern in the modern world when, at the height of their imperial power in the 1850s and 1860s, a positive frenzy for team sports had engulfed the public schools. It was defended partly on religious grounds – these were the days of Charles Kingsley's muscular christianity – and partly on patriotic grounds as the ideal training for future Empire builders. Sir Henry Newbolt's *Vitai Lampada* explained how, when 'the sand of the desert is sodden and red', the comradeship and selflessness that had won the school cricket match would also serve to vanquish England's foes:

> But the voice of a schoolboy rallies the ranks,
> Play up! Play up! and play the game.

By 1950 the role of policeman to the world had been taken over by the Americans and they too enrolled sports in the cause. 'The discipline and reliance on one another it teaches is so valuable . . . It merges the individual in the eleven; he doesn't play that he may win, but that his side may.' That could be an American explaining the merits of football, but in fact it is Tom Brown talking about cricket in *Tom Brown's Schooldays*, vintage 1857. Now hear President Kennedy in 1962: 'I sometimes wonder whether those of us who love football fully appreciate its great lesson: that dedication, discipline, and teamwork are necessary to success.'

The similarities must not be allowed to obscure a crucial difference between the two situations. In 1850 England was supremely confident of her ability to handle the task. There was no foreign power strong enough to threaten her militarily, and there was no international ideology for opponents to rally around. A comparatively small cadre of ex-public-school cricketers was all that was needed to run the Empire. America took over under very different circumstances, faced by the military might of Russia and the menace of communism, which appeared to be spreading like a plague. Making the worst of a bad situation, the Americans quickly developed a king-sized obsession that saw red agents at work all over the United States, attempting to destroy the country from within. Futile to imagine that a few football-trained officers of the type that Eisenhower so admired could cope with such a comprehensive threat. If football was to be of any use it had to be presented not just as a valuable adjunct to military training, but as an essential feature of the American way of life, something that *all* Americans could respond to. Thus was accomplished the final step in the apotheosis of football with the assertion that success on the football field meant certain success in the most American of occupations, business.

This blending of military, business and football interests can be seen in the National Football Foundation, founded in 1954 with a 'General MacArthur National Advisory Board' bristling with generals and top business executives. Starting from the premise that 'Football is more than a game. It is an American institution',* the N.F.F. seeks to 'help football maintain its rightful place not simply as a sport, but as an integral part of our nation's educational pattern' and 'as a vital force in preparing American youth for the competitive business of everyday life'. Alongside the glowing encomiums to football that populate the pages of the N.F.F.'s literature are persistent reminders that 'these are no ordinary times', that 'our country faces new and perplexing problems', or as the N.F.F. president put it in 1967, 'a critical time when the beatnik element participate in a breakdown of law and order'. The answer to the problems and the beatniks is, naturally, large doses of football, 'one of the principal organized training grounds of national spirit and morale. It is a ready-made "production line" not to be discounted'.

In 1969 the N.F.F. chose President Nixon as the recipient of its annual Gold Medal award. Nixon was not the first President to be so honoured – Hoover, Eisenhower and Kennedy were all previous medallists – but his selection was perhaps the most appropriate, because

---

* A premise that would have sounded familiar to Tom Brown, who said of cricket: 'But it's more than a game. It's an institution.'

9 President Nixon capitalized on his interest in football by attending games, telephoning coaches, even dropping in on practice sessions.

Nixon

he was the first President to make systematic capital out of what can be called the 'football vote', the political expression of the football mentality.

Football supporters, for the reasons given above, were known to be essentially conservative people who believed strongly in the preservation of the American free-enterprise system, patriots of the 'my country right or wrong' school. They were part of the Silent Majority and as such they provided a useful focal point within what was a rather vaguely defined concept. With a reference to football here, and attendance at a game there, Nixon could woo them in a way that was unmistakable, but not too overtly political. Before his election, he and his advisers had seriously considered asking Vince Lombardi to join the Republican ticket as vice-presidential candidate. The disadvantages – that Lombardi had no political experience and was a life-long Democrat anyway – would have made the suggestion derisory had he not also been the nation's top professional football coach. In the event it was Spiro Agnew (no Lombardi, but a keen football fan all the same) who got the call, but there was soon a football coach on Nixon's staff. One of his first appointments after his election was that of Bud Wilkinson, a top college coach, as one of his special advisers.

Nixon became the first president to attend a regular season game in professional football. He attended the college championship game in 1969 and made televised visits to both locker rooms after the game. He flew to Green Bay, professional football's spiritual capital, to attend a testimonial dinner to quarterback Bart Starr. When 250,000 anti-Vietnam-war protesters gathered in Washington in November 1969, Nixon reassured the Silent Majority by letting it be known that *he* would spend the afternoon watching the Purdue–Ohio State college football game on television. A year later, to disprove the allegation that he did not dare set foot on a college campus, he paid a lightning visit to Kansas State University – an institution without academic distinction, but one that was in the midst of a massive drive to create a winning football team (new $800,000 athletic dormitory, new 36,000-seat stadium, and a new coach at a $26,000 annual salary). It was a football-oriented campus, carefully selected as safe territory for Richard Nixon.

Nixon's assiduous courting of the football vote highlights the contradictory situation in which his administration found itself. For he was committed to ending the Vietnam war, which had always been supported by the football mentality – indeed, in a very real sense, had been *caused* by it. That mentality, with its strain of messianic Americanism and its view of life as a survival-of-the-fittest contest was bound to find the idea of slugging it out with the Commies appealing. Obviously, the Americans would win the fight because they were bigger and stronger and meaner and smarter, they were more disciplined, they had all that sophisticated technical gadgetry, and they had the right game plan. After all, these were the things that worked on the football field, so who could doubt. . . ?

It might have been objected that these things worked in football only because the sport had been specifically designed to make them decisive factors, but people blinded by the notion that football and America were one and the same thing were not likely to listen to that sort of talk.

They did not listen, and the United States embarked on the most clamorous mistake in its history. Vietnam gnawed away at America throughout the sixties, a constant and ever louder reminder that something had gone wrong. The football virtues, those virtues so vital to America – could it be that they were just simplistic slogans, dangerously misleading when taken away from the football field? As opposition to the war mounted, the football mentality and then football itself felt increasingly threatened by the wave of hostility. Defenders of the sport began to speak in shrill, beleaguered tones, none more so than Max Rafferty, the former California State Superintendent of Public Instruction, and a well-known espouser of right-wing causes, who had this to say: 'Critics of college football are kooks, crumbums and commies, hairy loud-mouth beatniks. Football is war – without killing. They are the custodians of the concepts of democracy. As football players, they possess a clear, bright, fighting spirit which is America itself.' In a speech to California's college athletic directors and coaches he dubbed the critics 'hairy loud-mouthed freaks of both sexes who infest our campuses today like so many unbathed boll-weevils' and the audience gave him a standing ovation.

With student unrest at its height just after the invasion of Cambodia in May 1970, an incident at San Diego State College brought passing joy to football minds all over the country. Student protesters wanted to lower the American flag to half-mast, but they were turned back by Bill Pierson, who stood defiantly at the foot of the mast for over three hours. The beauty of it was that Pierson was an ex-Navy man and a 6 ft 3 ins 245 lb member of the college football team. It was a parable for America. Football defending the Flag, and Pierson received a note from Vince Lombardi saying how proud he was.

Among the critics of football, none was more articulate or better informed than Dave Meggyesy. What he had to say carried considerable weight because he was a professional football player (six-one, two-thirty) who had turned sour on the sport and quit – not at the end of his playing days, but in the middle of a successful career. Meggyesy let his hair grow, sprouted a beard, played around with drugs, and wrote a book in which he called football a political-ideological game, and 'one of the most dehumanizing experiences a person can face'.* He lashed out at the brutality of the sport, alleged that he was given illegal payments while playing in college, accused professional football of widespread use of

* Meggyesy, Dave, *Out of Their League*, Ramparts Press, Berkeley, California, 1970.

stimulant drugs, and of fostering racism. He wrote: 'It is no accident that the No. 1 football freak in the country is Richard Nixon. The President is the typical football fan . . . Some people can use athletics to attain a feeling of competence, but the only way a football player can attain a feeling of competence is to beat the hell out of everybody. That is the crux of the world the Nixons and Agnews identify with.' Back in Solon, Illinois, the small town where Meggyesy had played football as a boy, the authorities at his former high school removed a plaque honouring him from the school wall.

The mounting criticism of football, the sport of the Consciousness II generation, is exactly what would be expected from Charles Reich's theory. The main theme of *The Greening of America* is that the technical society of Consciousness II has proved so unresponsive to real human needs, so mechanical, that it has unwittingly spawned a new and hostile Consciousness III. This is the youth culture that began to grow in the 1960s, the long hair, bell bottom, rock music, drug culture with its accent on freedom of individual expression. The idea of a way of life based on 'doing your own thing' was anathema (as it was meant to be) to the discipline and uniformity minded football mentality.* The Consciousness III kids, with their unabashed contempt for everything their parents held dear were the 'hairy loud-mouth beatniks' who so enraged the Max Raffertys of the sports world.

While it is too early to speak with conviction of a Consciousness III sport – Consciousness III itself is still in its early stages, and sport does not set trends, it follows them – the phenomenal spurt in the popularity of basketball during the late sixties gave a substantial hint that, inscrutably but perceptibly, tastes were shifting in the sports world. Actually, the popularity of most sports grew by leaps and bounds in the sixties, but the largest leaps and the biggest bounds belonged to basketball. Statistics were on hand to prove it: from 1965 to 1970, baseball attendances rose 16 per cent, football 39 per cent, and basketball . . . 185 per cent. In 1971, for the first time in years, the percentage of Americans naming football as their favourite sport declined, from 30 to 28 per cent. Football was still ahead, but it was beginning to look over its shoulder.

* The hostility between the youth culture and the football mentality was clearly stated in the report of the White House Conference on Youth, 1971, which declared 'the right of the individual to do his thing, so long as it does not interfere with the rights of another' to be 'crucial'. One of a number of grievances it listed was that 'Appeals to chauvinism, nationalism and militarism smother the individual right to conscientious free choice of action and belief'.

While the origins of baseball and football – even where they have not been overlaid with myth and falsification – are difficult to pin down with any certainty, those of basketball are known with scientific accuracy. The game sprang, almost fully formed, from the brain of Dr James Naismith in 1891. Dr Naismith was an instructor in physical education at the International Y.M.C.A. Training School in Springfield, Massachusetts, and he had this problem: when the severe New England winter made outside activity impossible, his students had to spend their time doing calisthenics in the gymnasium, a routine that was far from popular. He needed an indoor sport for them to play, a *game* that could be fun and provide exercise at the same time.

The basic equipment of his solution was a soccer ball and two round peach baskets. The baskets were attached to the ten-foot-high balcony, one at each end of the gymnasium (and also provided a name for the sport), and two teams of nine men tried to throw the ball into their opponents' peach basket. The players were not allowed to run with the ball in their hands, which would have made things too easy, they had to dribble it by bouncing it, or they had to pass it; and they were not allowed to tackle each other, which would have been inviting injuries on the hard floor. A further possible source of toughness was eliminated by having the baskets high above the floor, where a vigorously thrown ball could not possibly score. The ball had to be thrown in an arc to enter the basket.*

The dream of the early baseball men – an American sport invented in America by an American – came close to realization in basketball, spoiled only by Dr Naismith not being an American. He was Canadian, and had been educated at Montreal's McGill University, that same university that had played so large a role in the birth of football.

The nationwide chain of Y.M.C.A.s, which were devoted to the idea of physical fitness, was an ideal means of spreading Dr Naismith's fun game with peach baskets. In no time at all regional Y.M.C.A. tournaments were being organized, and within only four years of its conception, basketball was gaining a hold in high schools and colleges. It was impossible for Americans, having discovered an exciting sport, to play it just for amusement. The will to win asserted itself. The Y.M.C.A. found the trend distasteful, and quietly disbanded its teams and tournaments, but the sport now had a momentum of its own, and the players got together to form clubs. By 1898 there were even professional leagues

* A short description of the rules and action of basketball is given in the Appendices, page 269 ff.

operating around some of the large cities, notably Philadelphia, but this was very low-key professionalism. Nobody was making or even looked like making a fortune out of professional basketball, and most of the teams were financed by commercial firms as a form of publicity rather than as profit-makers.

Ultimately it was architecture more than anything else that decided the future of basketball. If the sport was to make money, it had to be played in large halls that could seat thousands of spectators. By the 1930s such arenas were available in several large cities. They had been built to cash in on the boxing craze of the twenties, but to make them profitable they needed to be used as much as possible. The new Madison Square Garden, for instance, opened in New York in 1925, offered boxing and track meets and six-day bicycle races and ice hockey and the circus, and it still had spare time to fill.

What brought Madison Square Garden and basketball together, goes a rather appealing story, was a ripped pair of trousers. They belonged to the *New York World Telegram* sports writer Ned Irish, and the damage was done as he climbed through a window, the only way he could get into a jam-packed gymnasium to cover a local college game. Such frenzied and chaotic conditions were a regular part of the New York college scene, where the enthusiasm for basketball was enormous, but the gymnasiums were not. Figuring that thousands of fans were being locked out, or were simply staying away because of the rough-house conditions, Ned Irish decided to leave the newspaper world and become a promoter of college games, to be played at Madison Square Garden where over 16,000 fans could see them. He put on the games in pairs and in 1935, his first year of operation, eight of these 'doubleheaders' drew an average of 12,000 fans each. Big-time college basketball – with all that it implied by way of highly paid coaches and high-pressure recruiting of high-school players – was on the way.

It was given a welcome, if rather unexpected, boost by World War II. While baseball and football were watching their best players disappearing into the armed services, many of college basketball's stars were being declared 'too tall' for military duty. In 1942, West Texas State College was able to bill itself as the World's Tallest Team, with an average height of 6 ft 6½ ins. Height always had been an advantage, but now began the systematic search for exceptionally tall players. DePaul University built a winning team around 6 ft 9 ins George Mikan, while Oklahoma A and M, led by 7 ft Bob Kurland won the college championship twice running in 1945 and 1946.

While the college game went from strength to strength, the professional scene languished. In 1946 there were two leagues, but they were second-rate affairs with teams in such un-noteworthy places as Oshkosh, Sheboygan, Wilmington and Jersey City. Not what might, by any stretch of the imagination, be called major-league cities. The anomalous situation almost demanded the attention of big promoters, for surely there must be a way of translating college popularity into professional profit? Convinced that there was indeed a way, eleven promoters – every one of them the owner of a large arena in a large city – got together in 1946 and formed the Basketball Association of America. The teams were thus owned by the arenas, which ought to have meant that they would not have any difficulty finding anywhere to play. It did not, quite, because professional basketball was not yet important enough for Madison Square Garden, who owned the New York team, to give it preference over the college doubleheaders. The New York Knickerbockers had to play most of their home games in an armoury.

In 1949 the B.A.A. swallowed up its only serious rival, and changed its name to the National Basketball Association. It now had all the top players, including the giant George Mikan, who was proving as big a draw in the professionals as he had been in college. The new league had seventeen teams, but not for very long. By 1950 it was down to eleven again. The millennium, evidently, had not arrived yet – but the ground was being prepared. In that same year of 1950, for the first time, black players appeared on N.B.A. teams, just one or two at first, the advance guard of what was to become almost an occupying force.*

Another key step in basketball's rise was the 1954 decision to introduce the 24-second rule. This was the sport's answer to the same problem that has bedevilled soccer in the sixties – negative, defensive play. A team that had the lead became more interested in maintaining possession of the ball than in attempting to score. The new rule stated that a team must make a scoring attempt within 24 seconds of gaining possession of the ball; if they did not, the ball was given to their opponents. The problem of timing the attempts was neatly solved with 24-second clocks placed at ground level at each end of the court, or suspended over the centre, with large illuminated numbers ticking off the seconds where

---

* There had never been, as there had in baseball, any serious attempt to belittle the talents of the Negro players. It would have been difficult to do so, with the example of the Harlem Globetrotters so close at hand. This all-black team, famed for its comedy routines, had frequently beaten professional teams, including the 1949 champions, the Minneapolis Lakers, George Mikan and all.

10 Wilt Chamberlain (left), at 7 ft 1 is the biggest of basketball's big men. By 1972 'Wilt the Stilt's' salary exceeded $300,000 a year.

fans and players alike could see them. An extra timekeeper was required to orchestrate the clocks, resetting them by pressing a button after each scoring attempt or when the ball changed hands. Designed to ensure an attacking, high-scoring game, the 24-second rule worked like a charm, and so it was a rather perverse twist that the man who came to dominate the game between 1957 and 1969, Bill Russell, was a defensive specialist. Russell, the best of the brilliant young black players who were now entering the game, joined the Boston Celtics after helping the United States win the 1956 Olympic title in Melbourne. During his thirteen years with the Celtics, they won the championship eleven times. The N.B.A.'s first 'big man', George Mikan, had regularly been among the leading scorers but Russell, who was the same height, never was. Leadership in that department went to another black player, the phenomenal Wilt Chamberlain. They called him Wilt the Stilt, and one look was enough to tell you why. His height was officially given as 7 ft 1 in, he admitted to 7 ft $1\frac{1}{16}$ ins, and there were plenty of people around willing to swear it was nearer 7 ft 4 ins. Chamberlain rewrote all the scoring records, especially in 1962 when he poured in 4,029 points while his nearest rival could manage only 2,495. Despite his assault on the record books, Chamberlain's professional career was not all that it might have been. He had disputes with several of his coaches, getting two of them fired by he-goes-or-I-do threats, and even though by 1973 he was reputedly the highest paid professional athlete in America (at over $300,000 a year) he had only twice in 1967 and 1972, been on a championship team. In seven of the remaining years he had run into Bill Russell and the Celtics, and lost each time.

In 1967 basketball got the traditional and unwelcome signal that it was now an established professional sport. A rival league appeared. The formation of the American Basketball Association (A.B.A.) had a sensational effect on players salaries which increased, in some cases, by as much as five times. It was painful to the N.B.A. owners, but at least it prevented a mass switch of stars to the new league. The A.B.A., with George Mikan as its Commissioner, staggered through its first two seasons without making much impression on anything (always excepting players' salaries) and played its games before dangerously low attendances.

Looming on the horizon, however, was a giant figure who, the A.B.A. felt, could act as a sort of *deus ex machina* and resolve all their problems for them. Lew Alcindor,* in 1969, was just completing his spectacularly successful college career, and if mouths were watering in the N.B.A.,

* In 1971 Alcindor changed his name to Kareem Abdul-Jabbar.

those in the A.B.A. were positively awash. With Bill Russell now retired, and Wilt Chamberlain nearing the end of his career, everyone was agreed that Lew Alcindor, at 7 ft 2 in, would be basketball's next superstar. If the A.B.A. could get him, their days out in the cold would be over, and excitement was heightened by Alcindor's statement that he would not, as had so many college stars, automatically join the older league. If the A.B.A. made him a reasonable offer, he would seriously consider it.

There was plenty of excitement in the N.B.A., too, notably, in the cities of Phoenix and Milwaukee, the teams that had finished bottom in the league's West and East divisions. One of these two would get the first choice in the 1969 draft, and obviously they would pick Alcindor. But which one? The N.B.A. resolved this by simply tossing a coin. The Phoenix Suns called heads, and got it wrong.

Poor Phoenix. They had spent the season being beaten by insultingly large scores. Their won-lost record was far worse than Milwaukee's, yet it would all have been worth it – if only they had got Alcindor. Their most crushing defeat thus came off court, the result of a mis-call on a coin toss. Considering what was at stake, it was just as well that it was their president who made the call. It meant that if Alcindor chose the N.B.A., he would have to play for the Milwaukee Bucks.

In their scramble to get Alcindor, the A.B.A. owners threw their own draft regulations out of the window, and announced that if he joined the A.B.A., Alcindor could choose which of the clubs he preferred to play with, the assumption being that, because his home was in New York, he would choose the New York Nets (who were not entitled to the first draft choice and, for further confusion, actually played in New Jersey). With their saviour almost in reach, the A.B.A. muffed it by offering him a lousy $1 million. Milwaukee's offer was $1.4 million, and so it was to Milwaukee that Alcindor went – a twenty-three-year-old who had not yet played one second of professional ball, but who already had a tax lawyer.*

The loss of Alcindor did not cause the A.B.A. to roll over and die, as some had predicted. It hung on until it was time for them and the N.B.A. owners to forget all about this competition stuff, and arrange a nice little

---

* Alcindor did all that was expected of him. Before he arrived, Milwaukee had a 1969 won-lost record of 27-55. In 1970, that was almost exactly reversed, 56-26. In 1971 it was 66-16, and the Bucks won the championship. For the tax lawyers, there was this: the year before Alcindor arrived, the Bucks lost $371,894 on the season. The very next year their home attendances jumped 50 per cent, and they made a profit of over $500,000.

merger, just as the two football leagues had done in 1966. But 1970 was not 1966. The basketball players, from both leagues, were wiser than the football players had been. They knew exactly what a merger was likely to do to their bargaining power, and hence their salaries. They went to court to block the merger.*

To account for the rapid way in which basketball had pushed its way into the major sports scene there were, to start with, two prosaically practical reasons: space, and money. Most Americans were now living in big cities, and basketball is the ideal big city game. It needs no grass and requires a minimum of ground space because, like the cities themselves, so much of its movement is vertical, not horizontal. A ball, a few square yards of concrete, a hoop attached to a lamp post or a wall are all that are needed. It is a godsend to schools and colleges without space for playing fields. It is also one of the cheapest sports to organize, with only five men to a team, and very little equipment needed, and this became a factor of increasing importance as education budgets were cut back in the late sixties.

Alongside the practical reasons working in basketball's favour are the less tangible social forces represented by the transformation of Consciousness II into Consciousness III. The coming of Consciousness III, says Reich, represents the end of man's subordination to the machine; its key 'lies in the concept of full personal responsibility'. Should these become the dominant trends in American life, as Reich suggests they inevitably will, it is difficult to imagine football – the most mechanical and the least individualistic of games – retaining its hold as the nation's leading sport.

Basketball is another matter altogether. It is a fluid, free-flowing game of constantly changing patterns, a game in which the players are called on to use their own judgement in almost every move they make. Gone are the helmets and padding of football, replaced by the scanty shorts and shirts that permit complete freedom of movement (for Consciousness III, says Reich, 'clothes express freedom)'. The basketball player is again a human being, recognizable both by his face and by the shape and movements of his body. The core of football is violently applied brute strength. That of basketball is subtly applied skill. Football's insistence on its patriotic and political merits has given it a relentless solemnity, an almost lowering quality that leaves no place for fun. Nothing light-

* A move that resulted in a good deal of legal activity and attempts to get Congress to pass special legislation permitting a merger. But the 1973–4 season was played with the two leagues still operating independently.

hearted ever happens on the football field. Basketball has so far managed to avoid being saddled with socially meaningful overtones. It remains a game, and one in which there is room for the expression of individual virtuosity and style. 'The individual is free to be inventive, playful and humorous', says Reich of the Consciousness III type, and while it is asking a bit too much of a professional sport to allow that degree of licence, the Harlem Globetrotters have shown that basketball and light-heartedness are not in any way incompatible. But what is amusingly irreverent in basketball would be sacrilege most foul in football. The very idea of a football version of the Globetrotters escapes the imagination. Religions are not mocked.

Maturing in an age when the youth culture had brought iconoclasm into style, basketball avoided locking itself into the traditional positions of the other sports. Where baseball and football worried about hair length and moustaches and some clubs even issued regulations stipulating an acceptable length for sideburns, basketball players were to be seen with beards, mutton-chop whiskers, and Afro hair styles. It was, to a large degree, the presence of so many black players (by 1970 they outnumbered whites) that accounted for basketball's freer attitude. Many of them were from the big city ghettoes and they knew from first hand experience all about the other side of the American Dream. Any attempt to sell them football-style discipline in the name of patriotism and the furtherance of the American way of life was doomed to failure.*

One of the more remarkable things about the youth culture is its internationalism, the way that the life style symbolized by long hair, bell bottoms and Beatles has taken root in places as culturally diverse as London, Saigon, Prague and Stockholm. It is a quality that has been conspicuously missing from American sport. Baseball and football both delight in calling their top teams 'World Champions', but it is a designation without much meaning. After an initial rush of enthusiasm around the turn of the century, baseball soon lost interest in spreading its gospel around the globe and of the major countries only the Japanese have shown enough interest to make it their No. 1 sport. Football is virtually unknown outside North America. Basketball is the first American sport to be taken up widely all over the world (it has been an Olympic sport since 1936), and the only one to offer the possibility of genuine international play. Even so, for a long time yet this is likely to be competition only for amateurs. The American professionals are simply too good.

* Football, of course, did try it, and found itself beset with problems. See Chapter 7, page 134.

7 Too Bad He's Coloured

All it took was a request for a cup of coffee in a Woolworth's store in Greensboro, North Carolina. The request was refused because the four customers were black and 'we don't serve coloureds here'. They sat there, four frightened but determined teenaged students, until the store closed. The news media the next day hardly bothered to notice the incident, but it made no difference. An idea's time had arrived. Suddenly, white America was given notice that Negroes were sick of their second-class citizenship. They had been waiting with a slowly diminishing patience since 1865, since the end of the Civil War when the North had conquered the South and the slaves were freed, and it looked as though that shining declaration of the United States Constitution, 'That all men are created equal,' was about to mean what it said.

Now it was 1960, nearly one hundred years later, and their patience had run out. It was still the back of the bus for the blacks, the menial jobs, the worst schools, the ghetto. They felt that white America was turning its back on them, was developing a society in which they were fast becoming superfluous. The Civil Rights Movement was born and America could no longer ignore the frightening fact that some 20 million of its citizens were dissatisfied and were making noises that sounded almost revolutionary.

As the sixties went by, those noises were to get considerably louder. Threaded through the debate that arose was the general opinion among both whites and blacks that there was one area, at least, where blacks had been treated without discrimination: sport. A quick look at the professional sports scene was enough to prove this. There were black stars – and highly paid ones at that – in football, baseball and basketball and the number of black players in all three sports was on the rise. The Washington Redskins football team was the only professional team with no Negroes. The owner of the club simply would not have them, and he was paying quite a price for his prejudice: between 1948 and 1960, a period when all the other football teams were using black players, the all-white Redskins were consistently one of the worst teams in the league, and they won nothing at all. In baseball, the Boston Red Sox had held out for years, but had finally signed their first black player in 1959. Compared with almost every other field, sport was in great shape as far as integration was concerned.

This was, however, a comparatively recent state of affairs – post World War II, in fact. The early days of professional baseball, at the end of the nineteenth century, had seen the beginning of a concerted movement to keep the blacks out. In 1887 there was a handful of blacks playing on white teams in the minor leagues. One or two had even played for a major-league team. But their acceptance by the white players was something less than eager. One of the most vehement opponents was Cap Anson, the captain of the Chicago White Stockings, and the greatest player of the time. Everyone wanted to see him in action – like the fans in Newark who flocked expectantly to an exhibition game despite the disappointment that their own star pitcher, Stovey, had been suddenly taken ill and was unable to play. Stovey was black, and it later turned out that he had not been ill at all. He had been taken out of the line-up because Anson refused to have his White Stockings play against a Negro. Feeding on quiet, spineless decisions of this sort, camouflaged by suitable lies, the anti-black movement grew. In September of 1887, there was further trouble over an exhibition game. Seven thousand people were already in the stadium at West Farms, N.Y., waiting to see an all-Negro team play the St Louis Browns, when a telegram arrived from the Browns' owner. The Browns had too many injured players and would not be able to play, it said. It was another lie. What had happened was that eight of the St Louis players had told their manager that they would not play against Negroes. Lest it be thought they were merely being lazy, they added, 'We will cheerfully play against white people at any time, and think, by refusing to play, we are only doing what is right . . . '

The attempt by the black man to play the white man's game was over. The International League, the most important of those that did allow blacks to play, had voted to 'approve no more contracts with coloured men'.

Banned from playing with whites, the few Negro baseball players who had made it returned to the professional and semi-professional all-black teams. Attempts to organize the teams into leagues met with little success. Clubs were not willing to be tied down by a regular schedule, they preferred to make their money by barnstorming, travelling all over the

11 Satchel Paige, the legendary figure of the black baseball leagues, styled himself 'The World's Greatest Pitcher', and there were not many players, black or white, prepared to dispute the claim.

12 Barred from professional baseball until 1947, black players quickly
established their worth throughout the 1960s. By 1970 one out of four
baseball players in the major leagues was black.

country, often arranging their games as they went. The subculture of black baseball was born.

The early black teams were almost all from northern cities, and played most of their games in the north, where the problems of discrimination were less pronounced. They frequently played against white teams, even against major-league teams. In Chicago, the White Sox and the Cubs would not agree to meet black clubs – they no doubt felt it would be of little merit to win such a game, and extremely embarrassing to lose it. Yet individual players from these teams, including some of their most prominent stars, regularly played against black teams; they simply lent themselves to another team, under a false name, and played in Sunday morning games.

There remained the problem of discrimination outside the ballpark. For black teams who did a lot of travelling, as most of them did, this could mean having to travel hundreds of miles without finding a restaurant that would serve them or a hotel that would put them up. It was a serious problem, and one of the first black professional teams came up with a solution of sorts. They changed their name from Athletics to Cuban Giants, the idea being that if they posed as foreigners they would get better treatment. On the field they chatted away to each other in a meaningless gibberish that they hoped the opposition would believe was Spanish.

For most black teams the life was one of almost incessant travelling and baseball. They went by rail, or by bus, or sometimes they had a team car. They stayed in the seediest of hotels, or they lodged overnight with black families, or if the worst came to the worst, as often it did, they slept at the stadium. They covered heroic distances in days when there were no highways, taking on any team that would play them. Black baseball was often more than just baseball. When the barnstorming teams arrived at small rural villages, it was an occasion for celebration, like the visit of a circus. The baseball team would form a parade to march through the town to the stadium before the game, and some of the teams specialized in clowning before and even during the games. Others were part of a carnival, travelling with the sideshows and the performers, challenging local teams to play, and rarely losing, probably because they also supplied the umpires. The All-American Black Tourists, formed in 1899, did their barnstorming with a deal of class, travelling in their own railway carriage, and parading through the streets in full evening dress, including top-hats. They even offered to play baseball so dressed if any of their opponents wanted it that way.

Another difficulty was that players rarely signed written contracts with their clubs, and were forever jumping from one team to another and back again. Spectators watching a game on Wednesday were likely to see quite a few of the players they had watched playing for different teams the Monday before. By Friday they might be back with their original teams again.

At the turn of the century, organized baseball (that is, the major-leagues and the system of minor leagues associated with them) was a totally white affair – well, almost so. For it seems that the big objection was not so much to skin colour, as to the American Negro. American Indians, for example, were acceptable. This led John McGraw, manager of the New York Giants, to concoct a neat deception in 1901. He discovered a fine black player named Charlie Grant, who, he decided, was just what the Giants needed. Grant was light-skinned, and McGraw announced that he had signed a 'full-blooded Cherokee' named Tokohama. Under this unfamiliar name, Charlie Grant prepared to enter the major leagues. He never did make it. The secret got out. One story has it that during an exhibition game in Chicago, hordes of his former fans turned out and greeted his appearance with a banner saying 'Our Boy – Charlie Grant', blissfully unaware that they were wrecking Tokohama's chances; another story says that the deception was spotted by another club owner who said that 'the Cherokee of McGraw's is really Grant, the crack Negro second-baseman from Cincinnati, fixed up with war paint and a bunch of feathers'. Whatever the reason, Tokohama was soon to be seen playing with the Columbia Giants – an all-black team.

It is thought that a few other Negroes, of light enough skin colour, probably did manage to pass as white or Indian and there were certainly one or two Cubans (light-skinned, of course) who played. But they were the rare exception, an oddity here and there, and it never for one moment looked as though they were preparing the way for the fall of organized baseball's apartheid.

In 1920 the Negro National League was formed, consisting of eight of the top Negro professional clubs. It was to prove the first viable league, but it did not in any way stop the clubs from barnstorming. These were teams that never stopped playing baseball. In between their league games, they went off on their traditional barnstorming tours, and when the winter arrived they headed South, a colourful swarm emigrating to the sun of Florida or California or – even better – to Cuba or Mexico, where they could play baseball without having to worry about discrimination.

Throughout the twenties and the thirties these sporting troubadours criss-crossed the United States, entertaining black and white alike. They had taken the white man's game and produced a wild and woolly black version of it. If white baseball was the classical version, then the blacks played it jazz style, less disciplined, more colourful and, of course, less profitable. The names of the stars have the same euphonious flamboyance as those of the early jazz musicians: Cool Papa Bell, Mule Suttles, Pee Wee Spencer, Cannonball Redding, Double Duty Radcliffe, Big Train Parker, Goo Goo Livingston, Buck Leonard, Buster Haywood, Popsickle Harris, Rab Roy Gaston, Bear Man Davenport, Steel Arm Davis, Black Bottom Buford.

No doubt the life had a glamorous free-swinging attractiveness about it, but black baseball, beneath that carefree surface, was at heart a tragedy. There were men playing for black teams who would have been stars, perhaps even superstars, in the major leagues. They were cut off from national fame and fortune, not because they were not good enough, but because their skin was the wrong colour. They did, from time to time, play against white all-star teams; they frequently won these games, and it was the opinion of many white players that the best black players were at least as good as their white counterparts. While Babe Ruth was being paid $80,000 because he could hit the ball further than anyone had yet hit it, the top black slugger Josh Gibson was making about $4,000 a year, and playing many more games. And there is weighty evidence that says Gibson was the more powerful hitter; he played several times in Ruth's home territory, Yankee Stadium, and hit the ball further into the centre-field seats than Ruth was ever to do. It was also claimed that he once hit a ball clean out of the stadium, something neither Ruth, nor anyone else, has ever done.* It made no difference. Gibson's main claim to fame is still that he was known as The Black Babe Ruth. It was the opinion of Walter Johnson, a top white player of the era, that any big league club would cough up $200,000 to get Gibson. 'Too bad this Gibson is a coloured fellow,' he mused.

Even if prejudice could be laid aside, there were still immense problems in assessing the performances of the black players. Records of

---

* It is said, as they say, that Gibson once hit a ball so hard and so high during a game in Pittsburgh, that it just took off and disappeared. The umpires searched the heavens for a while, and then awarded Gibson a home run. The following day Gibson was playing in Philadelphia and during the game a ball suddenly dropped out of nowhere and was caught by an opponent. 'Yer out!' said the umpire pointing at Gibson, 'Yesterday – in Pittsburgh.'

their games were patchy affairs, really rather ludicrous when compared with the welter of statistics that surrounded the white players. When Babe Ruth hit sixty home runs in one season, it was acclaimed as a superhuman feat that would never be equalled.* But Josh Gibson was said to have hit eighty-nine one year, seventy-five another. Alas, there was just no way of checking up, or finding out what sort of opposition he faced.

Looking back into Negro baseball history, even just a few years back, was like peering at a landscape in the gloaming when everything fades into formlessness on close scrutiny. It was the perfect atmosphere for the birth of myths and legends. Out of it, right on cue, came the fabulous Satchel Paige. By the 1930s, Paige's name was known to everyone who knew anything at all about baseball. He was a one-man show, travelling around the country pitching for any team that would pay him from $500 to $2,000 for three innings. He wore a uniform with the word 'Satchel' on it, and he billed himself as The World's Greatest Pitcher. Everyone who saw him, and the crowds flocked out whenever he was performing, knew it was the truth. He threw the ball harder and faster than seemed possible: To make contact, however slight, with a Paige pitch was quite an achievement; to hit one solidly could make one an instant hero.

Born in Mobile, Alabama, Paige soon fell a victim to southern justice. At the age of twelve he stole some toy rings from a store – and that was enough to land him in reform school for five years. That was where he learnt to pitch. Released in 1923, he played in semi-professional teams for a while, and began his professional career in 1926. Paige was recognized as something very special almost from the first pitch he threw. He won almost every game he pitched, and, as his fame spread, the fans came to expect him to be, at least, sensational. Usually he was. In some games, when he felt he was in good form, he would wave his three outfielders off the field, confident that no batter would hit the ball that far. Occasionally he would even send the infielders off as well, declaring to everyone that Satchel Paige needed no help from anyone.

For Paige was always completely his own man. He never really could get accustomed to the thought of regular schedules and playing for only one club. Throughout his career he bounced around from club to club in a way that was the despair of his managers. He could get away with it because his talent and drawing power were so enormous that he was

* It was – in 1961, when Roger Maris of the New York Yankees hit sixty-one.

always welcomed back. He was an unlikely shape for a super-athlete. He stood 6 ft 3 ins and was alarmingly thin, with all the solidity of a tooth-pick. The most impressive part of him were his feet, which were size twelve and flat. Nor did he behave like a star athlete is supposed to. The idea of strenuous exercise, particularly running, filled him with horror. In fact, it upset his stomach, which was the only part of him that Satch ever had any trouble with. 'I believe in training by rising gently up and down from the bench,' he said, and could not understand at all the training ideas of a manager who 'had me flyin' around, shakin' my legs and carryin' on until I very near passed. Now what did all that do for my arm?' Paige had his own way of looking after the fabulous arm – he rubbed it with a mysterious oil. This, he revealed, he had obtained from one Dorothy Running-Deer, a Sioux fan of his, whose father raised rattlesnakes. The oil was supposed to neutralize snake bites, but Paige found that it had a galvanic effect on his arm. It had to be diluted though. The first time, Paige used it neat, and later allowed: 'Man, it's a wonder my arm didn't fly outta the room.'

Paige played in Cuba where – shades of the New York Cuban Giants – everyone on the team really did speak Spanish and Paige could not understand a word. He pleaded: 'Speak English, Brothers, I is with you!' He played in Mexico, where, for the only time in his career, he developed trouble with his arm. He blamed it on the spicy Mexican food which he said upset his nervous stomach, from which the poisons spread to his arm. And, under rather James Bondish circumstances, he also played in the Dominican Republic. The call came in 1937, and it came from Numero Uno himself, the dictator Rafael Trujillo. That a head of state needed his services did not impress Paige at all, and he agreed to go only when the financial part of the deal became irresistible. Once again he deserted his club, and this time he induced nine others to go with him. His team was the Trujillo Stars, and it quickly became clear to Paige that he had landed himself in quite a predicament. It seemed that this was election year, a somewhat fictional affair that Trujillo was scheduled to win. His opponent, however, had been showing surprising and totally inexcusable popularity, mostly because he was the owner of an all-star baseball team that was going round the country playing superb ball and beating every-one. Paige and his Trujillo Stars were to put a stop to that at a special tournament featuring both teams in Santo Domingo. They were to win the tournament – those were orders. To make sure there were no second thoughts by any of the Stars, they were chaperoned everywhere by large contingents of Trujillo's army with fixed bayonets. It was all very bad for Paige's stomach gas, but he came through and the Stars won the tournament. They all left the Dominican Republic immediately afterwards, $30,000 richer, without waiting to see if El Presidente won his election.

By 1939, Paige's wanderlust seemed to have dried up; he joined the Kansas City Monarchs, and remained with them for the next ten seasons, age apparently powerless to interfere with his amazing right arm. Anyway, no one was really certain how old he was. His mother said he was born in 1903, his draft card said 1906, and *he* said 1908. Not that it mattered, for legends are not supposed to have birth certificates and Paige was unquestionably a legend. He had pitched more games, and won more games, and struck out more hitters and just done more of *everything* than any other pitcher, black or white, in history. The whites had kept him out of the big leagues, but at one time or another during his barnstorming games, he had played against most of the white stars in exhibition games, and there was hardly one of them who did not rate him among the greatest.

Paige's most outstanding performance was the game he pitched against Dizzy Dean's team of white all-stars, beating them 1–0. Dean, himself a candidate for 'greatest pitcher' honours, said later that Paige was the greatest of them all.

Paige made no secret of the things that were responsible for his greatness. Apparently anyone could do it – there were just six rules to be followed:

1. Avoid fried meats which angry up the blood.
2. If your stomach disputes you, lie down and pacify it with cool thoughts.
3. Keep the juices flowing by jangling around gently as you move.
4. Go very light on the vices, such as carrying on in society. The social ramble ain't restful.
5. Avoid running at all times.
6. Don't look back. Something might be gaining on you.

For over twenty years Satchel was the scourge of the Negro baseball leagues, pitching like a demon while avoiding fried meats, vices, and running, and, of course, never once looking back. But during those twenty years, there was shamefully little pressure for the admission of blacks to the major leagues. The whites did nothing while the Negroes contented themselves with occasional complaints in the black press.

It is a sad reflection on man's sanity in these matters that it took a hideously destructive war to bring about what could have been accomplished at any time by a simple decision of the baseball owners. As the formidable American armaments industry expanded in 1940 and 1941, the chronic unemployment that had lasted since the Depression began to decrease. But blacks could hardly help noticing that it was the whites who were employed first, and that it was the blacks who got the worst-paying jobs. When Negro leaders threatened a mass march on Washington unless this discrimination were stopped, President Roosevelt issued the famous Executive Order 8802 in 1941, that outlawed discrimination in the defence industries or any government employment. Ironically, segregation remained the rule in the biggest of the government-run defence operations: the armed services. The war, incredibly, made no difference to military thinking.

Jack Robinson was an intelligent young black, educated at the University of California, who was drafted into the Army in 1942. In 1943 he was commissioned as a lieutenant and put in charge of a tank battalion – an all-Negro battalion, that is – in Texas. One evening he boarded a bus, on the base, and was promptly ordered to 'get to the rear' by the driver – a white civilian. Robinson refused, and was later charged with being drunk, 'conduct unbecoming', and disrespect. The charges were eventually dropped, but only after an intense campaign by the black press and the National Association for the Advancement of Colored People (N.A.A.C.P.).

Such incidents could not be explained away. To ask a man to risk his life fighting against distant Nazi racism when he was a continual victim of racism right in his own country was too big and too obscene a contradiction.

The pressure on baseball was rising. In the spring of 1945, two black players did actually have a tryout for the Brooklyn Dodgers. They were turned down as not good enough by the Brooklyn manager, Branch Rickey. It looked like just another piece of proof that blacks would *never* be good enough for the major league. It was not. For Rickey, long one of the most adventurous minds in baseball (and therefore, something of a pain in the neck to his fellow owners) was already devising a scheme to break baseball's colour bar. He knew that if he blandly announced an intention to recruit Negroes for the Dodgers, he would immediately solidify all the opposing forces, particularly among the baseball owners, who believed that such a move would damage the sport, and hence reduce the value of their investments in it.*

* Rickey later claimed that at a meeting of the owners in 1945, he had brought up the question of allowing blacks to play, and that fourteen of the fifteen clubs present supported a resolution banning them. There is no official record of this

Rickey fooled them all by announcing that the Dodgers were going to organize an all-black team, the Brown Dodgers, and enter it in a newly formed black league, The United States League. He could now loose his scouts all over the country – and the Dodgers had one of the best scouting systems in baseball – to look at black players. Even the scouts themselves believed that they were recruiting for the Brown Dodgers, a team that Rickey had no intention of fielding. Ironically, while this subterfuge worked beautifully to allay the fears of the white owners, it provoked harsh criticism from many black sources, who did not want more white men running black clubs.

Rickey was not looking for black players. He was looking for just one – *the* black player whom he could trust to play the role of pioneer. This meant not just a superb player, but also a man of irreproachable personal life and great self-discipline. Rickey anticipated that the pressures on baseball's first black major leaguer would unsettle any but the most exceptional man.

The names of likely prospects for the Brown Dodgers came in from the scouts and from them Rickey singled out that of Jackie Robinson, then playing shortstop with the Kansas City Monarchs – the team with which Satchel Paige had finally settled down.

Robinson was twenty-six, a non-smoker and a non-drinker, and he was the same Robinson who had been ordered to the back of the Army bus in Texas. Rickey sent for him, and Robinson – somewhat half-heartedly – agreed to go to New York for an interview.

Within minutes of starting to talk, Rickey had told Robinson that the Brown Dodgers were a front, and that what he wanted Jackie to do was nothing less than single-handedly brave the slings and arrows of the white baseball world. Rickey spent the next three hours explaining to Robinson the sort of mental and physical abuse he would have to put up with – often acting the part of the tormentor himself, all the time assessing Robinson's reactions, trying to decide whether he would be able to turn a deaf ear to racial taunts and slurs. Robinson was amazed at Rickey's insight: 'He seemed to know more about the problems that Negroes face than any white man in my experience. He knew every taunt, dig, threat, and underhand device of the bigots. He shouted their damnable curses at me, then pulled up sharply. "Can you take it?" he demanded. "Can you take it without fighting back?"' Robinson had been sitting listening

---

because, says Rickey, all copies of the report containing it were collected and destroyed.

to Rickey tell him that opposing pitchers would throw the ball at his head, that base runners would try to run into him, and that when he did not retaliate – as he must *never* do – they would call him a yellow nigger. Then there would be umpires who certainly would not give him any breaks, and snotty hotel clerks and waitresses who would refuse him service. To all this provocation, Robinson's only answer was to be excellence as a player; he would silence his critics with his baseball skill. Not surprisingly, it took a great deal of effort by Rickey to convince Robinson that this was the only way it could be done. Finally Robinson agreed: he would play for Montreal, one of the Dodgers' farm clubs, in 1946. Here he would be groomed for his entry into the major leagues with the Dodgers – if all went well, in 1947.

Again criticism came from black sources, this time because Rickey had signed Robinson without paying a cent to his original club, the Kansas City Monarchs. This was quite legal, because Robinson had no written contract with the Monarchs; hardly any black players had contracts, they just 'agreed' to play for a certain club for a certain fee.

The expected furore from organized baseball never happened. No doubt this was partly because the major-league clubs knew next to nothing about the quality of black baseball; they believed that Robinson, trying to break into the game at twenty-six, would not be good enough, and that the experiment would quietly drop out of sight. But the quiet, if rather sullen, acceptance of Robinson was also an indication of slowly shifting attitudes. The feeling, however grudging, was that the time had come for change.

Before Robinson played his first game for Montreal, the club's manager Clay Hopper (he was from Mississippi) asked Branch Rickey 'You don't really think Nigrahs are human beings, do you?' with genuine puzzlement. Yet throughout the 1946 season Hopper treated Robinson fairly and when the season was over told him that he hoped to have him back in 1947.

He was out of luck. Robinson had performed spectacularly for Montreal, and was obviously ready for the Dodgers. Early in 1947, Rickey announced that Robinson was now a Dodger, the first black major leaguer in over fifty years. And immediately there was trouble among the other Dodgers. A group of them, mostly Southerners, signed a petition protesting against Robinson's signing and some of them demanded to be transferred. Rickey's talent for reasoning with people came to the fore; he talked with each player individually and persuaded them to accept Robinson.

Rickey had another problem to cope with before sending Robinson out to play with the Dodgers. He knew that New York's large black population would treat Robinson like a hero – and who could blame them – but he was worried that the player would become the centre of an adulatory social whirl that would affect his playing. There was also the possibility that an excessively triumphant attitude on the part of blacks would produce a white reaction. He discussed the matter with black community leaders in Brooklyn, who agreed to help cool matters should they look like getting out of hand. Their campaign used the slogan 'Don't Spoil Jackie's Chances'.

Even if things were settled in New York, and within the Dodgers, there was still the probability of trouble from other clubs. It was not long coming. Soon after the season opened, the *New York Herald Tribune* revealed that the St Louis Cardinals planned to refuse to play the Dodgers and were trying to organize a strike of all the other National League clubs against the Brooklyn Dodgers. The rumour brought a quick and stern response from the president of the National League, Ford Frick. His statement represents one of the few occasions when baseball took a firm stand on principle:

If you do this you will be suspended from the League. You will find that the friends you think you have in the press box will not support you, that you will be outcasts. I do not care if half the League strikes. Those who do it will encounter quick retribution. They will be suspended, and I don't care if it wrecks the N.L. for five years. This is the United States of America, and one citizen has as much right to play as another. The N.L. will go down the line with Robinson whatever the consequences.

There was no strike. There was, however, plenty of abuse for Robinson. In one notorious game, the Philadelphia players kept up a stream of such venomous insult that even the southerners on the Dodgers team publicly defended Robinson, knowing that he could not answer back himself. The episode aroused such general resentment, that the Philadelphia captain later issued a rather insipid apology.

It soon became obvious that Robinson was more than good enough as a player and as a man. Yet there was no great rush by the other clubs to sign blacks. The first to join Rickey was Bill Veeck (another maverick looked upon with distaste by his fellow owners) who, late in 1947, announced the signing of Lary Doby, and put him straight onto the Cleveland Indians team. The following year Veeck signed a black relief pitcher, and on 9 July 1948, when he was brought into a game for the first time, the Cleveland crowd of 20,000 stood and cheered and applauded for minutes on end as the tall long-legged figure ambled across the outfield towards the pitching mound. Satchel Paige had at last made the major leagues. At the age of forty-two (give or take a couple of years) he was still good enough.

The number of Negroes in baseball increased with painful slowness. Six years after Robinson's début, there were twenty blacks playing, but nine of the sixteen major-league clubs had yet to integrate. By 1957 the number was thirty-six, while the number of all-white teams was down to two. In 1959, the Boston Red Sox became the last team to integrate.

Slowly, without noticeable good grace, baseball was conceding the blacks' right to play. It had ignored them for over fifty years, something that can never be atoned for, and now, even as it started to put things right, baseball added one final injury to all the insults it had dealt the Negroes. The admission of blacks to the major leagues was to mean the death of the black leagues, who saw their best players siphoned off by the National and American Leagues, and their attendances slump. The Negro National League soon folded, and the Negro American League struggled on until 1960 when it too collapsed.

Professional football, coming on the scene fifty years later than baseball, never had that sport's colour bar. For professional football the problem was a lot easier because there were not masses of blacks playing the sport all over the country, forming their own leagues, and waiting for a chance to get into the majors. Professional football drew virtually all its talent from college teams, where there were only a few Negro players. Furthermore, those blacks who did manage to get into college in the first decades of the twentieth century had to be exceptionally intelligent. But there was prejudice in the colleges – even for the exceptional.

In 1915 the great Negro singer and actor Paul Robeson entered Rutgers College as a seventeen-year-old freshman. He had been an outstanding athlete at high school, but it was his academic brilliance that had won him a scholarship to the college, where he was the only black student. He thought he would like to try out for the football team, and the coach agreed to give him a trial. At once half the team objected – they would not play with Robeson. The coach gave in to their pressure until Rutgers met local rival Princeton – and lost 10–0. After that, the coach announced that Robeson was going to join the team, and those who did not like it could quit if they wanted to. The white players did not quit, they just gave Robeson a thorough working over during practice sessions.

They broke his nose, and several fingers and they dislocated his shoulder. Robeson withstood it all, and went on to become one of the finest college players of his time. Twice, in 1917 and 1918, he was chosen as an All-American – yet even this highest of honours did not help him when Rutgers played Washington and Lee U from Virginia in 1918. The southerners objected, the northerners bowed, and Robeson had to sit out the game. He did go on to play professional football for a short while, before moving on to London, *Ol' Man River* and world-wide acclaim. But even he, the most exceptionally talented black of his time, had had to struggle for acceptance in college football.

Integration in sport proceeded at gathering pace throughout the fifties, leading to the receptive sixties when it looked as though all barriers were collapsing. A seemingly inexhaustible stream of black athletes flowed into professional sport, and many of them rose to the top and superstar status. Willie Mays was hitting home runs like nobody had since Babe Ruth, and was on his way to becoming the highest-paid player in the history of the game. Jim Brown was being called the greatest football player ever and was setting new records every time he stepped on the field. In basketball, Bill Russell was revolutionizing the game by showing that defence was important, too, and was another greatest-ever candidate.

When *Time* magazine conducted a survey of the number of blacks playing professional sport early in 1970, it found that Negroes, who make up 20 per cent of the United States population, had moved into sport with a vengeance. The figures were: baseball – 25 per cent, football – 32 per cent, and basketball – 55 per cent. It looked as though the Promised Land had arrived at last, that the black athlete had attained equality with his white colleague.

It may have looked that way, but the appearance was deceptive. During the late sixties a new voice began to be heard from black athletes, a strident voice that tended to talk of things like *rights*, and to frame requests as *demands*. It had taken nearly twenty years, but the era of the 'good black', the athlete who would put up with abuse and discrimination just for the privilege of being allowed to play the white man's games, was over. The new discrimination was not the crude sort of nigger-baiting that Robinson had had to put up with, but a more subtle and insidious thing that was much harder to come to grips with. The *Time* survey gave a clue as to what it was all about. In baseball, 25 per cent of the players were black, yet when it came to selecting the all-star teams, the percentage jumped to 36 per cent. The discrepancy was similar for the other sports – football 32 per cent jumping to 44 per cent of the all-stars, basketball 55 per cent to 63 per cent. What did this mean? It could only mean that the black players were, on average, better than the white players, and it backed up a claim that blacks had been making for some time: that for a black to get into professional sport it was no good his being as good as a white player – he had to be better. Most teams are made up of three or four stars plus a bunch of average performers. It had long been the feeling among blacks that to break into professional sport, the black had to be or show the potential of a star. The clubs were not interested in the average black player; there were plenty of average white players, and they would almost always get the job. This would not be easy to prove – there could always be reasons, other than race – ostensibly valid reasons – for preferring a white player over a black.

There was also discrimination within teams when it came to playing certain positions, especially in football. The key position in football is that of quarterback. He is the man who runs the show, usually the one who decides what plays to call.* It calls for an intelligent performer, and it is a position that is hardly ever occupied by a black player. In professional football in 1973 out of twenty-six first-choice quarterbacks *not one* was black.

In the professional world, a black quarterback is decidedly a *rara avis*. A rather more common *avis* is the black cornerback. This is a position on the defensive team, and his job is to mark opposing pass receivers – it consists mainly of running full speed with the opponent, trying not to be fooled by all his weaving and zig-zagging, and preventing him from catching a pass should one come his way. It is not considered a position that requires much brainwork – just speed and agility.

Of course, there could be perfectly valid reasons why there are no black quarterbacks and a surplus of black cornerbacks. What is more likely is that this is just another example of the prejudice that has always surrounded the black athlete. It is based on the assumption that the Negro is unintelligent, and can only perform well those tasks that require mere physical effort.

When black athletes started winning Olympic medals for the U.S.A. in the thirties, it was quickly noted that they were unbeatable at the short sprints, and the wise heads nodded and said well, that was what you would expect, all they had to do was run like hell until they hit the tape. Now, in the longer distances, the mile and up, blacks were no good,

---

* So much so that 'quarterbacking' is another of those sports terms that have seeped into everyday usage. To quarterback an operation is to be in charge of it.

because you had to pace yourself. With the arrival of such as Keino and Bikila, one does not hear that sort of nonsense much any more.*

There has been a series of these myths, the white man's defence against the feared superiority of the black (he can't think, he won't submit to discipline, he's lazy), and one by one the black has had to overcome them. Perhaps the most pernicious of these slurs is the one that holds that blacks are quitters who give up when the going gets tough. There is not the slightest shred of evidence to support these views, yet they persist, and their persistence shows that somebody needs them. They have become part of the white man's way of looking at the blacks, a set of basic assumptions that make up the institutionalized racism of sports. So institutionalized, in fact, that it is probably entirely unthinking by this time.

It is not just the Negro's pride that is hurt by this sort of discrimination. His pocket suffers, too. Quarterbacks are the glamour boys of football, and they earn the largest salaries of any players; cornerback is just another position, and one at the bottom of the pay scale.† There are other ways in which the black athlete suffers financially. Most believe that their signing-on bonuses are not as high as those paid to whites, while in the field of advertising endorsements – which can be an extremely profitable game to play – the black athlete has, until quite recently, been virtually invisible. Television commercials for things like hair dressings, toothpaste, razor blades and deodorants, frequently feature star athletes, and the casting directors seem to have a strong preference for white faces. Many black players have found that, once their career is finished, they are back to being just another Negro whose talents are not wanted anymore. There has been a steady flow of white ex-athletes into business, encouraged by firms and corporations who believe, no doubt rightly, that it is good for their image to have nationally known stars working for them. For black athletes, the opportunities have been less easy to come by.

* What one does hear, and what is equally silly, is that blacks are not good swimmers. Again, it *might* be that they are not, but anyone who has read this far will almost certainly agree that a far more likely reason is the social factor: swimming and swimming pools tend to be middle-class affairs – and there is a great deal of touchiness on the subject of mixed bathing.

† To illustrate: the team is watching films of their last game, which clearly show a cornerback failing in his duty and allowing an opponent to catch a pass. The coach turns off the projector and turns to the offending player: 'You're being paid $18,000 a year to stop him catching those passes.' 'OK,' comes the answer, 'but he's being paid $30,000 to see that he does catch them.'

There is a feeling among black athletes – for many it is more than that, it is a certainty – that there will never be an all-black baseball or football team, even though the talents of the players might warrant one. They maintain that there is an unwritten agreement in force, a quota system, that limits the number of blacks that each club will play. The number varies according to the club (and particularly that club's geographical location), but, say the blacks, it will never be high enough to allow blacks to dominate a team. Why should this be so? Because, it is suggested, the white owners believe that all-black teams would be bad for business, and that white fans – who are the substantial majority, and are wealthier – would soon stop turning out to support black teams.

Basketball star Bill Russell spoke out in 1958 and accused professional clubs of having a quota system. It was denied in the same way that it has always been denied: coaches and owners expressed amazement at such a suggestion and insisted that, if a player was good enough, they would use him whatever his colour – white, brown, yellow, purple or striped. When Russell made his original complaint, professional basketball was in its early days. No team had more than three blacks. Things have changed enormously since then, and today the idea of a quota in a sport where over half of the players are Negroes is hardly tenable. As a basketball team consists of only five players, it was always the most likely sport to field an all-black squad. Ironically, when it did happen, in 1970, it was the Atlanta Hawks who did it – the only professional basketball team located in the South.

The dissatisfaction of the Negro athlete built up throughout the sixties, nurtured by the growing atmosphere of black revolt. The first inkling that the average American sports fan had that something was drastically wrong came shortly before the 1968 Olympics in Mexico City. On to the scene strode Harry Edwards, 6 ft 8 ins tall, dark glasses, bearded and wearing a beret – good heavens, the man looked like a radical. He talked like one, too. Black athletes, he said, should not run for the United States at the Olympics. Why should they win glory for a country where they and their brothers were frequently denied the most simple of civil rights? He started to organize a black boycott of 'Whitey's Olympics'.

Edwards's challenge did not go unnoticed, to put it mildly, in white athletic circles. He had obviously struck a very sensitive area. He was attacked as a traitor to his country, dismissed as a malcontent. Leaving his house one morning, he opened the front door to find his two dogs killed, hacked into pieces, and dumped in his porch. Those athletes who supported his idea – they included world record holders Tommy Smith and Lee Evans – received plenty of hate mail of the 'you are a fine nigger specimen . . . hope you and your followers get your heads bashed in' variety.

Particularly galling to his adversaries was the way in which Edwards had risen to his eminence. He had been born in the East St Louis ghetto, just another of thousands of black kids with no future, and had been able to get out by way of sport. He was awarded an athletic scholarship to San Jose State College on the strength of his discus throwing. Once at college, his 165 IQ took over, and Edwards abandoned athletics for studies. And now here he was, turning and biting at the hand that had fed him.

His plan for an Olympic boycott was meant to dramatize to the world that the United States was still treating her blacks as second-class citizens – it was not aimed at getting specific reforms within sport. There was no boycott,* but to say that Edwards failed would be to grossly misread the situation. His movement was centred on amateur athletes – which means college athletes. It injected a mood of sharp militancy into the college scene, the full force of which is only beginning to be felt. The years since 1968 have been increasingly difficult ones for those college athletic departments – the majority – who want to continue running things the way they always have done.

A book about Negro athletes had been published in 1939, an optimistic volume proudly listing all those blacks who had been sports stars and predicting much better things to come. It contained only occasional references to what it called 'the bar sinister', and bore the non-controversial title *The Negro in Sports*. Thirty years later, Harry Edwards published a book on the Negro in sports – and he called it *The Revolt of the Black Athlete*.† The difference in the two titles tells the story. For almost every page of Edwards's book was controversial. He was especially scathing of those big universities that recruit black athletes to build up a

---

* But there were protests. Tommie Smith and John Carlos, the gold and the bronze medallists in the 200 metres, took the victory-stand shoeless and wearing black gloves. When the United States national anthem was played they bowed their heads and raised their gloved fists in the air. They were promptly suspended from the U.S. Olympic team. In the 1972 Olympics at Munich, Vince Matthews and Wayne Collett finished first and second in the 400 metres; on the victory stand they chatted and laughed during the national anthem and were banned from further competition in the games.

† Edwards, Harry, *The Revolt of the Black Athlete*, The Free Press, New York, 1969.

winning football or basketball team: 'For the black athlete in the pre-dominantly white school was and is first, foremost and sometimes only, an athletic commodity.' He called their recruitment, 'the modern-day equivalent of the slave trade'. He pointed out that the campus life of the black student-athlete was often an unhappy one, because racism barred him from many activities, especially those organized by the fraternities, most of which would not admit blacks.

What happened down at the University of Texas at El Paso bore out many of Edwards's charges. In 1966 the university had won the national collegiate basketball championship. The game was nationally televised, and viewers all over the country had seen the all-black Texas team beat the all-white team from the University of Kentucky. As Texas Western (as it was then called) was virtually unknown in the rest of the country, most people assumed it was an all-black college. Far from it. The basketball team were part of a select group of Negroes, about 250, amongst a total white-student population of nearly 10,000.

The University of Texas at El Paso* was an institution with ambitions. It was expanding, seeking to become a nationally-known institution and, given the peculiar importance of sport in the American university, what surer way to instant fame than a championship team or two?

U.T.E.P.'s recruiters did their job well. They convinced enough blacks – many of them from the north east, 2,000 miles from El Paso – that U.T.E.P. was just what they were looking for, and awarded them athletic scholarships. If these blacks were under the impression that campus life would be undiluted bliss, their disillusionment was total.

Their resentment at the way they were treated grew slowly, but it eventually resulted in open rebellion. A group of them refused to compete. Their punishment was to have their athletic scholarships taken away from them – which meant the end of their university education. The atmosphere that had driven them to this desperate point was investigated by Jack Olsen in his book *The Black Athlete – A Shameful Story*.† It started with the almost incredible fact that most of the coaches persistently called them 'niggers', or sometimes, in that sly way that is considered both amusing and clever by certain southerners, 'nigrahs'.

As the coaches' own success depended heavily on the success of the black athletes, this terminology can hardly have been deliberate. It was,

---

* Not to be confused with *the* University of Texas, with its main campus at Austin, Texas.

† Olsen, Jack, *The Black Athlete – A Shameful Story*, Little Brown, Boston, 1969.

rather, part of a pattern of plain ignorance. Olsen's story revealed clearly that almost no one at U.T.E.P. had thought very deeply about the sort of life that a black athlete would lead once he joined the university. During recruiting, the inevitable questions about 'social life' had been glossed over by the recruiters. But the athletes soon found that there were hardly any black girls on campus, and woe betide them if they dated – or were even seen talking to – a white girl. The basketball players were expected to put in so much time practising, that they inevitably fell behind in their studies. They received none of the services from the University that they claimed were given to white athletes, such as help in finding employment for wives or in getting over financial difficulties.

It was not that the coaching staff was flagrantly racist. By Texas standards, they were probably pretty liberal – U.T.E.P. was in fact the first major college in Texas to field a black athlete – it was just that they were totally unaware that being a black athlete at a predominantly white university brought with it a special tension and a set of problems totally different from those faced by the white athlete. These problems were aggravated even further for many of the blacks, because they were very obviously not academically qualified to be attending a University, 'We were suckered into coming here,' one of the basketball stars told Olsen, 'I come from the toughest, blackest, poorest part of the Bronx (New York). I won't be unhappy to go back.'

The climax came early in 1968 when the black athletes were asked to compete in a track meet against Brigham Young University, to be held on that University's campus in Provo, Utah. Brigham Young University is run by the Mormon Church, and that faith has a decidely hard line on Negroes. They are held to be cursed, and as such although they can join the Church, they can never become members of the priesthood orders, something that is expected of all male members of the Church. Because of this, the blacks' place in the Mormon celestial kingdom of eternity is likely to be a familiar one – that of second-class citizen.

It does not seem unreasonable that the U.T.E.P. blacks should object to going all the way to Provo to perform before people who regard them as cursed. The U.T.E.P. track coach thought otherwise, and he ordered them to participate in the meet. When they refused, they were cut from the track team, and their scholarships were 'suspended'. It meant the end of their subsidized stay at the university, and it also doomed the chances of U.T.E.P. winning the national track and field championship. This had been a distinct possibility, for once again the U.T.E.P. recruiters had done their work well; the athletes involved included Bob

Beamon, who astounded the world later in 1968 with his 29 ft 2½ ins world record long jump at the Mexico Olympics.

The experiences of the black athletes at U.T.E.P. gave substance to Harry Edwards's charge that they were treated as a commodity. A group of outstanding black athletes, most of them not academically qualified to enter a university, had been cynically recruited to help bring national fame to U.T.E.P. Once at the university their special – and considerable – problems with their studies and their social lives had been largely ignored. Their job – and job it certainly was – was to win. An education, getting a degree, these were secondary matters. The 1966 U.T.E.P. basketball team did their job beautifully. They won the national championship. Yet when Olsen wrote his study two years later, he found that not one of the five starting members of the team had graduated.*

The troubles at U.T.E.P. were but the early stirrings of widespread unrest among black college athletes. A *New York Times* survey of the problem in 1969 concluded that most of the colleges where black athletes competed had felt the effects of rising black militancy, even remote places like the University of Wyoming, situated near Laramie, in deepest cowboy country. Here was another university that recruited blacks to build winning teams, another university where a handful of blacks, about 150, studied among some 8,000 whites.

In October 1969, fourteen black members of the university's un-defeated football team decided they had to do something to protest against the anti-Negro attitudes of the Mormon Church. Their method of protest could hardly have been milder – they all put on black arm-bands and went to their coach's office to discuss the matter. Coach Lloyd Eaton's reaction could hardly have been harsher – he dropped all fourteen from the team on the spot. They had, he said, violated two rules: they had participated in a demonstration and had formed a faction within the team. The sides formed along predictable lines. The students and the faculty supported the athletes, saying the coach should back down. The school administration and the alumni backed up Eaton in what they saw as his fight 'to maintain a consistent, stable institution regardless of angry, radical voices which, if heeded, could bring chaos and ruin to our esteemed university'.

The Governor of Wyoming was prepared to call out the National Guard if trouble developed on the campus. The truly troublesome thing

---

* A sad enough state of affairs, but that much worse when put alongside the record of the five white members of the beaten University of Kentucky team, all of whom had graduated.

proved to be that Wyoming, without its black players, started to lose games. It had won the Western Athletic Conference title in 1967 and 1968. It did not win it in 1969. Not much the National Guard could do about that. And in 1970 it finished dead last, having won only one game out of ten.

The University of Syracuse, long a hard-recruiting football power in upper New York State, came under attack early in 1970. Nine out of the ten blacks on the squad walked out of spring practice. They claimed they had been promised that the university would employ a black assistant coach – and had not done so. At the start of pre-season training in August, six of them were not invited to attend by coach Ben Schwartz-walder. The players enlisted the help of the local Human Rights Commission, and filed charges of discrimination against the coaching staff. In particular they alleged that black players were frequently shifted from their regular positions to ones with which they were not familiar. A compromise was sought: the blacks would sign a 'Code for Syracuse Athletes' (as would all the other players), pledging to give 100 per cent effort at all times, and to use an agreed set of procedures for airing grievances. In return all suspensions would be revoked. The blacks were not happy with the Code idea, because at no point did the university admit it had been guilty of discriminatory practices. Eight of them refused to sign it, and were automatically suspended by the chancellor of the university. Syracuse played its opening game without them, and was clobbered 42–16. Then the chancellor announced he would appoint a committee to look into the athletes' charges, and coach Schwartz-walder, after a meeting with the whole team, reinstated the players. It was a decision that did not sit well with some of the white players on the team, who said it had been forced on them by fear of violence. For by now the suspended athletes had gained a firm support amongst the substantial black population of Syracuse. The police were preparing for possible riots at the stadium when the university played its first home game. The day before the game, student groups on campus called for it to be cancelled, and for Schwartzwalder to resign. Neither of which happened.

But it was not a happy day for Syracuse or for football. The stadium was picketed, and 200 armed and helmeted police were on hand, some stationed atop nearby buildings, to see that law and order prevailed. It did, just. It was, said a police captain, the biggest security opera-tion since Richard Nixon was there during his 1968 presidency campaign. The blacks did not play, and to complete a sad afternoon for

Syracuse they lost 31–14. The police eventually had to use tear-gas to break up the crowd that had blocked one of the approach roads to the stadium.

Although the athletes had officially been reinstated, they refused to accept such a move. They did not play at all during the season, which Syracuse finished with a 6–4 won-lost record, not too bad everything considered. The 'everything' by now included charges from former Syracuse star and more lately Hollywood actor Jim Brown, who said that the university deliberately flouted college regulations by giving their players *sub rosa* payments. It was some fifteen years since Brown had played at Syracuse – but a more contemporary charge soon followed. In his book *Out of their League*, Dave Meggyesy, another former Syracuse star (1959-62), who had left professional football in 1969, charged that Syracuse players were given as much as $120 a game.*

The chancellor's committee spent ten weeks investigating the dispute and taking 604 pages of testimony. Their report, published after the close of the season, criticized the athletic department of the University in general terms for their insensitivity to the problem of the black athletes. But the committee was at pains to point out that the racism they found was not the result of any deliberate policy. It was simply *there* – in many cases felt deeply by the blacks, but in all cases almost totally invisible to the white coaches. The assumptions on which it was based went so deep that no white was aware of them. Said the report: 'Racism in the Syracuse athletic department is real, chronic, largely unintentional, and sustained and complicated unwittingly by many modes of behaviour common in American athletics and longstanding at Syracuse University.'

The turmoil that black athletes were producing on campuses throughout the United States spread hardly at all to the South. The reason was not too difficult to discern, for there was hardly a black face to be seen on the athletic teams of the large southern universities. Until the mid-sixties there were *no* blacks at all. Then, as the southern universities started with painful slowness to integrate, an occasional black athlete got his chance. The first to play at first-team level was Perry Wallace, who turned out for Vanderbilt University at basketball in 1967. During the three years that he played, Wallace was a model of good behaviour, voicing no complaints and playing brilliantly. In his last year he was even voted the Most Popular Student on Campus. With his final season

* Meggyesy's book and his indictment of football are discussed in Chapter 6, page 124.

behind him, Wallace spoke out, and the words were the familiar ones: 'I have been a lonely person at Vanderbilt . . . It was not so much that I was treated badly, it was that I wasn't treated at all.'

There had been sharp individual incidents, like the time he was asked, politely, not to attend church services lest his presence reduce the collection, but the main complaint was, again, that this was a closed white society and no one had made any attempt to help him adjust to it.

The recruiting of southern blacks by southern universities was a half-hearted affair. In 1970, out of some 500 football players in the Southern Conference, only seventeen were blacks – just over 3 per cent in an area of the United States where Negroes make up some 40 per cent of the population. At the University of Alabama the Afro-American Association took the football coach, Paul Bryant, to federal court, charging that he did not recruit blacks with the same diligence as whites. The hearing of the suit was postponed to allow the university to demonstrate its goodwill by recruiting a number of blacks. The university claimed that it had been trying to find black athletes, but had not been successful. While their efforts were, no doubt, far from all out, there are two very real difficulties for the southern university trying to find black athletes. Firstly, black high-school education in the South is so poor that the number of black students who qualify academically is woefully small. Secondly, there are not many blacks who *want* to attend the southern schools, whose record in the field of enlightened race relations is not exactly exemplary.

Although the black protests vary in detail from campus to campus, the underlying theme is always this: college sports belong to the white man. If he wants the black to play them – and he very obviously does, or he would not recruit him so assiduously – then he should be prepared to make some alterations in the structure of them to allow for the blacks' different background. It is, in short, a plea (or in the most militant of the protests, a *demand*) for understanding. Sadly, most black athletes seem to have given up on the idea that a white coach can understand black problems. The most common of the athletes' requests is for the appointment of a black coach – someone in authority to whom they can relate.

The pressure of the protests has brought action, and black coaches, usually at the assistant level, are becoming slightly more common in university athletic departments. There is evidence that the generation gap is at work too. The black coaches required are *not* wanted if they merely do the same thing as the white coaches. They must, in addition to knowing about football, be aware of the modern young blacks' burgeoning pride. Part of the trouble at Syracuse arose when the University appointed the wrong sort of black – Floyd Little, a former player at the university who had gone on to the professionals. It was his statement that 'I've never known coaches to mistreat anyone here', that set off the spring-training walk-out. The athletes responded, not by attacking Little's skill as a player or a coach, but by implying that he did not understand that they were not willing to put up with things that he had never questioned: 'Floyd Little has never grown as a black man' was their comment.

Perhaps the last group to feel the winds of change were the very ones who had been among the first to demonstrate just how good the black athletes were – the Harlem Globetrotters. As black militancy increased and as black athletes poured into pro basketball the Globetrotters were left behind, no longer able to attract any of the top black players. In addition, their act was viewed with distaste by many of the new black athletes, who saw it as an acting-out of the white man's view of the black man: amusing, but not to be taken seriously. In 1971 news came from Port Huron, Michigan, that the Globetrotters, in the midst of their never-ending city to city travels, were on strike. They wanted all the things that the pros were getting but that they were not – better salaries, a pension plan, better insurance, meal money. It even came out that the players were responsible for washing their own uniforms. Their long-delayed protest had a familiar sound to it: 'We just want,' said a Globetrotter 'to be treated as men and given our human dignity.'

The brouhaha that black athletes have been causing on campus has inevitably bred its own reaction. More than one coach has been heard to remark that recruiting blacks is now more trouble than it's worth – unless the athlete happens to look like a superstar in the making. There is also a sinister suggestion that any black who takes an activist role in college protests may be jeopardizing his future as a professional. He may find that when the time comes for him to be drafted by the professional team he is not chosen. For a good college player to be passed over by *all* the professional teams would have to be more than coincidence. It suggests concerted action; deliberate blackballing. Jack Olsen recorded the case of Bobby Smith, a defensive back at the University of California, an above-average performer in whom a number of scouts had shown interest. At the beginning of 1968 the black athletes of the University revolted, demanding that the basketball coach be fired because of his racist attitudes. Bobby Smith was one of the leaders of the uprising which was successful – the basketball coach resigned. But when the professional draft was held shortly afterwards, not one club expressed any interest whatsoever in Bobby Smith.

Those black college players who are drafted into the professional leagues find that, in many areas, discrimination persists. It is still true that they are in a white man's world. The top brass in professional sport – the owners, the managers and the head coaches – are almost exclusively white. At the end of his book *Revolt of the Black Athlete*, Harry Edwards listed all the black owners, managers, and head coaches in professional sport. Of a possible 225, he found only two – both head coaches, both in basketball. That was in 1969, but the situation has changed little since; in 1973 there were one black manager and two coaches – all in basketball.

The more overt acts of racism that blacks on the first integrated teams had to contend with have mostly disappeared – things such as segregated hotels and restaurants, racist taunts from fans. When Bill Russell first played for the Boston Celtics in 1956, he heard the shouts from the fans in St Louis 'Coon! – Go back to Africa you baboon! – Black nigger!', and he experienced plenty of trouble in hotels, mostly when the team played exhibition games in the South.*

Russell, who was one of the first of the prominent black athletes to speak out, experienced no racism from his playing colleagues. This, of course, was in basketball, the sport in which the Negro presence is greatest. In football and baseball there have been instances where friction between the black and white players has seriously damaged a team's performance.

When Dave Meggyesy – who is white – joined the St Louis Cardinals football team in 1963, he was quickly made aware that the team contained a vociferous group of white racists. According to one of them the professional football clubs were doing Negroes a favour because 'niggers were generally too dumb to play professional football'. He was also told that he would certainly get on to the team, because the competitors for his position were 'so stupid they have trouble tying their shoes'. The group also assumed the right to order the Negro players about. Negroes who did not complain were 'decent niggers'. Those who protested were getting above their station.

---

* Before one such game, Russell personally telephoned the hotel in Miami to make sure that all was O.K. The hotel said it was, but Russell persisted. Finally he was told: 'Yes, you can stay here. You may use the diningroom and the swimming pool. We ask only one thing. Be inconspicuous.' Russell, apart from being black, is 6 ft 10 ins tall and wears a beard.

The situation got out of hand because the St Louis coaching staff (all white) did nothing to restrain the white racist group. In 1967 the Cardinals, who had all sorts of talent on paper, finished next to last in their division. Near the end of the season, every black on the squad signed a petition to the head coach, charging that an atmosphere of discrimination pervaded the club, and naming one of the assistant coaches as largely responsible. Such are the subtleties and misunderstandings of the black-white encounter that the coach concerned was genuinely shocked at the charge. Convinced that he had not discriminated, he was nevertheless honest enough to admit that there had to be something in an accusation signed by every black on the club.

For Dave Meggyesy, a sure indication that the coaching staff had little idea of what was going on came at the end of a meeting held to discuss some of the black grievances. The head coach tried, naturally enough, to minimize the friction and ended by suggesting that everybody should go down to 'The Lantern', a nearby bar, for a few beers. He did not even know that 'The Lantern' was a white haunt – the blacks, by some unwritten, unspoken agreement, never went there.

The situation on the St Louis Cardinals was extreme, but it was symptomatic of a widespread, if less virulent, *malaise* that affected most professional teams. Rarely are the issues as clearly defined as at St Louis. They usually revolve around difficult-to-prove suspicions – perhaps that the white quarterback is not passing as often to the black player as to the white, or that a black player would be earning more money if he were white, or the feeling that a black player is acceptable only so long as he is playing well. Baseball slugger Reggie Jackson, himself prone to spells of indifferent play, said, 'Everything's fine when the black player is doing good, hitting home runs and winning games and all that. But let something happen, let a problem come up, and the black player is going to be up against it.' Nebulous feelings, perhaps, but every bit as hard to refute as to prove.

There was one team that became something of a legend in its own time for being free of racial troubles. This was the Green Bay Packers of the early and mid sixties, coached by Vince Lombardi. That the Packers were sweeping all before them no doubt helped, things always go smoother on a winning club, but Lombardi was evidently a person without prejudice who treated all his players – black and white – alike. He was, for example, unlikely to accuse blacks of being lazy, because it was his conviction that *all* men were lazy. He was glad that he was not prejudiced, he said, because it is wrong to feel that way, and because 'it's good football not to feel that way'.

When all the minuses have been put alongside all the pluses, a clear verdict on the Negro in sports remains elusive. The recent mood of militancy has been bitterly resented by many whites, who believe, many of them no doubt sincerely, that when compared to that of other trades, businesses or professions, sport's record of accommodating Negroes is beyond reproach. They point to the black superstars earning over $100,000 a year and ask: 'Where would they be without sport?'

They do have a point. In many ways sport *has* been good to the Negro. Ignoring the early days of discrimination, when baseball was certainly acting no worse than society in general,* sport has on the whole been pursuing a course leading to total integration. The knowledge that sport, if not exactly falling over backwards to employ blacks, was not overtly hostile to them, made it an occupation about which the young black could dream, around which he could fashion the hope – so taken for granted among the ruling classes, but so desperately lacking in the ghetto – that one day he might amount to something. Add to this the peculiar structure of American sport that requires a top player – especially in basketball and football – to attend college, and sport becomes a vehicle for many poor blacks to get an education they could otherwise never have acquired.

Education, fame, money – none of them to be sneezed at. Yet the accolades for sport dim somewhat with the realization that the opportunity for all three ought never to be lacking in the first place. It should not be necessary for a black to have to excel at sport to get to college – yet in far too many cases that is the way it is.

Sport has also helped the black cause by providing – in many cases unwittingly, and almost always reluctantly – respected men to speak out on black affairs. This is something that has caused the sporting establishment to become increasingly hot under the collar as the level of black militancy has risen. For black sports stars to talk of how sport had given them everything they had was one thing, but when they started criticizing and throwing charges of racism all over the place, well, that was quite another matter. The early black stars never spoke out about anything; they knew they could not, they had to remain 'good' if they were to be accepted at all. They were courageous men who suffered immensely

---

* Baseball started integrating in 1947. New York's Metropolitan Opera did not introduce a black singer until 1955.

in silence to make sure that they did not queer the pitch for future black athletes. Their self-control was mistaken for docility, and that was just what was wanted.

Against the opportunities that sport has provided for Negroes has to be set everything that the Negro has done for sport. For if sport has been good to the blacks, it has certainly benefited enormously from their presence. Many – probably a majority – of the professional sports' best and most exciting performers are black. They bring in the fans, who bring in the money, which is what professional sport is all about.

Even if, as seems quite likely, the Negro has put more into sport than he has got from it, there is a much more serious indictment of sport's role in the life of black Americans. It is that the Negro's involvement and success in sport has, paradoxically, been damaging to the black struggle for equality. It is a matter of image, of the way in which blacks are viewed by whites. There is a dark and tenacious thread that runs very deep in the subconscious of white Americans (and probably of all whites): the feeling that the Negro is lower on the evolutionary scale than the white man, that he is inherently less intelligent, that he is more animal than human.

The feeling seems to run rather less deeply in sporting circles, and from time to time comes openly to the surface.

There are coaches who use the word 'animal' when they yell at their black players, but not when they yell at the whites (during his college athlete days, Harry Edwards overheard a coach refer to him as a 'terrific animal'). At the University of Detroit, where the entire 1970 basketball team demanded that coach Jim Harding be fired, one of the black players complained: 'My parents came to watch us at practice. He called me a son-of-a-bitch in front of them, and said I was an animal who should be locked in a cage.' Even in the arts the bias is there. Reading the programme notes before giving a 1971 concert with the Los Angeles Philharmonic Orchestra, the black conductor James DePreist was surprised to see himself described as a 'former college football star' – a game he has never played in his life.

But blacks are supposed to be football players, not conductors, and there can be no denying that for the Negro to show excellence in sport while not making much headway in the professions provides *prima facie* support for the theory, if 'theory' is the correct term for unthinking bigotry. The truly sad part of all this is that the Negro has been trapped by the white man's view of him and his place in society. Logically, the white man has arranged this society so that the Negro is more or less obliged to act out the white man's version of him, if he wants to get anywhere at all.

The Negro is considered to have meagre intelligence, so that it is rather a waste of time and resources to provide him with an elaborate education. In the early days after the Civil War, when northern missionaries arrived in the South and set up schools for ex-slaves, the southerners found the idea of *any* education for blacks incomprehensible. As time went by, they softened their attitude somewhat, and accepted that certain types of education were suitable for the Negro – specifically, those that would turn out skilled labourers. Once again, the blacks had to go along, though the enthusiasm with which Booker T. Washington, one of the most important black leaders of the period, embraced the scheme was regrettably excessive. His famous Atlanta Exposition speech of 1895, in which he endorsed the idea of 'industrial education' for blacks, had, and continues to have, disastrous consequences. There grew up in the South a string of all-black colleges, where 'learning' in its traditional sense was a secondary item and where the students were taught how to be mechanics or farmers or cooks.

The anti-intellectual atmosphere of these institutes impressed itself sharply on the black sociologist Dr E. Franklin Frazier, when he taught at one of them during the World War I. He received a reprimand from the dean for walking across the campus with some books under his arm – if the whites saw him, they might get the idea that the students were being taught to think rather than trained to use their hands.

The Negro's place was established for him: mechanic, farmer, cook – nothing that was likely to lead on to fame and fortune. To escape from these paths, the young black had to be of truly exceptional quality. Paul Robeson had a father who insisted that he study the classics. Robeson was a brilliant student and after graduation from Rutgers he went on to study law at Columbia University. During this post-graduate work, Robeson had to pay his own way. He earned the money by doing the jobs that Negroes were supposed to do, by working as a post-office clerk, or as a waiter, or coaching basketball. It was only his outstanding determination that kept him from being channelled into athletics where great opportunities awaited him. He played professional football for a while, getting as much as $1,000 a game. And he was approached by people in the fight game who were sure they could turn him into a boxer good enough to challenge Jack Dempsey for the heavyweight title and earn maybe $1 million while doing it. Outside of sport, even for a black of Robeson's qualifications, opportunities barely existed. He did get a job with a distinguished New York law firm, but it was not long before hostility to his presence surfaced. When it was suggested that perhaps he might like to open a Harlem branch of the firm, Robeson quit law for good. He was eventually able to realize his vast talents as a singer and an actor – but he had to move to England to do it.

There are very few people, black or white, with Robeson's talent and tenacity. Most are willing to settle for what is available. For the American Negro the idea of spending his life struggling towards a goal he will almost certainly not be allowed to reach has never had much sense. In Bill Russell's words: 'Like most Americans, Negroes are practical. If a Negro studied to be a biochemist and became a pullman porter because he could not get any other job, then he is not going to encourage his son to study biochemistry.'

After World War II, when professional sport began to admit Negroes, there was the possibility of making real money in a glamorous career. Naturally enough, the vision of sports stardom came to dominate the outlook of black youths – usually at the expense of everything else. Sitting in his office in Newark, a crumbling mostly-black city that was ravaged by riot and burning in 1967, a young black social worker reflected on his efforts to keep boys in school, to keep them out of the hands of the drug pushers: 'I don't know what I'd do without the basketball programme,' he said, 'It's the only thing that keeps them coming here. It's something they do beautifully.'

It is indeed, but black communities like Newark do not need more sports stars. They need educators and doctors and lawyers and administrators. What sport has done is to provide a more exciting alternative to the struggle for academic recognition. Today's black youth is the product and the prisoner of the sports-hero complex. His horizons, restricted enough as it is, have been further narrowed by the blinding brilliance of a career in sport, the possibility of becoming another Willie Mays, a second Wilt Chamberlain.

It is the sort of cruel trick that, throughout history, has been the lot of have-nots. The beckoning mirage of sports stardom is just that – a mirage – for all but a select few. It is the black youth's Siren, and there is no Orpheus around to sing a sweeter song. The great majority of Negroes who follow the call of a sports career never make it. They are left, early in life, with nothing but crumbled dreams; and in the harsh terms of the modern technological society, a black athlete *manqué* is a singularly useless individual.

For those who make it to college on an athletic scholarship there await some or all of the disillusionments discussed earlier in this chapter.

The survivors enter the professional ranks, where further tribulations await. For sports stardom is an ephemeral thing, maybe five or six years at the top, then what? For many white players the answer is to continue in sport, in non-playing roles like coach or manager. For Negroes this type of job has been notoriously difficult to land. They are usually obliged to leave sport – often the only field in which they have any experience – and find a new way of making a living at the age of thirty plus. For the least fortunate, in Harry Edwards's words, 'only the ghetto beckons and they are doomed once again to that faceless, hopeless, ignominious existence they had supposedly forever left behind them'.

Sport, then, has been something of a mixed blessing for the American Negro. While raising a few to national fame and riches, it has proved a damaging dead end for many more. Sport has enabled many under-privileged blacks to get to college on athletic scholarships; and it has also been the main reason why so many of them fail to graduate. The black man has shown that he is as good as, and probably better than, the white man at the sports that the white man devised. In one of the disgracefully few jobs where he has been allowed to compete on something like equal terms, he has shown himself anything but inferior to the white man.* Yet, ironically, the better he performs, the more he lays himself open to the snide dismissal of his achievements as 'just what you would expect' from Negroes.

At the beginning of the seventies, there were signs that some at least, of the problems were being tackled.† But the black athlete's frustrations are merely reflections through the sporting mirror of what goes on in society as a whole. And the closest and most depressing parallel between the two is the slowness with which anything is done about them.

---

* In a paper written in 1943 in the *Psychoanalytic Review*, Dr Laynard Hollo-man summed it up like this: ' . . . the supremacy of the Negro athlete in competition with the white group can be accounted for on the basis of his hatred and desire for revenge, his efforts to compensate for his feelings of inferiority, and his desire to overcome his oppression by identification with the majority group.'

† Baseball's Hall of Fame, for instance, at last decided that it would honour the famous players from the Negro leagues, even though they had never played in the major leagues. On 9 August 1971 the first player to be so honoured ambled to the podium in Cooperstown to give his acceptance speech, jangling a little as he went, and not looking back. It was Satchel Paige.

8   The College Professionals

It is twelve o'clock midday on a cold, winter's afternoon in Columbus, Ohio. Groups of people, some young, some not so young, are walking across a windswept field near the Ohio State University campus. On that field, two hardy teams are playing a soccer game in 20 degrees weather to the shouts and cheers of a few chilled substitutes huddled on the side-lines. Occasionally some of the passers-by stop for a moment to watch, but the majority go hurrying on without a second glance. Though most of them would claim to be rabid supporters of O.S.U. they are not interested in the O.S.U. soccer team. It is the O.S.U. football team they want to see, and so they keep walking, another 300 yards or so, until they are at the gates of the University's massive two-tier stadium. It will cost them up to $6 to get in, but by game time at 1.30 the stadium is a roaring cauldron bubbling with over 85,000 people. Outside, the wind and the lightly falling snow have the soccer field all to themselves.

Both the soccer game and the football game are examples of American college sport, but there is obviously a world of difference between them. From being what one might expect it to be – a means of enjoyment and exercise for students – college sport ranges ever more commercially upward until it reaches the bigtime, as typified by the O.S.U. football set-up.

Let us return to the O.S.U. stadium for a moment. A huge marching band is performing on the field, and despite the snow and the sub-freezing temperature, scantily clad girls are going through their baton-twirling and cheer-leading routines. There are television cameras on both sidelines, getting ready to transmit the game live all over the U.S.A. In the stands the spectators browse through printed programmes, or perhaps the local newspaper where the game is all over the front page, taking up more space than the South-East Asia crisis and the latest moonshot combined. One does not have to know that the total enrol-ment at O.S.U. is 40,000 to see that the majority of the 85,000 present are not students. They have come from miles around, some of them hundreds of miles by car, some by private plane . . . to see a game of college football.

They come every time O.S.U. plays at home, six times a year, and their loyalty adds around $500,000 a year to the coffers of the O.S.U. athletic department. And that is what makes bigtime college sport bigtime. Money.

The National Collegiate Athletic Association, which is the controlling body of collegiate sports, lists seventeen sports played in more than 650 colleges. Of these seventeen, only football and basketball as played at some 200 colleges make up the bigtime sports programmes. The rest – such as wrestling, ice hockey, soccer, fencing, baseball, lacrosse – even though they may involve large numbers of students and much expensive equipment – are not in the same class.*

A survey conducted in 1969 by the University of Missouri revealed that the 118 universities adjudged to have bigtime football programmes spent an average of $670,000 each on the sport and took in $960,000.† A profit of nearly $300,000 a season is welcome enough, but this is only a part of the monetary significance of a bigtime sports programme. There is nothing like a football team, a *successful* one that is, for attracting donations. When the old school team is winning the pride of the alumni swells and in flows the money – the lifeblood for colleges that rely on private donations for financing. For state universities such as Ohio State the bulk of their money comes not from private donations, but from public funds granted by the state legislature, and here again a winning football team is a substantial asset. 'Legislators and alumni measure their support for a school by the success of its athletic programme,' says the athletic director at the University of North Dakota. A team that can enhance the glory of the home state by crushing rivals from other states almost certainly makes legislators more munificent.

The glory to be garnered from a winning football team had a natural appeal for the flamboyant Huey Long during his term as Governor of Louisiana, and when he announced that he wanted money for Louisiana State University to strengthen its football team, his compliant legislators

* In addition to these sports, and the bigtime sports, there is a third category of college sport. Where a college has no official programme for a particular sport, but where there are enough students who want to play that sport, they may form a team on what is known as a 'club' basis. It will be controlled entirely by the students, and it will be up to them to find ways to finance the team.

† As in professional sport, television is a major contributor. In 1973 the A.B.C. network paid the N.C.A.A. $13.5 million for the rights to televise college football games.

hastened to oblige. In his determination to make L.S.U. a top football power, Long was forever appearing at practice sessions and games with detailed instructions for the coach and the players. Despite, or more probably because of, his efforts L.S.U. did not produce a team that was the envy of all.

It was a different story for Notre Dame, a small Catholic college in South Bend, Indiana. By 1931, when Huey Long was trying to upgrade L.S.U.'s football image, Notre Dame was already a household word all over the U.S.A. It had gained such widespread recognition, not because of its academic fame as a centre of learning, but because it consistently had the strongest college football team in the land. Throughout the 1920s the fortunes of Notre Dame's team, the Fighting Irish under their coach Knute Rockne, were avidly followed every autumn by hundreds of thousands of Americans who had never been within a thousand miles of the college. Jokes circulated about the Notre Dame Football Factory, and one New York journalist announced that he was going to South Bend to investigate the rumour that there was a university there. It was there all right, and it was growing, largely thanks to the money (as much as half a million dollars each year) and fame that the football team was bringing. Today, Notre Dame is a university of considerable academic repute, a sort of Catholic Harvard, conclusive proof that strength can come through football. It now has one of the world's largest university libraries, and it still has one of America's strongest football teams.

It stands to reason that college football could not attract over 30 million paying customers a year unless it were offering them top-class entertainment. While the standard of play is not up to that of the professionals, neither is it much below it. In fact, in almost every way, the bigtime college sports of football and basketball have the air of professional operations. With all that money to be made, it could hardly be otherwise. Professional coaches are employed at substantial salaries of up to $30,000,* and frequently have a large squad of assistant coaches.

The players themselves, like their professional counterparts, undergo rigorous training schedules and do an extensive amount of travelling for away fixtures. A college player could almost imagine himself a professional, were it not for one thing: where a professional might be getting

---

* A coach's salary does not, by any means, tell the whole story about his income. He is likely to be receiving also such benefits as rent-free housing, free cars, fully paid-up life insurance and, in football-mad areas, a weekly television show worth, say, $1,000 a week during the season. In this way he may gain an extra $20,000 a year.

$30,000 a year for his efforts, the college player, for very similar efforts, is getting paid precisely nothing. He is an apprentice learning his profession, and apprentices have never exactly been among the big wage-earners. Lodging, meals, and a small allowance has usually been their lot. And lodging, meals and a small allowance is exactly what the apprentice-athlete gets, plus one more item: a free education. He gets all this in the form of an athletic scholarship, awarded to him by the university, which entitles him to free room and board, $15 monthly for incidental expenses, and the four years of free tuition.* Virtually every bigtime college athlete attends college on a 'scholarship' of this type, given to him not because of any intellectual promise, but because of his ability to run with a football or to put a basketball through a hoop.

There is a fair amount of logic in the practice. It has been frequently remarked that American universities tend to serve as technical schools, training personnel for work in business, banking, accounting, salesman-ship, journalism, and so on – the lucrative jobs of the modern society. Professional sport can certainly be added to this list, making its 'study' a legitimate university activity. So why not sports scholarships?

Yet the athletic scholarship had its beginnings in the decidedly non-American mind of Cecil Rhodes. Howard J. Savage, in his study of American college athletics†, traced the origins of athletic scholarships to one of the conditions that Rhodes laid down in 1902 for the award of Rhodes Scholarships to Oxford University: that the student should show a fondness for and 'success in manly outdoor sports, such as cricket, football and the like'. At the beginning of the century athletic scholar-ships were a step in the right direction, representing a more honest approach to the matter of subsidizing football players than the virtually open paying of 'tramp athletes'. These were football players who moved from school to school selling their talents to the highest bidder. Some-times they were quickly and fraudulently registered as students, some-times – as with the seven non-students who played on the University of Michigan 1893 team – they were not.

Initially limited to covering part or all of a student's tuition fees, athletic scholarships gradually extended their benefits until, shortly

---

* This is a full athletic scholarship. There are also partial athletic scholarships, awarded mostly for minor sports or at smaller colleges, which cover only some of the student's costs, or which require the student to spend part of his time working for the school's athletic department.

† Savage, Howard, J., *American College Athletics*, Carnegie Foundation for the Advancement of Teaching, Bulletin No. 23, New York, 1929.

before World War II, the full scholarship was introduced. The concept of the athletic scholarship is today firmly implanted in the mind of every high school boy possessed of some sports talent. He knows that, if he plays his cards right, he can obtain some sort of athletic scholarship from some college, somewhere. There is prestige value in it, too, such that even a boy who can afford to pay his own way feels obliged to try for a scholarship. Neither is it unknown for boys to shop around among colleges looking for the one willing to offer them the most attractive deal.

For those who were outstanding high-school football or basketball players there will be no need to go looking for a college. The colleges will come to them, right to their doorsteps – literally. There is no way that a high-school star, who will already have received considerable local publicity, can avoid the embraces of the college recruiters. They come in many different guises, these recruiters. It may be a local scout for good old Bountiful U, it may be the chief coach from Bountiful U himself, or one of his assistants, or it may be a wealthy and famous Bountiful U alumnus. Whoever it is, the aim is to grab the kid before the other colleges can.

What happened in 1970 to Leslie Cason, a seventeen-year-old school-boy from East Rutherford, New Jersey, is typical of the colleges' great annual talent hunt. When the word was out that the 6 ft 10 ins Cason was the nation's top high-school basketball player, over one hundred colleges got in touch with him, each trying to convince him that theirs was the place for him. He was getting as many as thirty telephone calls a day, so many that his mother thought about changing the number, then decided that 'it wouldn't have done any good. The schools would have found us somehow'. To Cason, it seemed that he could not come out of a classroom without finding a scout waiting for him. The college that eventually succeeded was Long Beach State in California, about 3,000 miles from New Jersey. Cason had made two expense-paid trips to Long Beach where he met not only the coach and the players, but also 'all these important people', that is, local businessmen, one of whom told him: 'You come to Long Beach State and you work hard and get your degree and we can help you in the future.' When Cason had made up his mind, the Long Beach State coach flew into East Rutherford, and they held a press conference to make the announcement.*

* The Cason case highlights one of the pitfalls of aggressive recruiting. Long Beach State had recruited Cason before his final year of high-school competition. That final season proved to be a big let-down, and Cason never did go to Long Beach State.

High-school athletes are the essential raw material of the bigtime college sports, and recruiting them is a deadly serious and highly competitive business. The top football universities spend over $100,000 a year on recruiting, and Ohio State runs up a phone bill of $10,000 making nationwide calls to likely high-school athletes.

The lengths to which recruiters will go to get their boy stretch from what is permissible under N.C.A.A. regulations through a grey area of dubious practices into what is specifically forbidden. Take, for instance, the business of paying the prospective student-athlete (as he is known in the N.C.A.A. regulations) his travelling expenses so that he can visit the university campus. This is permitted by the N.C.A.A., provided that the student is not given 'excessive entertainment' while on the visit. Entertainment must be 'at a scale comparable to that of normal student life', and that does not include providing a car for the boy to drive around in. No cars then, but what about girlfriends? The setting-up of dates with pretty co-eds (it is an unwritten rule of American journalism that co-eds are *always* pretty) is an accepted recruiting practice; officially, the girls are acting as hostesses, and there are even schools that recruit comely girls for this purpose. At Kansas State University, where the football coach is Vince Gibson, they are called Gibson Girls, while at Florida State, where the football team's nickname is the Gators, they are called Gator Getters.

Presumably sex cannot be objected to on the grounds that it is not part of 'normal student life'. But there are plenty of other inducements that far transcend such a standard. A 1970 *Wall Street Journal* story on recruiting told of 'an outstanding athlete who requests anonymity because he fears reprisals for rocking the boat' who claimed that the University of Arizona offered him a Chevrolet Stingray convertible; the University of Colorado found a ranch-style home it was willing to rent him for $25 a month, and Columbia University offered a degree 'no matter what' his actual scholastic aptitude turned out to be. Other under-the-counter ploys include offering the prospect unlimited use of charge accounts at, e.g., clothing stores or gasoline stations, free long-distance phone calls, scholarships for his girl friend or brother, free air travel for his family to and from all the college's home games. In those cases where money is involved, e.g., the charge accounts, the bill is paid, not by the university, but by 'interested alumni'. According to ex-professional Dave Meggyesy the alumni of Syracuse University, which he attended on an athletic scholarship, showed their interest in a much more direct way. After a game, one of the coaches shook Meggyesy's hand: 'He said, " Nice game". I thanked him and began to walk away when I realized he had put a $20 bill in my hand. He saw the startled look on my face and told me "It's all right, Dave, an alum asked me to give it to you" '. Meggyesy claimed that the stars of the Syracuse University team at this time (the early sixties) were getting from $20 to $50 a game. A star college-player summed up the situation in 1952 with the remark that he was not sure whether he could afford the cut in salary, but he was going to turn professional anyway.

For a young boy barely out of high school, and in many cases not even that, all this fawning attention is likely to make an anything but healthy impression. It lets him know that his athletic ability is measured in terms of money, that colleges are willing to outbid each other for his services, that they are willing to connive and cheat and bend the rules, and that he is expected to close his eyes to all this. Is it to be wondered at if some of the prospective student-athletes develop a rather cynical attitude; if, for instance, a boy accepts a college's offer of a free trip to their campus merely for the sake of making the trip, and with no intention whatever of attending that college, (the California colleges, no doubt because of the fine weather and so on, seem particularly susceptible to this). Or if a boy applies to colleges all over the country and, by accepting their offers of free campus visits, is able to spend his summer vacation touring the U.S.A. entirely at the expense of colleges in which he is not the least bit interested?

Any satisfaction there might be in seeing the colleges hoist with their own petard is quickly dissipated by a look at the damage that getting drawn into this ethical vacuum can do to the student's own values.

At the beginning of 1951 the dangers were exposed with tragic clarity by a series of scandals in college basketball. They began on 18 January with the arrest of two Manhattan College players and three gamblers, all accused of conspiring to fix games, and the web of guilt spread remorselessly for the next nine months until thirty-three players from seven different colleges had been arrested along with nine gamblers. The players had agreed, for sums ranging up to $1,500 a game, to help the gamblers by controlling their team's winning margins. Thus, in a game which, according to the bookies, their team was favoured to win by ten points, they would play to win, but would make sure – by bad shooting late in the game if necessary – that the victory was by a margin of less than ten points.*

* For an explanation of the point-spread method of betting on basketball games, see Chapter 9, page 203.

The players involved were not unknowns from obscure colleges. They included several of the country's top players. Two of them had been on the United States team that won the gold medal in the 1948 Olympics in London; another had been named Player of the Year by the *Sporting News* in an issue mailed before the scandal broke, and yet another had his photograph on the cover of the 1951 Collegiate Basketball Guide – the official publication of college basketball.

This was merely embarrassing; the truly appalling thing about the scandals was the glaring fact that nearly every single one of the players approached by the gamblers had agreed to go along with the scheme. Either one had to credit the gamblers with uncanny ability to pick susceptible students, or there was some more general *malaise* at work. It was around the nature of this *malaise* that a national controversy, accompanied by much heart-searching and hand-wringing, revolved. Were the players, as the President of the University of Kentucky suggested 'inexperienced victims of an unscrupulous syndicate' or was this a case, as others warned, of a weakening of the nation's moral fibre? No doubt there was a little of both, but the main culprit was the bigtime college sports atmosphere. In a March 1951 speech calling for moral revival in government, Senator William Fulbright indicted the colleges for helping to spread a cynical attitude towards honesty:

Our colleges, under extreme pressure from the alumni, have become so intent upon winning football and basketball games that they use any means to gain their ends. They hire players who are not *bona fide* students and thus make a mockery, a farce of the whole concept of amateur sport for the health and entertainment of our young men. They corrupt not only the hired players but also the entire student body who learn from their elders the cynical, immoral doctrine that must win at all costs.

When the 1951 scandals came to their melancholy end in a courtroom in November of that year, Judge Saul Streit placed the blame squarely on the colleges: 'To put it bluntly he [the athlete] is bribed in the first instance to choose one college over another.' He went on to list in detail the irregularities he had found in the colleges' recruitment and treatment of athletes. A constant theme was the acceptance by colleges of athletes with quite dismal academic records. One of them had an IQ of 82; he had spent six months at Villanova University where he did poorly in his studies. He left there and was accepted by Long Island University, where he suddenly started to obtain passing grades, in subjects such as music seminar, oil painting, rhythm and dance and public

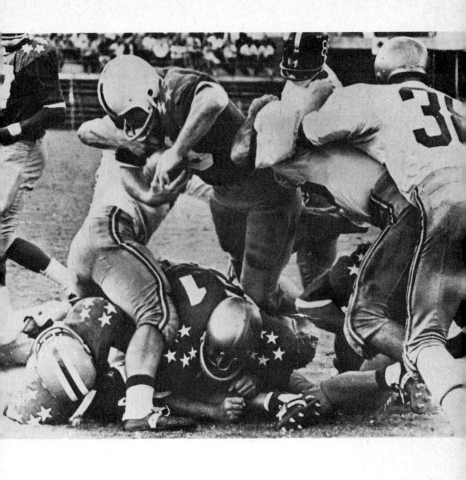

& 14 To millions of Americans an autumn Saturday afternoon means one thing: college football. In 1973 college games drew over 31 million fans.

speaking.* Another athlete had a high-school average of 70·43, too low for admission to New York City College. Yet there he was, enrolled as a student at City College. A look at his records, held by the College, revealed that his high-school average had somehow been entered as 75·5.

Outright falsification of academic records is one way of making sure that the not-too-bright athlete remains in school, but there are other, slightly more subtle methods. The sort of thing that James Thurber described in *University Days*, where he talked about a student in the economics class:

He was a tackle on the football team, named Bolenciecwcz. At that time Ohio State University had one of the best football teams in the country, and Bolenciecwcz was one of its outstanding stars. In order to be eligible to play it was necessary for him to keep up his studies, a very difficult matter, for while he was not dumber than an ox he was not any smarter. Most of his professors were lenient and helped him along. None gave him more hints, in answering questions, or asked him simpler ones than the economics professor, a thin, timid man named Bassum. One day when we were on the subject of transportation and distribution, it came Bolencie-cwcz's turn to answer a question. 'Name one means of transportation,' the professor said to him. No light came into the big tackle's eyes. 'Just any means of transportation,' said the professor. Bolenciecwcz sat staring at him. 'That is,' pursued the professor, 'any medium, agency, or method of going from one place to another.' Bolenciecwcz had the look of a man who is being led into a trap. 'You may choose among steam, horse-drawn, or electrically propelled vehicles,' said the instructor. 'I might suggest the one which we commonly take in making long journeys across land.' There was a profound silence in which everyone stirred uneasily, including Bolenciecwcz and Mr Bassum. Mr Bassum abruptly broke this silence in an amazing manner, 'Choo-choo-choo,' he said, in a low voice, and turned instantly scarlet. He glanced appealingly around the room. All of us, of course, shared Mr Bassum's desire that Bolenciecwcz should stay abreast of the class in economics, for the Illinois game, one of the hardest and most important of the season, was only a week off. 'Toot, toot, too-tooot!' some student with a deep voice moaned, and we all looked encouragingly at Bolenciecwcz. Somebody else gave a fine imitation of a locomotive letting off steam. Mr Bassum himself rounded off the little show. 'Ding, dong, ding, dong,' he said hopefully. Bolenciecwcz was staring at the floor now, trying to think, his great brow furrowed, his huge hands rubbing together, his face red.

* Courses of this sort, full of meaningless subjects, are referred to as Mickey Mouse courses.

'How did you come to college this year, Mr Bolenciecwcz?' asked the professor. '*Chuffa* chuffa, *chuffa*, chuffa.'

'M'father sent me,' said the football player.

'What on?' asked Bassum.

'I git an 'lowance,' said the tackle, in a low, husky voice, obviously embarrassed.

'No, no,' said Bassum. 'Name a means of transportation. What did you *ride* here on?'

'Train,' said Bolenciecwcz.

'Quite right,' said the professor. 'Now, Mr Nugent, will you tell us . . '.*

The professors who are lenient with athletes are still around. They are said to employ the A-B-C system of marking: A for Athlete, B for Boy, and C for Co-ed.

The N.C.A.A. has a rule that, to be eligible to play, a student-athlete must maintain a certain level of marks in all his subjects. If he does not, he will not be allowed to play – but he may still be doing well enough to remain a student at the college, in which case he is still entitled to his scholarship, but the poor athletic department gets nothing in return. A four-year full scholarship is worth around $12,000. The bigtime school, awarding twenty-five such scholarships a year, will at any given time, have one hundred student-athletes on campus, representing an investment of over $1 million. Which is why athletic departments do not at all like the idea of losing the services of an athlete merely because his academic grades are not good enough. To protect their money, many athletic departments now employ a new type of coach, the 'brain coach', whose task it is to see that the athletes are attending classes regularly and doing their homework properly. For those whose grades are consistently poor, tutors are made available, as at the University of Texas, which retains twenty part-time teachers at $3.50 an hour.

When talk turns to all the extravagances and the absurdities and the irregularities of bigtime college sport, a handy euphemism is used: over-emphasis. The N.C.A.A. has for years been trying to eliminate or at least hold down the abuses that over-emphasis gives rise to. It has, for instance, succeeded in imposing minimum academic standards for student-athletes, and in paring away some of the more outrageous recruiting excesses. That is to say, it has established rules about these things; how successfully they can be enforced is another matter. There are, for instance, the regulations that limit the number of times that a

* Thurber James, 'University Days' in *The Thurber Carnival*, Penguin Books, 1971.

coach may interview a high-school athlete. This is systematically evaded by a practice known as 'bumping' – the boy just happens to turn up on campus and who should he bump into but, of all people, the coach. Sheer coincidence, of course, and no amount of legislation can eliminate coincidences.

The ridiculous extremes of some recruiting practices inevitably elicit almost equally ridiculous regulations:

Whenever an aircraft (other than a commercial airplane or one owned personally by one individual) is used for purposes of transporting a prospective student-athlete, payment for its use must be at the established charter rates at the airport where the craft is based and the institution must be prepared to demonstrate satisfactorily that such payment has been made.

Aside from the problems of policing what is, in practice, almost unpoliceable, the N.C.A.A. runs into difficulties when its desires (i.e., the desires of the majority of its 656 member colleges) are in conflict with what the majority of bigtime schools want. It has for years been the practice at some of the 'football foundries' to build special dormitories exclusively for the use of student-athletes. This gets all the football team under one roof and makes the coach's job of supervision so much easier – they know where to look for their players, and they find it easier to check up on who is not in bed by the specified time. Athletic dormitories are frowned upon by the N.C.A.A. but there are plenty of them around. Such facilities often have a distinctly luxurious flavour. At Iowa State the dormitory is air-conditioned and has wall-to-wall carpeting. At the University of Alabama, where the football coach's name is Bear Bryant, they call the athletic dormitory the Bryant Hilton.* At Louisiana State University the athletes all have colour television in their rooms. In August 1973 Southern Methodist University in Dallas moved thirty-six students out of one of its best dormitories so that the building could be used exclusively by football players. The members of the team were also given separate eating facilities in the cafeteria. This was all necessary the football coach said, for 'control, morale and a prideful atmosphere'.

The objections to this sort of thing are that it divides the student-athletes from the rest of the students, making it embarrassingly obvious that they are athletes first and students second. This flies in the face of the N.C.A.A.'s unflagging efforts to promote the idea that the term

---

* There is an equally impressive dormitory on the campus of the University of Arkansas. Among the ordinary students it is known as the monkey house.

'student-athlete' has the priorities in the right order and that the prime idea behind an athletic scholarship is to give the holder an education.

Without doubt athletic scholarships have enabled large numbers of boys to attend college who otherwise could not have done so. But what does this prove? 'You hear a lot about how football scholarships allow poor kids to attend college,' says Dave Meggyesy. 'This may be true, but it isn't anything to be proud of. It's pretty obvious that this country could, if it wished, give everyone a chance to go to college.' There remain several other questions. Do student-athletes occupy university places that ought to go to other boys who are more academically worthy, but who are no good at games? Do student-athletes take advantage of the educational opportunities of college, are they truly interested in getting their degrees or are they merely treating college as so much unavoidable time-wasting until they can get into professional basketball or football? Most seriously of all, are the colleges sincerely interested in giving student-athletes an education, or are they treating them as hired mercenaries whose sole function is to win games and keep the money rolling in?

There is plenty of evidence to suggest that studying for a degree comes off second best in the student-athlete's activities. Even with the Mickey Mouse courses and the special coaching for examinations, the proportion of student-athletes who graduate is not exactly impressive. One survey conducted in the mid-sixties revealed that between 40 and 50 per cent of professional football players who had been in college for at least four years did not have degrees. In 1970 the *New York Times* sportswriter, Robert Lipsyte, found that of 124 players leaving college that year and entering professional football, only sixty-six were graduating. Boys' High School in Brooklyn, New York, has long had a reputation as a producer of basketball stars – forty-four of them, in fact, have been snapped up by the colleges and given athletic scholarships. Only one of them got his degree. It is true that many students, not only student-athletes, find it difficult to graduate in four years, but the student-athlete's task is that much greater because of the time he is required to spend on his athletic activities. He may even find himself in trouble with his coaches if he burns the midnight-oil studying. He is permitted, under N.C.A.A. regulations, four years of playing eligibility. When they are over the athletic department is likely to lose interest in him. His scholarship is terminated, and if he has not yet got his degree he will have to pay his own way if he wants to complete his courses. Some athletes do return to college, attending summer courses after they have signed as professionals, but it is a strong-willed individual who, once he has entered the well-paid ranks of the professionals, is willing to go back to school.

Which brings up the question: why should a college star bother to play out his four years of college eligibility when after, say three years, he has made a name for himself and could quit and make a fat salary as a professional? We are here once again in one of those murky areas of American sport where a convenient (but clearly illegal) agreement has been worked out between the people who run things. In this case, the professional football and basketball leagues have entered into an agreement with the colleges – the so-called 'four-year rule' – that they will not sign, or even approach, any player before his class graduates, i.e., four years after he enters college. Before his *class* graduates, that is, not before the player graduates. If the player does not graduate with his class, as many do not, he can be signed anyway, and his name will be on that year's college draft list from which the professional clubs select those players they wish to sign.*

There are clear financial advantages for the colleges in this set up, for it means that their money-spinning teams will not be prematurely broken up by raids from the professional clubs. On the other side of the deal, the professionals are even more amply rewarded. They are, in effect, relieved of the enormous expense of running farm teams, of having to spot, develop – and pay – their own future players. In football and basketball† the colleges are able to function as farm teams for the professionals, *and* make a considerable profit, because they do not pay their players.

There is one very obvious disadvantage for the player, in that control of his future career is taken out of his own hands, and his potential for earning money is severely restricted. The four-year rule applies regardless of whether a player stays in college or not. Thus, if he quits after his first year, no professional club will sign him for another three years – no matter how good a player he is. He may be capable of earning, say, $20,000 a year for those three years as a professional, but he will not be allowed to. Similarly, a player who reaches a peak in his playing ability during his third year at college is not permitted to bargain with the

---

* See Chapter 3, page 25.

† Unlike football and basketball, where the professional.leagues were formed only after the sports had achieved considerable popularity at the college level, baseball established itself as a professional sport quite independently of the colleges. The vast majority of professional baseball players learn their trade, not at school, but in the sport's minor league and farm teams.

professionals at that time. He must wait another year – a year during which there is always the possibility that his form will drop off, or that he will suffer a serious injury.

By agreeing to honour the four-year rule the colleges and the professional leagues not only limit competition among themselves, they also restrict the athlete's right to work, a combination almost tailor-made to attract the attention of that old sports nemesis, the anti-trust law. In March 1971 it did just that. The four-year rule had its day in court and was summarily declared to be a *per se* violation of the anti-trust laws, meaning that, whatever the circumstances, there was no justification for such an agreement. Yet, because the illegal rule had certain advantages for everyone involved, it continued to be observed. It was just another part of the legal tangle in which sport was enmeshed at the beginning of the 1970s.

The new decade brought two other, more pressing, problems for the administrators of college sport. One of them was money, of which there was not enough. The other was student activism, of which there was too much.

Financial crisis was suddenly a common ailment of colleges all over the country. 'The financial situation of higher education grew considerably worse during the last year (1970),' said Dr Frederic W. Ness, President of the Association of American Colleges, and in the ensuing atmosphere of austerity large athletic budgets began to look less and less defensible. In fact, 400 of the 656 N.C.A.A. colleges were losing money on their athletic programmes. Between 1960 and 1970, forty-two colleges gave up inter-college football because of its expense. Even the much less costly basketball suffered. New York University, reporting that it had a deficit of $4·5 million, decided in April 1971 to drop its basketball team. 'The decision was very serious,' said the university president Dr James Hester. 'The competition for athletes is keen and costly, and the money can be used better in other ways to maintain the quality of the university.'

This was exactly what the critics of bigtime college athletics had been saying all along, but unfortunately for their arguments it was precisely the bigtime schools, the football foundries, that were best placed to withstand the squeeze.*

---

* Louisiana State University's football programme made so much money for the athletic department that by 1969 it had amassed a surplus of $2·3 million. When the university found itself in financial need, the athletic department very kindly loaned it $400,000 at 6 per cent.

Adding an extra football game to their fixture list was one quick and easy way to increase income. Another was to rent out their huge stadiums to the professionals for exhibition games. When the Detroit Lions played the Baltimore Colts at the University of Michigan's stadium in 1971, 92,000 people paid $546,000 to watch the game, of which the university's share was $200,000.

These extra sources of income were needed to cope with rising costs, and also because there was an unwelcome possibility that formerly secure money might be snatched away. Students at colleges – all students, not just student-athletes – are required to pay an annual 'activity fee'; the amount varies, but $50 is about the average. In many universities the activity of athletics has always claimed the lion's share of this money. The University of Kansas athletic department, for example, got $180,000 a year in this way. Until January 1971 when the student senate at the university voted against giving any student-fee money to support the major sports.

The Kansas students were not the first to vote against athletics; a similar vote had been cast the previous year at the University of California demanding that the '$309,000 in student fees given to the department of intercollegiate athletics be re-allocated in a manner more broadly representative of all students', the point being that only 700 male students took part in the athletic department's programmes out of a total enrolment of nearly 28,000.*

That the students themselves should do anything to hamper athletic programmes was tantamount to a revolution. The time-honoured image of the American college student was a care-free, overgrown boy (clean cut, naturally, and white) who divided his time between conducting panty raids on the female dormitories and cheering his school football team to victory. What had happened to that? It was an image that had been fading rapidly during the 1960s as student activism, awakened primarily by the iniquities of the Vietnam war, but also by the problems of racial injustice at home, captured the campuses. Nevertheless, amongst all this turmoil, if there was one area of college life where the old image had persisted, where these new trends had been resisted, it was the athletic departments. It was always assumed, not without reason, that athletes constituted the most conservative, most conformist, least politically-active section of the student body. Among the reasons for this

* San Francisco State College voted $15,000 to the Third World Liberating Front, $22,000 to the Black Students Union, and precisely nothing to the athletic department.

belief, none loomed larger than the figure of the coach, the man to whose care the athletes entrusted themselves.

When the sports psychologists, Drs Bruce Ogilvie and Thomas Tutko, conducted tests on college coaches throughout the U.S.A., what they discovered led them to describe coaches as one of the most authoritarian groups in the country. Discipline is the key word of the coach's vocabulary. He issues commands, and he expects them to be obeyed without question. He is totally in charge of the football or the basketball team. The student-athletes are there to do as he says, even the captain of the team who is captain in name only.

Examples of the military-style rigidity of college coaches were given in Chapter 6 (page 119), but the demand for unquestioning subservience is not limited to games or practice sessions. It reaches out to cover much of the athlete's off-the-field behaviour, such matters as the hours he keeps, whom he dates, and the way he dresses. The tone of athletic departments, set by the coaches, has always been one of conformity to the traditional values, with the athletes as conservative in attitude as the department requires them to be in appearance. But the 1960s were an anything but conservative time on the American college campuses, with radical groups and liberation movements springing up on all sides, and the tight little world of college athletics did eventually feel the effects of the changes that were taking place.

In view of the coaches' obsession with 'clean-cut' appearance it will come as no surprise to learn that an area of bitter confrontation, as so often in the sixties, was . . . hair.

The athlete must at all times be neatly attired, clean-shaven, well-groomed and have an acceptable haircut. (By acceptable, we mean that it must be acceptable to the head coach of the given sport. If there is a question, acceptability will be determined by the director of athletics.) Any mustache is to be short, well-trimmed and not to extend beyond the mouth line. Beards are not permitted. Sideburns are not to extend below the bottom of the ear and must be neatly trimmed.

That is an excerpt from the Colorado State University Athletic Department 1971 Rules of Personal Conduct. It is typical of most such regulations, and more liberal than many in that it does allow short moustaches and sideburns. For many coaches, even that was too much. When the Oregon State University football coach, Dee Andros, spotted one of his players with a small moustache and beard, he ordered him to shave them off, even though the football season was still months away.

The athlete, who was black, refused and a *cause célébre* developed. All eighteen black athletes at the university left their teams, protest rallies were held both for and against the coach, and an English professor showed his contempt for the coach's rule by ordering his students to come to class wearing beads and feathers. A student faculty commission spent eight weeks studying the case, and decided that neat moustaches were O.K., but that beards were doubtful. Despite all the furore, coach Andros did keep his job. At Coe College in Iowa, the athletic department was asked by the college president to come up with a less strict grooming code 'which takes due account of the changes all around us'. Whereupon the football, baseball, track, wrestling, and basketball coaches all resigned. High-school coaches were just as adamant as their college colleagues. In Somers, New York, three coaches left when the State Education Commissioner ruled that school athletes could wear their hair long provided 'it did not present a health or safety hazard'. A dispute in San Francisco ended up in Federal Court, where several long-haired high-school athletes, backed by the American Civil Liberties Union, tested their school's grooming rules. The judge ruled against them, using the sort of language that was doubtless sweet music to coaches' ears: 'In these perilous, troubled times, when discipline in certain quarters appears to be an ugly word . . . '

But as the seventies progressed it became clear that the struggle to keep athletes clean-shaven and crew-cut was doomed to failure. Moustaches, beards, and shoulder-length hair were a regular part of the scene, and even football players from such a citadel of southern conservatism as the University of Texas were seen with hair over their ears. The new generation of athletes had more in common with their own generation of students than they did with the traditional sports' values of their coaches.

Of deeper significance than long hair, and much harder to combat, was the questioning attitude of the new athletes. They no longer bowed down to the autocratic authority of the coaches. They dared to ask 'Why?' about coaching methods and if they were not satisfied with the answer, they might even decide that they no longer cared for sport, and simply stop playing. To the coaches that was quitting, one of the dirtiest words in their vocabulary. To the athletes, like Bob Ryder, a Princeton basketball player, it meant becoming 'a student and a person again', not being continually afraid of making mistakes during a game, not having to put up with bellowed reprimands from a furious coach. Ryder's problem, according to his coach, was that he got caught up in the intellectual currents at Princeton, and from the coach's point of view, that is an awful thing to happen to a student-athlete.

Being a student at one of the Ivy League schools, Ryder did not lose his scholarship when he quit, for at Ivy League schools (alone among the major college groups) financial assistance is issued solely on the basis of the student's need. There are no athletic scholarships.*

But the possibility of losing a scholarship did not prevent non-Ivy-League athletes from speaking out and protesting. Many coaches believed this new-found independence was directly ascribable to the ease with which athletes could now get financial aid; they no longer valued it because 'just about anybody who is warm and has a pulse rate can get a scholarship in some sport somewhere'.

Long hair and intellectual currents were menacing enough, but they were the lightest zephyrs compared with the tornado of black liberation that swept through the nation's athletic departments during the 1960s, resulting in upheavals like the ones that convulsed Syracuse University and the University of Texas at El Paso (see Chapter 7, page 154). Then there was Women's Lib pointing an accusatory finger at the male-dominated athletic departments and their programmes – programmes devoted exclusively to sports for men, but often supported in part by money from women students. Ultimately, there was the Jock Liberation Front 'to prove that an alternate form of athletics for people can exist'. One of the leaders of Jock Lib was Jack Scott, a former university athlete turned radical, who continually needled the coaching fraternity by calling them 'soulless, back-slapping, meticulously-groomed, team-oriented efficiency experts', by telling them that their primary responsibility was not to win games but to be educators, by rating them among 'the least intelligent and least educated people in the university', and by suggesting that their aversion to long hair on males was caused by their own latent homosexuality. When lecturing at the University of California, Scott began his course on 'Intercollegiate Athletics' by entering the classroom dressed as a typical coach, complete with the mandatory whistle around his neck. 'I blew my whistle,' he said, 'and told people to line up for seat assignments ... actually my whole get-up was a put-on to demonstrate that athletic coaches operate with a kind of dictatorial authoritarianism that students would not tolerate in their professors.'

* The Ivy League is the name given to a group of eight colleges in the north-eastern United States. It includes the most hallowed and oldest universities in the country – those likely to have ivy-covered walls: Harvard, Yale, Princeton, Brown, Columbia, Pennsylvania, Dartmouth, and Cornell.

Indeed they would not, and the message of the sixties was that they were increasingly disinclined to put up with it from coaches. Change was in the air, and the *New York Times* sports columnist Arthur Daley had a modest proposal: 'Why not use students on athletic teams? . . . Once upon a time the members of all athletic teams were students who attended college primarily for an education. After class each day they engaged in sports just for the fun of it.' And the funny thing was that a swing towards true amateurism did seem a real possibility – not because the colleges had decided that was the way they wanted it, but because the costs of the quasi-professional bigtime set-up were swelling to prohibitive levels for all but a select few colleges.

9 Shadow of the Black Sox

Given New York's insatiable compulsion to tear down its most distinguished buildings, the most surprising thing about the Ansonia Hotel is that it is still there. Built just after the turn of the century, the massive seventeen storey chateau-like structure was the work of Stanford White, second only to Frank Lloyd Wright among American architects. Majestic turrets, ornamental balconies and elegant windows adorn its upper floors, but the ground floor has succumbed to progress and presents a ghastly vista of cheap shop-fronts and garish neon signs. The Ansonia has the air of a dignified old lady in psychedelic sneakers. One look tells you that it has known better times. Indeed it has.

It was built for the elite, and it had private elevators, and carpets and tapestries in the hallways, and it had a driveway. And it had tenants to match. Millionaires and personalities – the long-serving superintendent will dredge names out of his memory: 'Yeah, there was Theodore Dreiser, and we had the opera people, Melchior and Pinza, they both had apartments here, and Paul Gallico's father, and Jack Dempsey's wife, and who was that guy in the corner on the sixteenth floor? – yeah, he was a big shot. And Babe Ruth – he had an apartment here.'

It is ironical that the hotel that housed Babe Ruth, the man who to many *was* baseball, should also have been the scene of a meeting that nearly resulted in the death of the sport. In 1919, the hotel was a popular place for visiting baseball teams. In September of that year the Chicago White Sox were in town. They were not just any old team – not by a long way. This was the most formidable side in the land, bristling with batting, pitching and fielding stars. They had already won the American League that year, and were getting ready to start the World Series against Cincinnati, the National League Champions. The White Sox were overwhelming favourites to win the best of nine series, probably in five straight games.

But meanwhile, back at the Ansonia, Chick Gandil, the club's first baseman, was talking with seven other White Sox in his room. The topic was as appalling as it was appealing. They were agreeing to throw the World Series, to deliberately lose. Gandil had already been in touch with some of his gambling pals, and had been promised $80,000 if the Series were lost. He had managed to interest the other seven to go along with the idea.*

Gandil was a rough sort of character who had been around, mostly on the fringe of criminal society, and his involvement with gamblers was a pretty natural one. But what of the other seven? How was he able to convince over half the team that it was OK to betray their club, and their fans? There were two factors here that certainly helped Gandil. Firstly, he was well aware that the White Sox were a pretty disgruntled bunch, because of the stinginess of their owner, Charles Comiskey. They were the best team in baseball, but they were also one of the most poorly paid.

Just that season, 1919, Comiskey had cut all their salaries, pleading poverty because of falling attendances. Because of baseball's reserve clause, the players had no answer to this. They could like it, or they could lump it. So they lumped it. But as the season went on, and as they went on winning, they could hardly fail to notice that the crowds were pouring out to see them everywhere, and they knew that Mr Comiskey must be making a fat profit. And there were petty indignities: on nearly all the other clubs, the *minimum* meal allowance was $4 a day, while Comiskey allowed a flat $3. Not infrequently the White Sox took the field in grubby uniforms, and that was because Comiskey had decided the laundry bills were too high. For many of the put-upon White Sox, the coming World Series was, if not the last, certainly the penultimate straw. Their opponents, the Cincinnati Reds, were a small-town club whose players were, by general opinion, inferior to the White Sox. Yet the Reds were better paid, *much* better paid. Gandil, for instance, got $4,000 a year, while the Reds' first baseman got $9,000 So, no doubt, it occurred to some of the White Sox that there was something to be said for a scheme that at one and the same time would make them some $10,000 richer and deprive old skinflint Comiskey of the prestige of a World Series winning club.

Gandil had something else going for him. Simply that fixed games were not exactly a rarity. Baseball had for some time been living uneasily with the knowledge that bribes were being offered by gamblers, and that

* I am indebted to Eliot Asinof's remarkable book *Eight Men Out*, Holt, Rinehart and Winston, New York, 1963, for details of the background of the 1919 World Series scandal.

some players were accepting them. The players knew it was going on, and the owners knew it was going on. But more important, the players knew that the owners knew – and they knew that the owners were doing nothing about it for fear of a scandal that might damage organized baseball. Under such conditions it quite obviously did not pay to be honest. Where corruption grows unchecked, cynicism is sure to follow. It was cynicism that enabled the White Sox to accept Gandil's plot without shock or moral outrage. Fix the World Series? Yeah, why not?

When the Ansonia Hotel meeting broke up, it had been decided: the World Series would be fixed. The offhand, almost fatalistic way that the players accepted this is evident for they decided little else – no details of how they were to fix the games, or which games, or even more astonishing, of how they were to get their money. Gandil was to arrange it all with the gamblers.

Gandil's arrangements, however, were also pretty slapdash. He was dealing with two groups of gamblers. One of them had promised $80,000, the other $100,000. He had met only with underlings, but he had received assurances that both offers were backed by someone who was known to have the wherewithal: Arnold Rothstein, an almost legendary figure among East Coast gamblers. Actually, Rothstein had agreed to put up the $80,000; the $100,000 deal was being put across by a group using Rothstein's name.

As people in the know began to pile up money on Cincinnati and the odds against them shortened, the rumours built up that the Series was fixed. Everybody – the fans, the sportswriters, even Charles Comiskey – heard them, but hardly anyone believed them. The World Series was an almost holy event, the national pastime's yearly high mass; how could you imagine for one moment that it could be soiled by gamblers?

Arnold Rothstein had already bet heavily on Cincinnati to win, but before he put down any more money, he wanted some sign that the players were fulfilling their part of the bargain. He sent word from New York that the first game, in Cincinnati, was to be lost by the White Sox; but, more than that, he wanted a clear sign, early in the game, that all was going to go according to plan. He commanded that the White Sox pitcher deliberately throw at and hit the first Reds batter to come to the plate in the first inning.

This was 1919, well before television, and even before radio – the first commercial radio station did not start broadcasting until the following year. In 1919 they spread the news by telegraph to halls throughout the United States, where fans sat and followed the play. They had such a room set up in the Ansonia Hotel, and if Arnold Rothstein was there, he quickly heard what he wanted to hear. The White Sox failed to score in their half of the first inning. When the Reds came up to bat, their leadoff hitter was hit square in the middle of the back by the very first pitch. It looked like Eddie Cicotte, the White Sox pitcher, had thrown a wild pitch. But Rothstein and a few other gamblers knew better. And Cicotte knew that far from being a wild pitch, it was an extremely well-aimed one; he had already received his $10,000 to lose the game, and he proceeded to do just that. The Reds won it 9–1, and they went on to win the Series by five games to three.

The gamblers, of course, cleaned up. The players did not do quite so well. Instead of the expected $180,000, they got only $40,000 between them. Four of them had jeopardized their baseball future for a measly $5,000 each, Cicotte and Gandil had $10,000 each, while two of them had received nothing at all.

The 1919 baseball season was over as far as playing games was concerned. But it was to cast an ominous and ever darkening shadow over the 1920 season. Comiskey, who by now was sure of the worst, received a letter from one of the players involved offering to tell all he knew. Comiskey simply buried the letter, fearful of exposing the whole mess, hopeful that it would soon be forgotten. Seven of the eight fixers were still playing for the White Sox, who were again leading the American League and looked like winning it.

But by now too many people were involved in the fixing of games for it to remain even semi-secret. A newspaper story in September 1920 alleging that $500,000 had been bet on a fixed game between the Philadelphia Phillies and the Chicago Cubs, started the exposure. A Grand Jury, convened in Cook County, Illinois, to investigate the charges, decided that it might as well investigate the 1919 World Series while it was about it.

Slowly at first, then with gathering impetus, the activity of the gamblers was exposed. Now all the interest was centred on the 1919 World Series, and within three weeks enough had been uncovered for the Jury to return indictments against the eight White Sox players, who were now being called the Black Sox. Three of them had signed confessions. Comiskey, forced to act at last, suspended all seven who were still playing for the White Sox – a move that ruined the club's chances of winning the League.

The players who had confessed explained how they had thrown the games – a bad pitch at a crucial moment, a sudden hesitation when going to field a ball, a second's delay in making a throw – all actions so close to a legitimate play that they would be undetectable. One of them made a terrible mess of trying to catch a high-hit ball; he was, he claimed, *really* trying to catch it, but he dropped it, and after the game one of the other Black Sox, who thought the whole episode looked a trifle too theatrical, told him to be more careful how he dropped catches in the future.

The players were charged with an assortment of conspiracies – conspiracy to defraud the public, conspiracy to commit a confidence game, and conspiracy to injure the business of the American League and of Charles Comiskey. But where were the gamblers? True, there were five of them charged with the players – but these were minor figures. The big names were missing – in particular there was no mention of Arnold Rothstein, even though his name had kept bobbing to the surface during the Grand Jury inquiries.

The big-name gamblers may have been absent, but the big-name lawyers were out in force, particularly on the defence side. This was somewhat odd, for certainly the players could never have afforded such high-priced legal aid. Who, then, was footing the bill? The suspicion was that organized baseball itself, which ought to have been concerned in exposing the players' activities, was now doing its best to protect them. None of the Black Sox took the stand, which meant that there were no awkward revelations about the way Comiskey ran his ball club and treated his players. Strangest of all, several of the White Sox who had not been involved in the fix, but who had realized what was happening and were thus in a position to give damning evidence about the conduct of the thrown games, took the stand – and revealed nothing.

The trial lasted just over two weeks, but it took the jury less than two hours to reach a verdict – Not guilty. The prosecution had failed to prove the conspiracy charges, and everybody – gamblers and players alike – went scot free. The accused players had no doubt that they were now totally exonerated, and would be able to play again the following season. They were quickly and rudely disabused of this notion.

The very next day a statement was issued by the recently elected Commissioner of Baseball, Judge Landis, saying, in effect, that organized baseball cared not one fig for the court's verdict; these players had been shown to be the associates of gamblers, and as such, they would never be permitted to play in professional baseball again.

For one of the players the decision was particularly hard to take. Buck Weaver, the third baseman, had been at the original meeting in the

Ansonia Hotel, and had agreed to go along with the fix. Later he had changed his mind, and had in fact played honestly throughout the Series, and he had not accepted any money. Yet he was implicated in the confessions of others and had to stand trial. The not-guilty verdict was his vindication – and then came Landis's banning. Weaver spent the rest of his life protesting his innocence, repeatedly trying to have his case reviewed, to get back into baseball. He never made it. Neither did any of the other Black Sox.

The move by Landis sealed the triumph of organized baseball. It had survived the trial without any really damaging revelations emerging. And now it had shown itself to be even more stringent than the law. Landis had been appointed Commissioner of Baseball only eight months before, at a time when the baseball owners were coming under increasing pressure to clean up the sport. His first official act had been to suspend the Black Sox, and now he had banished them altogether. Gambling problems later led him to tangle with two of baseball's superstars, Ty Cobb and Rogers Hornsby, both tough outspoken characters used to getting their own way. Hornsby, perhaps the game's greatest-ever right-handed hitter, was known to bet heavily on horses. Landis summoned him to a meeting, and told him he was gambling. Hornsby said yes he was, and so what, and if Landis was playing the stock market then he was gambling too. Maybe that struck home – no action was taken against Hornsby. With Ty Cobb, the stormiest of baseball's stormy petrels, Landis was even less successful. In 1926 Cobb unexpectedly resigned his post as player-manager of the Detroit Tigers. Some months later a statement from Landis made it clear why: Cobb had been accused by another player of rigging a game back in 1919, good old vintage 1919. The evidence against Cobb was pretty strong, and it included a damning letter in his own handwriting. Nonetheless, Cobb did not take any of this quietly. He denied everything and sent an icy shiver through organized baseball by announcing that while he had never been involved he certainly *knew* a heck of a lot about crookedness in baseball, and some of it involved owners, rather than players. Cobb had his hand on the corner of the rug and the baseball owners acted quickly to stop him from lifting it. Too much had been swept under there. Landis, under the impression that he had quietly eased Cobb out of baseball, had to retract. He declared that Cobb had never been found guilty of fixing games, and that 'no decent system' could ever find him so guilty, and that therefore, Cobb was free to play baseball when and where he wished. Cobb died in 1961, the same year that he published his autobiography; in it he revealed that his lawyer had written the conciliatory statement published over Landis's name.

The schizophrenia of the baseball magnates, who wanted a pure sport but did not want to expose the dirt, was but an extension of a similar conflict among the fans. They wanted a sport free of gamblers – but they wanted to gamble. And how they wanted to gamble.

The Australians usually claim to be the world's greatest gamblers, but the record suggests that the Americans have an equal, if not greater, claim to the title. It would hardly be exaggerating to say that at no time since the Mayflower deposited the pilgrims at Plymouth has America been lacking in people looking for a wager. Even the North American Indians, who had discovered America some 25,000 years before the Pilgrims, were inveterate and inventive gamblers. The Onondaga had a type of dice game in which they used plum-stones ground down to a rectangular shape, with the sides painted in different colours. They staked their blankets and their beads and their hatchets, and when things got desperate, even their squaws. The Naragansett Indians of Rhode Island had things well organized, with a special area of their land set aside specifically for gambling.

The Indians had no playing cards, but they did have a variety of card-type games, in which they used straws and sticks. When it came to gambling the Europeans could teach the Indians very little. But they brought one thing with them, what Henry Miller once described as 'the blight of Christianity'. The Puritans, of course, were ferociously opposed to gambling. They were in charge, they made the laws, but they also were a minority, and it seems pretty certain that the majority wanted to gamble. The almost incessant string of denunciations from pulpit and bench would hardly have been necessary otherwise.

The city of Boston was only seventeen years old when, in 1647, the authorities found it necessary to pass a law forbidding all types of gambling – a great deal of which was going on in the taverns over such games as shuffleboard, and bowling, and cards. In the milder moral climate of the Southern Colonies, gambling had struck even earlier, and at the·very citadel of morality. A 1624 law of the Virginia Assembly was aimed at stopping gambling among . . . clerics. In New England the Puritans were ready with a theological argument against gambling; they said that it was a usurpation of God's power. Cotton Mather, never at a loss for words when it came to condemning something, ruled that lotteries were 'God sitting in judgement', so that they were not to be used by man. In 1670 the Massachusetts legislature banned dice and cards as 'a great dishonour to God', and the constables were given full power to root out all sorts of 'gameing meetings' even to the extent of entering private houses. By the beginning of the eighteenth century the gambling problem was being felt in Philadelphia, and the mayor himself was empowered to enter any building where gambling was suspected. In New York, the taverns became more and more the centres for all sorts of games on which bets were placed – games that were encouraged by the landlords as they were good for business. In 1788 a law was passed to curb gambling in New York State, one of its requirements being that only ready cash could be staked.

In the South, the attitude towards gambling was less severe, no doubt because most of the leisured class who ruled were rather keen on having a flutter now and then. Many observers of the southern scene commented that the two main interests of the people seemed to be horse racing and cock fighting, and that a considerable amount of betting was done on each. The plantation owners had rapidly acquired wealth and the independence that goes with it. Their non-Puritan consciences did not bother them in the slightest as they gambled away their money or their goods or their slaves.

The obsession of the early colonial governments with devising ways to stop gambling had its ridiculous side. For many of these administrations were prompt to organize lotteries whenever they needed money. One of them – the Virginia Company – had been partially floated on a lottery held in England in 1612. In America lotteries were held to raise money for the construction of roads, bridges, public buildings, even churches. Education was helped, and funds were raised in this way for Yale, Harvard, and Columbia Universities. In dour little Connecticut, of Blue Law fame, lotteries were banned, as you might expect. But the ban was only on the sale of tickets for lotteries organized outside the state. Too much money was leaving the state, and Connecticut's own lotteries were suffering. The Continental Congress tried to raise $10 million for the war against England by means of a national lottery, knowing that at this time 'every city and town large enough to boast of a court house and a jail' also boasted of a lottery wheel. Privately run lotteries, which were open to all sorts of dishonesty, were banned early, and by the end of the nineteenth century the last of the State lotteries—in Louisiana – had disappeared. But not for good. In 1966 New Hampshire inaugurated a state-wide lottery, and in 1967 New York State, over the opposition of church leaders, started a lottery to raise funds for education. By August 1973 New York State education had benefited by over $460 million and several other states – New Jersey, Massachusetts, Pennsylvania, Michigan and Ohio among them – had started their own lotteries.

After the War of Independence, gambling quickly re-appeared, if indeed it had ever gone away. It re-appeared most of all in the South, but the new gambler was a very different figure from the rich southern gentleman of pre-war days. With the opening of the western frontier, the migration into the Ohio and Mississippi valleys, and finally with the Louisiana Purchase in 1803, the stage was set for the Golden Age of American Gambling, and the emergence of the professional gambler. He certainly had some of the elegance and some of the manners of the old southern gambler – but that was about all. His capital was New Orleans and he did his work on the riverboats that paddled their way up and down the Mississippi River. By the 1850s it is estimated that some 2,000 of his kind were working the boats. They played – occasionally honestly, but usually not – card games and dice games, and they invariably won. If they lost, then the veneer of civility was likely to evaporate and a gun might appear from somewhere among the elegant clothes.

Out on the frontier, the gambler lived a less ordered but even more adventurous life. He moved from town to town, staying long enough to find and fleece likely victims, or maybe until he was run out of town. For a while following its founding in 1879, Tombstone became the gambling capital of the South West, a wild and raucous centre of 15,000 people and countless gambling dives. The climax of its days of lawlessness was the famous gunfight at OK Corrall, when Wyatt Earp and professional gambler Doc Holliday shot it out with the Clantons.

The flamboyant Mississippi gamblers and the Doc Hollidays disappeared abruptly with the arrival of the twentieth century. Law, of a stringent, and ironically, almost puritanical intensity came to the South West. The new territories like Arizona and New Mexico enacted severe anti-gambling laws as they sought statehood and admission to the Union. From that point on, it was almost all uphill for those who wanted to wager. A wave of anti-gambling legislation rolled over the country after the Civil War, as state after state introduced or reinforced laws banning gambling.

Over the years, the laws against gambling have increased both in number and complexity. Each state has its own laws, laws which may be varied by local authorities within the state. They run from a total ban on all forms of gambling, through legalized gambling at horse-racing tracks (and certain other sports, e.g., dog racing in Florida) to the leniency of Nevada, the one state where gambling is legal, the one state where bookies can operate without fear of arrest. What the laws have *not* done is to stop gambling. The Black Sox scandal showed that pretty clearly in 1919, and the situation is not much different today.

The Black Sox did do one thing though. The scandal, the first big one in professional sport, came right at the top. If the World Series could be fixed, then quite obviously any sports event could. Professional sport developed a Black Sox Complex and became hypersensitive about the possibility of gamblers being involved in sports, or even of being on friendly terms with sports people – owners or players. When Bill Cox, the owner of the Philadelphia Phillies baseball club, was reported to be betting on baseball games in 1943, he was hauled before Commissioner Landis and bounced out of the sport for good. With players suspected of betting or associating with gamblers, the treatment has not always been that strict.

In 1963 it looked like the Black Sox all over again. Appropriately enough the rumours started in Chicago again, but this time the sport was football. Some big names were being bandied around in the headlines, and the Commissioner of Football, Pete Rozelle, admitted that his staff was investigating. One of the stars under suspicion was Alex Karras, of the Detroit Lions, whose extra-curricular activities included part-ownership of a bar, an interest that the Lions had been trying to get him to sell. Karras said he had $45,000 invested in it, and he was not going to sell. The Detroit police, however, were able to liven things up with reports that Karras and other Detroit Lion players had been associating with 'known gamblers and hoodlums'. They told of a private bus, owned by an underworld figure, and fitted out with a bar and bunks, that often toured around Detroit with a complement of roistering mobsters and their girls. It turned out that Karras and another Detroit player had travelled back from an away game in Cleveland aboard the bus. They were aboard as guests of Karras's business partner, who said that there were not any women on the bus, and that they spent the journey playing gin rummy and drinking, ahem, lime juice. Karras appeared in a television interview. Some of his answers were surprising, to say the least. When he was asked if he bet on ballgames, Karras said yes. As if that was not bad enough, he said 'yes' to the next question, too: 'Have you ever bet on a ballgame in which you were playing?'

The football establishment had just about regained *terra firma* when Karras was back on television, busy explaining that when he said 'bet', he meant that he wagered a packet of cigarettes or cigars, that sort of thing, and only with close friends. He certainly never bet with a bookie,

'I don't even know any bookie,' he said. Commissioner Rozelle had heard enough; he had a long meeting with Karras, and very little was heard from the Detroit player after that. The attention turned to Paul Hornung, of the Green Bay Packers, one of the game's superstars, a good-looking blond known as the Golden Boy. Hornung also had a meeting with Rozelle, and admitted that he too had bet on football games. His betting history had started back in 1957, when he 'met' one Barney Shapiro who turned out to be a gambler. Shapiro owned various gambling machines in Las Vegas, and he had Hornung out there to try them out. Hornung lost $500 on them, but it seems that a showgirl was part of the deal, and Hornung had a fine time. By 1959, he was getting Shapiro to place bets for him on professional and college football games, sometimes on games that he was playing in – but always to win. The amounts ranged up to $500.

Hornung and Karras both eventually paid the same price for their dalliance with the gamblers. They were suspended for one season. Karras, who loved football and was desperately anxious to get back into the game, sold his interest in the bar. But there seems to be something about bars, and owning them, that appeals to football players, for this was not the last of football's bar problems. The most spectacular of them came in 1969, and it involved the man who was then the No. 1 football player in the land – Joe Namath, the outspoken, swinging mod quarter-back of the New York Jets. Early in 1969, Namath had done what almost everyone agreed could not be done – he had led the New York Jets to victory over the Baltimore Colts in the Super Bowl. He had done it in *his* way, with no modesty or shyness or glowing praise for the other team. He said from the start: 'I guarantee you we're going to win – we're the better team.' Win they did, convincingly, and Joe Namath came home to New York to a ticker-tape parade and a greeting from Mayor Lindsay. The season was over, and that was all from Namath for the moment – until June 1969, when the pre-season training was about to begin. Then Joe hit the headlines again with one of the most celebrated press conferences in the history of American sport. Before a massive assembly of microphones and television cameras, Joe announced that he was retiring from football, and again it was high drama, for Joe was openly crying as he spoke, breaking up, wiping away the tears. Commissioner Rozelle had told Namath to sell his interest in Bachelors III – a smart little bar on New York's swinging East Side. Rozelle had been informed by the F.B.I. that the bar was a hangout for gamblers and other undesirables. Namath at first agreed to sell, but changed his mind at the last minute. 'I'm not selling – I quit,' he said. 'They said I'm innocent. But I have to sell. I can't go along with that. It's principle.' Namath's point was that he was a victim of guilt by association. Namath had a meeting with Rozelle, and was shown photographs of nine men; he claimed he recognized some of them as customers at Bachelors III, but that he knew none of their names. It was the 'backgrounds and habits' of these customers that was troubling Rozelle. Who were they? According to *Life* magazine, they included a choice set of Mafia types, a gang boss here, a triggerman there, plus a fugitive bank robber and a gangster or two. The magazine named them all. Then there was a revelation that the man who was managing Bachelors III had over the past ten years been associated with several bars known to be popular with gamblers and mobsters. *Sports Illustrated* said the real trouble was not the bar, but Namath's apartment where, it alleged, dice games were held attended by loan sharks, bookmakers, mobsters – and athletes. The police had the bar and the apartment under observation, and had been tapping the phones at both places. Namath stuck to his principles for seven weeks, then he changed his mind. There was a press conference again – tears were absent this time, but Commissioner Rozelle was very present. 'Joe has agreed to sell his interest in Bachelors III,' he said. Namath still insisted that he had done nothing wrong, but the agreement he had with Rozelle contained a tacit understanding that, in the future, he would be considerably more careful about whom he made friends with.

What the Football Commissioner had done in the case of Hornung, Karras, and Namath was, on the surface, beyond reproach. He had – before there was any question of any legal action – taken positive and, considering the stature of the players involved, quite drastic action to put his own house in order. As far as it went, it was fine. But it left one matter – perhaps the most important matter – completely untouched. Had any of the players been approached, or bribed, to throw games, and if so, had they thrown any? This was the really explosive stuff, and there was some suspicion that – as in the Black Sox case – it was being cleverly concealed by all the dust raised in a sanctimonious house-cleaning. This suspicion was given something pretty substantial to feed on early in 1970 when a major baseball scandal erupted. Denny McLain, a pitcher for the Detroit Tigers, had won thirty-one games during the 1968 season. Winning twenty games in a season is considered good for a pitcher; no one had been a thirty-game winner since 1934. Primarily on the strength of McLain's pitching, the Tigers took the American League pennant, and went on to score an upset win over the St Louis Cardinals in the

World Series. Then in 1970 came the almost incredible revelations that during the 1967 season McLain had not only been associating with gamblers, but he had actually been a partner in a bookmaking set-up. This was bad enough but apparently it was by no means all. Because at the end of the 1967 season the American League had come to the very last day of the season with three teams still having a chance of winning the pennant. One of these teams was Detroit – playing a double-header against the Los Angeles Angels, and needing to win both games. They won the first. The starting pitcher for the second was Denny McLain. He lasted only three innings and gave up three runs; the Tigers lost the game 8–5, and they lost the pennant. McLain was playing his first game in two weeks, having been sidelined with a toe injury. *Sports Illustrated* reported rumours that said that the injury had been caused by one of McLain's mobster associates stamping on his foot; and it quoted 'gang-land sources' as saying that the same mobsters had bet heavily against Detroit. It was, for Denny McLain, a decidedly sticky wicket. He was promptly suspended indefinitely by the baseball Commissioner while an investigation was conducted. This lasted for six weeks, when Commissioner Kuhn announced his decision: McLain was to be suspended for half a season. It was a curious verdict. Alex Karras, the football player who had suffered a full year's suspension for betting, pinpointed the anomaly: 'I must have been a bad, bad boy in 1963. What's this mean, anyway? If you can win forty games, can you kill somebody?'

Kuhn, obviously, had not based his rather light sentence on McLain's brilliance as a pitcher. Rather, he said, it was because McLain had in fact been duped by his bookmaking partners. McLain had coughed up over $5,000 to the operation, and thought that he had thus become a bookmaker. Not so. His wily associates apparently pocketed the money. So, reasoned Kuhn, McLain never had been a bookmaker, he only *thought* he was one. And as you do not punish attempted crimes as severely as committed ones, McLain would be invited to sit out only half the 1970 season. Kuhn also pointed out that there was 'no evidence to indicate that McLain gave less than his best effort at any time while performing for the Detroit Tigers'. The old Black Sox suspicions were suddenly very much alive again. For Kuhn admitted that throughout the investigation, one of the chief factors he had in mind was the possible damage that this incident might do to baseball. But surely the main object – the only object of an inquiry – ought to be to establish the truth, the whole truth. What would happen if the truth conflicted with an acceptable baseball image? If there was evidence suggesting fixed games or bribes, would it be followed up, or would it be quietly pushed aside?

Some would reply that the first question to be asked is: can a game be fixed anyway? How many players would have to be involved to make it a certainty? And would it be worth it? The Black Sox proved that games can be fixed – though there were seven players actively involved. To show just how tricky it can be to fix effectively, one need only refer to the frustrating experiences of Lee Magee, who used to play second base for the Cincinnati Reds. He was also on transaction terms with gamblers, and in July 1918 he was playing in a game which he and one other player had agreed to dump. It had obviously not been easy to do, for the game went into extra innings, with the score tied at 2–2. It was in the thirteenth inning that tragedy, or justice if you like, struck. The Reds were batting, there were two outs, and Magee was at bat. Naturally he was not about to get a hit – and he played the ball on the ground, straight at the shortstop for what ought to have been an easy out. Except that the ball hit a bump or a pebble or something, jumped in the air and hit the shortstop full in the face. It broke his nose. And it gave Magee all the time in the world to get to first base – he could have crawled there on his hands and knees and still have been safe. With the next hitter up, Magee was given the perfect chance to retrieve his unwitting error. He was ordered to steal second base; all he had to do to mess it up was to start slowly and late, and he would be thrown out easily before he made it into second. So he started half-heartedly for second base – and the opposing catcher winged the ball hard for second base; hard, but not very true – it sailed yards wide of the waiting secondbaseman and flew way out into centre field. Again poor Magee had so much time to get to second, it was ridiculous – so much time that he had to go on to third, to avoid making the whole thing look too obvious. And then the roof really fell on Magee – for the Reds' hitter smashed a home run. This is rather like a tidal wave, sweeping all majestically before it; it meant that Magee had to trot slowly and, no doubt, agonizingly, down to home plate. The second he trod on home plate, the score was 3–2, and the Reds had won. Magee lost $500 of his own money right there, and his gambling friends were somewhat out of pocket too.

Knowledgeable gamblers would point out that Mr Magee and his friends were doing it the hard way. The way to fix a baseball game is to get the pitcher on your side. He is the key man. Any deliberate mistakes he makes would be extremely difficult to detect, and, as he is in on every play when his team is in the field, he has much more opportunity to select the critical moment.

In football, the key position would be the quarterback, the man who initiates and directs every offensive play. Subtle mistimings in his handling of the ball, passes slightly over or under-thrown, would, theoretically, be all that was necessary. It would almost certainly not be enough. There are now so many players involved in a football game – possibly as many as forty in one game, that the chances of just one of them controlling the outcome of the game are remote. Then there are the game films, which are studied almost *ad nauseam* over and over again after each game, to find out just what went wrong or right. The feeling is that to really do an effective job of dumping a game, a player would have to be noticeably off-form. Such a player would be replaced by a substitute from the bench very quickly. Finally, there is the not inconsiderable factor of money. Most of the game's stars – and these would include a high percentage of quarterbacks and other key players – are extremely well-paid and would supposedly find no temptation in a bribe.

With football and basketball, however, 'fixing' a game does not entail deliberately losing it. Both these games are ones in which large numbers of points are scored: an average basketball score might be 104–98, a football score 24–14. In betting on these sports it is not so much who wins or loses that matters as the margin of the victory or loss. For each game, bookmakers quote a 'line' telling which team is favoured, and by how many points. Thus: New York six pts over Baltimore. Meaning that, if you bet on New York, they have to win by *more than* six points for you to collect. If they win by six, there is no bet, and if they win by less than six, you lose. If you chose Baltimore and they win, then quite obviously you have won your bet; but you can also win your bet, even if Baltimore lose – provided they lose by *less than* six points. (If they lose by six, then there is no bet.) The 'point-spread' is thus the important thing. It opens up sophisticated possibilities for the crooked gambler. He need not ask a ballplayer to dump a game – all that is required is that the player, while making sure that his team does win, also makes sure that they do not win by more than the point-spread. Point-shaving, as it is called, is a pernicious little wound in the morality of sport, one that is extremely difficult to diagnose, almost impossible to heal. The player who shaves points is, after all, not selling out his team-mates, or betraying the public. He is working for a victory just as much as anybody. What terrible damage is done if a basketball player, with his team ahead – and certain winners – by six points with 10 seconds to go, deliberately misses a jump-shot? His team wins anyway – by six points instead of eight. The only people who get hurt are those who bet on his team to win –

gamblers, you see. This sort of reasoning gives the point-shaver an almost holy air when contrasted with the dumper. The big point-shaving scandals have been in college basketball. There are, alas, all too logical reasons for that. Basketball is played by teams of only five men, so that one man's contribution is twice as important as, say, in eleven-man football, while college players are less mature and less wealthy than professionals. Plus the extra that some colleges, by over-emphasizing sport, might well impart to their players a feeling that honesty is not always the best policy.*

The point-spread system can produce some curious reactions at the stadiums, too: like the time, in December 1962, during the National Football League championship game. The New York Giants were trailing the Green Bay Packers by seven points to sixteen, with under two minutes left in the game. Suddenly, the stadium was making more noise than it had all afternoon, roaring the Giants on to score. Which was very strange, because, even if the Giants did score, they would still be behind, 14–16. The yelling, it seems reasonable to assume, was primarily from those Giant fans who had bet on their team, with a point-spread that said the Giants must not lose by more than six and a half points. They were behind by nine – a score, any score, even a three-point field goal, would not win the match, but it would mean a loss by less than six and a half points, and consequently plenty of salvaged bets. A knowledge of the points-spread is sometimes the only way to understand crowd reactions towards the end of a game. For instance, if, at the end of a basketball game, with say 20 seconds left, a player chooses to dribble away the remaining time rather than risk a shot, with his team already leading by six, he may be assailed by what sounds like totally unwarranted booing. If so, it probably means the point-spread for that game is seven points.

All three major professional sports prohibit players and owners from placing bets. It might seem innocent enough – even a good thing – for a player to bet on his own team to win. It should make him all the more determined to win. The trouble is that if he bets, he will almost certainly – unwittingly – be giving valuable information to gamblers. This is because his bets will vary from week to week.

If he bets $500 on his team for three weeks running, and then on the fourth game reduces the wager to $100, or does not bet at all, he is telling his gambling friends that he is not feeling nearly as confident about that

* See Chapter 8, page 174.

fourth game. This 'broken-pattern' betting is inside information, just what the gamblers want. It is for this reason that they are anxious to befriend players. In the vast majority of cases, there will be no crude attempts to bribe a player to fix games, and there may well be no straightforward requests for information. But the hope is that the player will let fall some small gem of news that the crafty gambler will recognize as significant; the quarterback has been rather grumpy lately, the star pass-catcher has had a row with his girl – anything that the bookies did not know about when they were setting the line.

Bookmakers, obviously, are not at all happy about that sort of thing. They are not in the business to take risks. They like to balance their book. If they can get an equal amount of money bet on both teams of a football game, then they are doing just fine. They cannot lose, because of the 10 per cent commission they take, variously known as the 'juice' or 'vigorish'.*

What it means is that to win $10 you have to bet $11. Thus, if the bookie has $50,000 worth of bets on Team A to beat Team B, and $50,000 on Team B to beat Team A, whatever happens he is going to make 10 per cent of one side of the bet, i.e. $5,000. The bookie, then, is a conservative type and, in his own illegal way, rather law-abiding. He does not like the thought of a fix – as he is the one who is going to get hurt.

Professional football, basketball, and baseball all have regulations designed to keep them free of gambling and fixes. When a football player, for instance, signs his contract, it includes the following clause:

Player acknowledges the right and power of the Commissioner (a) to fine and suspend, (b) to fine and suspend for life or indefinitely, and/or (c) to cancel the contract of, any player who accepts a bribe or who agrees to throw or fix a game or who, having knowledge of the same, fails to report an offered bribe or an attempt to throw or fix a game, or who bets on a game, or who is guilty of any conduct detrimental to the welfare of the League or of professional football.

All three professional sports also employ security agents. In football there are two full-time agents, who work out of the League's headquarters in New York, plus part-time agents in each of the cities where the

---

* The derivation of this last term is interesting: Webster's *New World Dictionary* says it probably comes from a Russian word *vyigrysh*, meaning winnings or profit. Not so, say knowledgeable gambling acquaintances, it is a corruption of 'vicarage', meaning the salary of a vicar, which used to be made up of tithes – which were 10 per cent taxes on the produce or income of local landowners.

League has teams – one for each city, except New York which has the doubtful honour of needing two.

In charge of the security operation is Jack Danahy, who had twenty-seven years' experience with the F.B.I. before joining professional football. Many of the part-time agents are also ex-F.B.I. men. The operation costs football $250,000 a year and is, says Danahy, 'geared to prevention – to stamp out fires before they blaze up'. The aim is to protect the image of football, to make sure that no one connected with the sport, whether owners, players, officials, or minor employees, is involved in a scandal that could damage it. To this end Danahy and his men will investigate the background of possible new owners and officials, check on business enterprises in which players and others want to become involved, protect players by warning them off from association with known criminals or other undesirables.

Important as they are, these activities are secondary to the problem of 'betting coups'. At its worst, a betting coup would mean a fixed game. At best it would mean that someone had been able to get hold of inside information that affected the playing of a game. This would usually consist of finding out about an injury – possibly only a minor one – to a key player, that was being hushed up by the club to prevent it giving a psychological boost to their next opponent. This sort of situation was once quite a problem until professional football passed a rule that all its member clubs must issue to the Press, twice a week, a list of all their injured players, with details of the injuries and an estimate of how long the player is expected to be sidelined. There remains the possibility of a late injury, or even of one that the player himself is trying to keep quiet about. Gamblers have been known to go to considerable lengths to get hold of this type of information. There was a period when the managers of clubs had to be very careful about telephone calls they received from people claiming to be 'journalists', and asking apparently innocent questions about the championship races, then slowly getting on to more specific details about the next game. Birdie Tebbetts, manager of the Milwaukee Braves baseball club in 1962, told of 'spurious telephone calls that plague us all over the country. They come from gamblers. They want some little bit of inside information that will give them an edge. Usually they try to conceal their identity by saying, "This is the A.P." or "This is the U.P.I."* One guy even has a typewriter pounding in the background while he's talking. Mostly they want to know the probables –

* The two major news wire services in the U.S.A. – Associated Press and United Press International.

who is going to pitch the next day. And they do not want to wait for the newspapers. By getting the information in advance, there's a slight edge, even if it is infinitesimal.' The direct phone call is a rather crude approach, and it is fairly obvious from another of Tebbetts' comments that the gamblers have other sources of information. A call came through asking who his starting pitcher was to be, 'I told him I had already announced it – Willey. Know what is answer was? "But Willey has a bad hand. Aren't you starting Spahn instead," he said. Where he got it I don't know, but he was right.' There can be two possible sources: either the gamblers have struck up a close relationship with one or more of the team's players, quite probably unknown to the players, or they are paying some one working within the club to relay them last-minute information.

The digging up of titbits of information on team fitness and so on, is also of interest to bookies in setting an accurate line for each game. The bookies work by trying to encourage approximately equal amounts of money to be bet on both teams in any game. If Team A has been made a six point favourite over Team B, and too much money goes down on Team A, the line may be changed, making them a seven or eight point favourite. This would encourage betting on Team B by those who feel that A, while good enough to win by six, will not win by eight points.

The funny thing about the line is that nobody seems quite certain where it comes from – or nobody is telling. There is general agreement that it is centrally prepared, and distributed – sold, that is, – to a network of the top bookies who, in turn, sell it to the smaller fry bookies. Depending to some extent on who you ask, you will find out that the line originates in Las Vegas or St Louis or Cincinnati or Minneapolis and so on. To many newspapers, the line is simply a way of selling more copies – they publish it, even though they may also publish editorials condemning gambling. This is a practice that has drawn a great deal of criticism from police, and particularly, college authorities, who say that it encourages gambling.

With his line set, the bookie can begin receiving bets. If he is in Nevada he can do it legally.* Anywhere else he cannot, and his methods of accepting bets have to be cloaked in various shades of secrecy. At the bottom of the betting hierarchy are small-time bookies, possibly store-owners or barmen, or elevator operators, who accept small bets where

---

* Though even in Nevada there are restrictions: betting by telephone, for example, is illegal.

they work – these are strictly part-time amateurs. Above them are street-corner bookies who meet bettors at specified times and places to receive and pay out money. Other bookies employ runners who, for a percentage of the bets they collect, do all the leg work. Or the bookie may set up his headquarters in a back room at, say, a candy store – which is likely to be uncommonly busy during the hours when the bookie is in residence.

Most of the big bookies rely on the telephone. While some claim they can, by payment of the appropriate 'fee', get a line guaranteed free from police surveillance, others prefer to use one or another of several dodges to avoid detection, like the call-back system. The bookie signs on with a telephone-answering service, telling them – if they are curious enough to enquire – that he is an insurance agent or a stockbroker or whatever. He gives them a false name, Mr Smith say, and a false address. This class of bookie will have his regular clients, accepted after personal recommendation from other trusted clients. To each of them he gives the telephone number of the answering service and the hours when he will be accepting bets. Each of the bettors uses a code name and gives the bookie at least one telephone number where he can be reached – his office or his home, for example. When a bettor wishes to place a bet, he calls the answering service during the stipulated hours and leaves a message that Mr Smith should call him 'at home' or, if he happens to be using a phone the bookie does not have the number of, he leaves the number with the answering service, but garbled in some pre-arranged way, e.g., with the first and last digits reversed.

All the bookie needs is a pocketful of dimes and a public pay phone. He calls the answering service and notes down all the 'messages' that have been left for him. Then he calls each one back and records the bets. When that batch is completed he makes another call to the answering service and receives a further list of names to call. In this way the bettors can expect to be called back pretty promptly after their original call.

The callback system offers considerable protection for the bookie. He can use a different phone every day, so that he has no permanent wire that can be tapped. His telephone number, should it fall into the hands of the police, turns out to be that of an answering service to whom he has given a false name and address and whose bills he has been paying with untraceable money orders. Furthermore, the answering service has no information about the bettors either, just notes containing false names, messages to 'call at home', and possibly some garbled restaurant or public call-box numbers.

But there are also disadvantages to the callback system; for the bettor, who may find it inconvenient to wait around for the return call, and for the bookie, for whom the system is really only practicable if he makes his living from a comparatively small number of large wagers. For the bookie handling large numbers of bets the system would not work. He has two alternatives: either to risk a direct line (and it is a substantial risk – sooner rather than later the number is turned over to the police, usually by a desperate wife), or to use some form of technical trickery to conceal the physical location of his telephone.

There is, for instance, the method known as cheeseboxing. The bookie rents two apartments within two or three blocks of each other. He applies, under different names, for a phone to be put in each. This gives him two separate numbers – ABC-1234 in Apartment A, and XYZ-5678 in Apartment X. As far as the telephone company is concerned, there is absolutely nothing to link the two. For the bookie, Apartment A is a dummy apartment. It will contain only the telephone ABC-1234 and the cheesebox, a complex piece of gadgetry that is connected to the phone and that automatically converts all ABC-1234 calls into XYZ-5678 calls.*

The bookie gives out his number as ABC-1234. Bettors dial this direct, but their call is received – after the cheesebox has re-routed it – on the XYZ-5678 number in Apartment X where the bookie has set up his office. One other piece of equipment is essential to the working of the cheesebox: a detection device in Apartment A that will ring, buzz or otherwise notify the occupants of Apartment X the moment that any attempt is made to enter Apartment A. When this happens the assumption is that the police have traced the ABC-1234 number. The bookie immediately collects together all his trappings and disappears from Apartment X. He is then out of business for a day or two until he can set up two more apartments – he may even have them already rented and waiting.

The actual handing over of money and collecting of winnings is done either on a person-to-person basis, with the bookie or his runner appearing at a fixed rendezvous at a fixed time, or, in the case of the bigger bookies, by sending money orders through the mail. If a gambler, or a bookie, takes a heavy loss and decides to welsh and just disappear, there is not much that can be done about it. The whole business is illegal anyway. In practice, it happens a good deal less than one might suppose.

* It is called a cheesebox because it is about the same size and shape as the once well-known Philadelphia Cream Cheese pack.

The ambiguous American attitudes to gambling produce their most perplexing anomalies in the field of law enforcement. The anti-gambling laws are by their very nature extremely difficult to enforce. This, plus the fact that enormous numbers of perfectly respectable Americans gamble, and do not consider it a crime, can hardly encourage the police to adopt a fervid moral attitude against gambling. No bookmaker using runners, or working out of a store, or using a direct telephone line, can operate for very long without the police becoming aware of what is going on. What is the policeman to do who knows that gambling is going on all around him, but who also knows that the community he is supposed to be protecting does not regard it as particularly sinful, and that the laws he is supposed to enforce are inadequate? All too often, what he does is to adopt the time-honoured solution: if you can't beat them, join them.

It is often said that no bookie can operate without police assistance, and certainly grumbles about the high cost of protection figure prominently in bookies' conversations. The payment of protection money is also probably the biggest cause of police corruption. The extent of the problem was revealed in 1950 when bookie Harry Gross was arrested in New York City. An investigation into official corruption had been proceeding for some time and had already resulted in the downfall of the Mayor of New York, William O'Dwyer. Two weeks before Gross's arrest, O'Dwyer had been suddenly and opportunely translated to distant spheres. President Truman had appointed him Ambassador to Mexico and O'Dwyer (who less than a year before had expressed unshakeable devotion to the mayoralty: 'I shall serve the four years to which I was elected. Nothing but illness or death can prevent me from that.'), now found that his country needed him. 'There's nothing I can do but go,' he said, adding that his new job was one of 'vital importance to our nation's interest.' It all seemed a trifle overdone. After all . . . the ambassadorship to Mexico? O'Dwyer left behind him the festering scandal of wholesale corruption in the police department that came dramatically to a head with the arrest of Harry Gross.

Along with Harry came a little address book. It contained, in addition to a list of all his bookmaking associates, the names of over 100 policemen. After some initial hesitation Gross cooperated with the authorities to the extent of implicating over 200 policemen. Gross, the star witness at the trial of many of these officers, was asked: 'When did you start corrupting police officers?' His reply was an indignant, 'I didn't corrupt them. They corrupted me. They looked for me – I didn't look for them.'

Gross had a point. It was impossible to tell whether what was being investigated was bribery by the bookie or a shakedown by the police. It was evidently a mixture from which both sides benefited. Harry Gross prattled on with his quite remarkable memory, bringing out name after name, identifying policemen in court, and recalling the various services he had done for them. By the time he had completed his astonishing performance, the Commissioner of Police had resigned under a cloud and the new Commissioner had demoted every one of the 355 plain-clothes-men in the city back to uniformed patrolmen. Fifty-two police-men were dismissed from the force after investigations of their conduct and during the period of approximately one year between Gross's arrest and the end of the trials an exceptionally large number of policemen – over 400 – had found it necessary to retire or resign. The cops turned off the force were by no means all patrolmen, they included captains, sergeants and lieutenants.

During his own trial Gross revealed that he had been paying about $1 million a year to the police. The most appalling part of the Gross case was the clear indication that the taking of graft from bookies had become an accepted practice among large numbers of New York policemen of all ranks.

Despite the scandal and the massive attempt to clean things up, the graft went on. Ten years later the *New York Post* ran a series of articles on the subject. A police official told them: 'If you knew the actual amount of money involved, you wouldn't believe it. And even if you did, the *Post* wouldn't dare print it. It's that big.' The stories touched off an investigation that went on for nearly four years before coming up with conclusive evidence. Ten policemen were dismissed and the entire squad of forty-eight men primarily responsible for enforcing gambling laws was transferred to other duties. The squad, said its chief, had 'lost its effectiveness'. In other words, corruption had reached the epidemic level of the Gross days.

After another ten-year span the seemingly inevitable link of gambling and police corruption surfaced again as a New York cop went on trial for lying about his connection with gamblers. The prosecutor said that the testimony would show 'the corruption of almost an entire police unit, the 7th Division plain clothes unit'. The unit, whose task was to suppress gambling in a limited area of the Bronx, consisted of nineteen men.

Police corruption is only one of the arguments against the anti-gambling laws, and it is by no means the strongest. The worst part of the illegal gambling situation is that, ultimately, it is controlled by organized crime – the Mafia, or the Syndicate, or Cosa Nostra, or the Mob, call it what you will. It is variously estimated that the amount bet *illegally* by Americans each year is between $20,000 million and $50,000 million.* Whatever the figure, about one third of it goes as profit to the Mob.

The anti-gambling laws help finance organized crime. They foster police corruption, they make criminals out of millions of Americans who see nothing wrong with an occasional bet, and they are extremely difficult to enforce. So why not legalize gambling? There are, of course, strong religious and moral objections to that, but powerful opposition also comes from a somewhat unexpected source: professional sport. Baseball, football and basketball have all let it be known that they are against the legalization of gambling on their sports. 'It would be chipping away at the integrity of the sport,' said football commissioner Pete Rozelle. 'We are a symbol sport. We have heroes. Any legalized betting would raise suspicion about performance.'

The tide of opinion nevertheless seems to be running in favour of legal gambling. In 1971 the New York Police Commissioner, Patrick Murphy, announced his support on the grounds that 'it would cut off organized crime from a chief source of revenue and eliminate a main source of police corruption'. But there was another motive beginning to be heard, one that had a much wider appeal: tax relief. City and state governments started to turn to lotteries as a source of revenue that would help keep taxes down. The biggest dent in the gambling laws came on 8 April, 1971. That was the day that the City of New York went into the book-making business, with the opening of its first two Offtrack Betting (OTB) shops. New York City thus became the first place outside Nevada to allow betting on horse races at a location other than the track itself. By 1973 there were 113 OTB shops operating throughout New York and some $240 million had gone into the city's treasury.

The success of OTB had little effect on illegal gambling, which

---

* Not all of this gambling money comes from sports betting. Particularly in the big city ghettoes the preferred form of betting is the numbers game, in which bets as low as 5 cents can be made. The bettor picks a three digit number between 000 and 999, thus accepting odds of 1,000–1 against winning. He can also bet two digit numbers at odds of 60–1, or one digit numbers at 6–1. The winning number varies from system to system, but is always one that the bettor can him-self check in the newspapers. It may, for example, be the last three digits of the daily balance in the U.S. Treasury. In 1970 the New York Police Department estimated that the numbers game in New York City employed some 10,000 people, grossed over $250 million a year, and was almost entirely under the control of organized crime.

offered three key services that OTB did not: betting on sports such as baseball, football and basketball; exotic 'if cash bets' such as round robins and parlays; and credit. When OTB announced that it was going to seek legislation allowing it to take bets on sports other than horse racing, the Commissioners of baseball and football immediately threatened court action to stop them. In the meantime, the friendly neighbourhood bookies continued to flourish.

10   A Foreign Affair

Having thought up two sports – baseball and American football – that the rest of the world finds unacceptable, the Americans, logically enough, have shown little interest in the one sport that everyone else enjoys: association football. There is, first of all, the matter of the name to be settled. Americans believe that they do play football. Europeans, like Nabokov's Professor Pnin, will never understand or accept this:

> . . . Pnin entered a sport shop in Waindell's main street and asked for a football. The request was unseasonable but he was offered one.
> 'No, no,' said Pnin, 'I do not wish an egg, or, for example, a torpedo. I want a simple football. Round!'
> And with wrists and palms he outlined a portable world. It was the same gesture he used in class when speaking of the 'harmonical wholeness' of Pushkin.
> The salesman lifted a finger and silently fetched a soccer ball. 'Yes, this I will buy,' said Pnin with dignified satisfaction.

But Americans, it seems, will not buy soccer. Later in Nabokov's book, when it becomes clear that Pnin's American-born son is not interested in becoming a 'footballist', the unwanted soccer ball is thrown out of a window and drifts away in a brook, a symbol of American disregard for the sport.

It has always been an anomaly, this. After all, the sport has enslaved people as different as the English, the Russians, the Brazilians and the Turks. Why on earth should Americans be resistant to its charms? It is all the more puzzling when one considers the enormous growth in sports interest that occurred in the U.S.A. during the sixties. By the middle of that decade, baseball, basketball, football and ice hockey were all falling over themselves adding extra teams to their leagues, with an occasional pause to count up the profits. They were often staggering. Professional sports franchises offered one of the few remaining opportunities for spectacular capital gains. Even at $13 million, a baseball franchise was still considered a worthwhile buy. But the really mouth-watering stories concerned those owners who, for a few hundred dollars, had purchased franchises in the early days of the leagues and had watched them become worth millions. Now, if only there were a new league starting up . . . And thus, suddenly, in 1965, the cries of Eureka! sounded all over the U.S.A. The investors had discovered soccer.

Here was the Golden Opportunity – a sport that was hardly organized at all in the United States; whoever was first to set up a league would have a huge untapped market at his mercy and could arrange things to his own convenience. And here was a sport with the biggest potential audience of all, with enormous international possibilities that none of the other American sports possessed.

The blinding vision of soccer as the answer to an entrepreneur's dream appeared almost simultaneously to several people. In no time at all three separate groups had been formed, all hoping to be the first to get a fully-professional coast-to-coast soccer league going. There was, however, a formality to be completed before the money could start flowing in. If they had not known it when they started, all three groups soon found out that there was, after all, some organization to this soccer business. They would have to get the approval of the United States Soccer Football Association (U.S.S.F.A.) if they intended to operate. Without that, they would be considered outlaws by all the rest of organized soccer throughout the world, and thus unable to partake of all that alluring foreign competition. That would defeat one of the main attractions of soccer.

In the fall of 1965, there arrived in the New York offices of U.S.S.F.A., three letters – one from each group – requesting sanction to form a professional league. A most intriguing and, for the sport of soccer, very nearly disastrous confrontation was in the making.

On the one side was U.S.S.F.A, formed in 1913, controlling body of soccer in the United States. That is, in theory. In practice, the powers of U.S.S.F.A. were more illusory than real. In a country where the sport was not taken very seriously, U.S.S.F.A. had little to offer that would make membership worthwhile. It had struggled along for years on very little money, run mostly by part-timers, men dedicated to soccer who devoted their spare time to running it. If they had anything in common, besides their love of soccer, it was that they were mostly foreign-born. Their continued devotion to the sport of the old country was a measure of the extent to which they had resisted becoming Americans, had refused to go along with the American values.

In 1965 there were plenty of amateur and semi-pro teams operating, mostly around the Eastern seaboard area. They tended to have names like Philadelphia Ukrainians, New York Hungarians, Blau-Weiss Gottschee, Newark Portuguese, and they played in leagues like the German-American League, or the Lega Italo-Americana di Calcio. If Americans thought of soccer as a foreign sport, there was a good reason for it. By and large, even within the U.S.A., it was a foreign sport. If you turned up to watch a German-American league game, for instance, you were likely to be regaled with announcements in German over the public-address system. Over in Harrison, N.J., they made them in Ukrainian. U.S.S.F.A. was run by the representatives of these ethnic groups. They were not, to put it charitably, men who were used to dealing with large sums of money, or with much experience in the world of big business. They had but one full-time employee, their Belfast-born secretary Joe Barriskill, who had worked for many years without pay, and was now seventy-six years old. They also had an office of sorts, a dingy, dusty, Dickensian shambles in midtown Manhattan to which they were ashamed to take anyone.

It was decidedly embarrassing, because they were about to suffer from a surplus of people who wanted to visit them. People who were used to plush carpets, and secretaries and intercoms and everything else that spells Big Business. The list of new soccer promoters read like a *Who's Who* of top sports promoters. There were those indefatigable sportsmen Judge Roy Hofheinz, Lamar Hunt, and Jack Kent Cooke, breath-takingly wealthy all three. There were top corporations, like Madison Square Garden in New York, and the R.K.O.-General Corporation; there were men who owned or were part owners of franchises in other sports. In football, there were the Detroit Lions, the Los Angeles Rams, the Pittsburgh Steelers, the St Louis Cardinals, and in baseball, the Cleveland Indians, the Atlanta Braves, the Baltimore Orioles,* plus the Boston Bruins from ice hockey. Just how much any of them knew about soccer remained to be determined, but they were all resolved to make of it an American major league sport.

U.S.S.F.A. found itself landed with a kingsize problem. Having spent over fifty years trying to spread the popularity of the sport and having got

---

* The fact that many of the new soccer promoters were also owners of major league baseball clubs did not go unnoticed among the other baseball owners. They asked which sport was to come first – baseball or soccer? If soccer were to succeed, it must do so – at least partially – at the expense of baseball, whose season it was usurping. And if it failed, the owners would have lost money that they could have spent improving baseball.

nowhere, they viewed the enthusiasm of the new devotees with some scepticism. At the most, there might be a chance for one league – but here were three groups all wanting to form separate leagues. What to do? U.S.S.F.A. did the safe thing, they appointed a committee to study the proposals. It consisted of three people, a Scotsman, a German, and a Rumanian. One part of their task was to look into the backgrounds of all the applicants and recommend who should be accepted. The other part was to tell the applicants the terms under which U.S.S.F.A. would accept them. It amounted to this: each accepted franchise would have to pay U.S.S.F.A. $25,000 plus a percentage of its gate and television receipts. This was not bad for an organization that had, up to that moment, an annual income of around $40,000. But U.S.S.F.A., which had been so impoverished for so many years while it kept the sport of soccer alive, was not going to miss this opportunity to augment its finances.

The millionaires professed shock at the terms. Their lawyers turned up the information that there was already an ostensibly professional soccer league operating in the eastern United States. It was called the American Soccer League, and it was paying U.S.S.F.A. precisely $25 a year to operate. The A.S.L. was a semi-professional league playing low-calibre soccer in second-rate stadiums. U.S.S.F.A. felt that the new league aimed at something better than that, and felt they should pay for it. In fact, for all the outrage expressed by the entrepreneurs, the sum of $25,000 for a franchise was hardly exorbitant. As it happened, one of the prospective owners, Jack Kent Cooke, was in the process of buying a hockey franchise: it cost him $2 million. Jack Flamhaft, a lawyer and a member of the U.S.S.F.A. committee found it amusing: 'It makes me laugh – here come in some sixteen millionaires who own some billion-aire businesses in other sports and fields – people who are in *big* business – did *they* want a franchise for $25?'

Apparently they did, or at least they wanted to bargain over it. This was difficult because of the resentments on each side. John Pinto, a vice president of R.K.O.-General and leader of one of the groups, found the U.S.S.F.A. Committee extremely difficult to deal with: 'They had the attitude that we were guys with an awful lot of money and they were not going to let us come in and reap the benefit after they had been working for years – we were going to have to pay for it. In other words, they were *selling* us a franchise, this was not entry into the thing, it was a highhanded attempt to make us pay when it should have been a spirit of co-operation.' Highhanded? Well, strange to relate, that was exactly how

Flamhaft saw most of the applicants: 'They came with a chip on their shoulder, they were saying "We're going to invest X millions of dollars – shouldn't we have the right to tell you fellows how to run this game?"'

Then the U.S.S.F.A. Committee had a sensible thought. Why not, they suggested to the three groups, take the best from each group and combine them into one really strong league? It was also an astonishingly naive thought. It was turned down flat in no time, each group convinced that it already was the best. There would be no deserting of colleagues.

For U.S.S.F.A. there was nowhere left to turn. Either it recognized all three groups and faced the certain disaster of competing leagues, or it had to single out one of them for recognition. In any case, the final decision would have to be made by U.S.S.F.A.'s full convention, to be held in July 1966 in San Francisco – though, of course, it was unlikely that the convention would vote against the Committee's recommendations.

Representatives of all three groups trekked to San Francisco to plead their case, and to hear the verdict. The convention went along with the Committee, and chose to recognize only one group, that led by Jack Kent Cooke. The reason for the choice was the obvious one that this was the only group that had agreed to U.S.S.F.A.'s terms.

While the Cooke group was busy congratulating itself, the other two groups quickly realized that all their efforts and dreams were about to add up to a big fat nothing. They had had the door slammed in their face, and they were not the sort of people to put up with that. Even before the convention was over, they got together – these two groups who had told U.S.S.F.A. they would not get together – they got together and decided they would make one last joint effort to obtain U.S.S.F.A. approval. They formed the National Professional Soccer League, with ten cities represented, and at a meeting with U.S.S.F.A. in New York announced that they were now ready to accept the terms. They even produced a check for $250,000 to prove it. The problem now was the U.S.S.F.A. contract with the Cooke group which gave that group the *exclusive* rights to operate a professional soccer league. The N.P.S.L. offer had to be rejected. The door was now not only slammed, but bolted too.

It was now August 1966, and on the 23rd the N.P.S.L. dropped its bomb. They announced that they were going to go ahead with their planned league without U.S.S.F.A. sanction, and furthermore that they would start operations the following April – just eight months away.

This was a decidedly nasty jolt for the N.A.S.L. people, who had thought they had the field to themselves, and who did not plan to start playing until 1968. But there was always this fact to reassure them; the N.P.S.L. was an 'outlaw' league, not recognized by U.S.S.F.A., and therefore not by F.I.F.A., the international controlling body. This was the key point. For everybody had realized right from the start that if a professional soccer league was to amount to anything at all, it would have to be stocked – at least initially – with foreign players. There were no American players of the necessary calibre. Here was the rub for an outlaw league. A chain of obstacles would be erected against them: U.S.S.F.A. would inform F.I.F.A. that it did not recognize the N.P.S.L. and that it was a non-sanctioned league. Finally each national F.A. would inform all its players that, if they agreed to have anything to do with the N.P.S.L., either by signing for any of their clubs or arranging fixtures against them, they ran the risk of being suspended from world-wide organized soccer.

Such a possibility presaged trouble for the N.P.S.L. when they started to comb the world for players. They had ten teams to build up, and would need at least 150 players. It seemed highly unlikely that they would be able to find that many top-class footballers willing to risk their career for a league that might not last out the season.

The N.P.S.L. bosses were not discouraged. They believed that if they were the first league to start playing games and if they did nothing to outrage world soccer opinion, then F.I.F.A. would be forced to re-cognize them. They had by this point virtually given up hope of trying to deal with U.S.S.F.A. and were bypassing them in favour of direct contact with F.I.F.A. They were encouraged by what F.I.F.A. told them, which amounted to private assurances that the N.P.S.L. would gain recognition. In public, F.I.F.A. issued statements expressing hope that the situation would be satisfactorily resolved.

Since the first approaches had been made to U.S.S.F.A., two things had happened within the United States that had made the millionaires even more sure that they were on the right track. The 1966 World Cup Final between England and Germany had been televised via satellite, all across the U.S.A. Despite the fact that it came on at 12 noon in New York and 9 A.M. in Los Angeles the viewing figures had been spectacular – eight million. Then in August 1966, an independent promoter in New York had staged an exhibition game between Santos of Brazil and Inter of Italy, and nearly 44,000 fans had turned out. Obviously, soccer's time had arrived. A mood of wild optimism had the owners in its grip. Many were expecting what Lamar Hunt called 'instant major league', with sellout crowds right from the start. So confident were the N.P.S.L. owners, that they took out a ten-year lease on an expensive office space in New York for their league headquarters, and voted an annual salary of $75,000 for an as yet unnamed Commissioner to head the operation.

Over in the N.A.S.L., the complacency that came with U.S.S.F.A. sanction had worn off, and it was realized that the N.P.S.L. really meant what they said about starting the following April. Well, they could not be permitted to get away with that unchallenged. For a start, the N.A.S.L. changed its name 'to avoid confusion' with the other league. Now it was the United Soccer Association, a meaningless title, but one that gave the familiar acronym U.S.A. Its members got together and decided that they had to operate in some shape or form in 1967, or the N.P.S.L. would establish a definite advantage. There was not time to assemble their own teams, so they hit on the idea of each league city adopting a foreign team for the season. They determined to bring in eight of the top European and South American teams who would put on a show that was bound to be of a much higher standard than anything the N.P.S.L. could provide with their fledgling teams.

The process of building up these teams was already under way. The N.P.S.L. obviously was having difficulties signing players, though fewer than it feared and, no doubt, the U.S.A. had hoped. The word had gone round that anyone doing business with the N.P.S.L. faced suspension, and had been topped with a rumour of dubious origin that announced that any player going to play in America stood a very good chance of being drafted into the Army and sent to Vietnam. It was not true, but it did not help the N.P.S.L.'s cause. But there were things working in their favour. The most important was that there evidently were more than enough players who found the lure of America and the dollar more than enough to offset the 'outlaw' label. The N.P.S.L. agents, genuinely believing that their league would soon be recognized, were able to reduce its effects even more. The *New York Times* started to print tiny little three-liners announcing the signing of players. They were all made to sound like superstars: 27 January 1967 . . . 'An outstanding soccer player from Africa, Sammy Zoom, has signed to play with the Atlanta Chiefs of the new National Professional Soccer League.' They were, almost all of them, total unknowns. Occasionally a big name would appear, but always it was a star in the twilight of his career. No matter – to the publicity people who wrote the releases, they were stars, one and all. The St Louis club pushed this to its logical end, and called itself the St Louis Stars. The press releases were absolute gems of misinformation;

there is no particular reason to believe that the people who wrote them were trying to mislead. It was just that, like the editors who occasionally printed them, and the fans who read them, they did not know of what they talked. For the majority of the people involved in the league, Sammy Zoom just *might* have been the second greatest soccer player in the world (even they knew that Pelé was the No. 1) – not only could they not be sure, but there was no simple way for them to check up.

This was no mere credibility gap – it was more fundamental than that. It was a knowledge vacuum. The vast majority of the new owners, in both leagues, had absolutely no experience whatever of soccer. Most of them did know about the way that baseball, football, basketball, and hockey were organized, and it was assumed that this, plus their undoubted success as businessmen, would be all that was necessary. They started in with all the assurance and the arrogance of men who are used to winning, to being right, to knowing all the answers. In soccer, it turned out, they barely knew what the questions were, never mind the answers. The existence of U.S.S.F.A., and above them F.I.F.A., meant that the new owners could not be a law unto themselves. They had to comply with the national and international regulations, and they found that for all their millions invested, their hands were tied on many important matters. Whether they realized this would be the case before they entered is moot; it seems likely that many of them were somewhat vaguely aware of it, but never really seriously imagined for one moment that they could be bossed about by a bunch of part-timers from U.S.S.F.A., even less so by F.I.F.A., which was not even American. In the United States the rights of the individual businessman to run his own affairs rank with the national anthem and the oath of allegiance as foundation stones of the Republic. In short, they probably knew what the form was, but they assumed that any bothersome restrictions would simply melt in the face of their entrepreneurial drive and their money.

Little did they know the hornets' nest they had jumped into. Bob Wolff, the newly appointed president of Madison Square Garden's newly minted soccer club, the New York Skyliners, got the message very quickly: 'I must have been getting twenty phone calls and visitors a day – all claiming to be soccer experts, all suggesting players I should sign, all with the magic formula that was going to spell success. They were coming out of the woodwork.' Wolff was finding out, with a rush, that the world of soccer was full of contentions, of theories, of national rivalries, of personal opinions. Unfortunately for him, the United States – and New York in particular – had become a gathering place for all of them. A

Brazilian would visit his office and tell him – convince him – that the
only sensible thing to do was to sign all Brazilians, because they played
the most artistic, attacking soccer, and this was what Americans wanted
– more goals, high scores. He would be followed by an Italian who
pooh-poohed such nonsense and pointed out that the Italians, indeed,
were the world's best, and that there was a huge Italian population in the
New York area, that always turned out *en masse* for Italian teams. While
Wolff was mulling that over, a German or Yugoslavian would arrive
with the unassailable truth that what was wanted was some hard rugged
play with body contact, that was what Americans always wanted to see,
so he should sign the tougher German or Yugoslavian players. Nonsense,
said the next visitor, why, didn't he know that England had just won
the World Cup? Obviously the English way is the best, and anyway if he
wanted to avoid all sorts of niggling problems, he should certainly sign
players who can speak English. The thing to do, said another, is to take
a few players of each style and nationality – this way he would get the
best of everything and would attract fans from each ethnic group, and
weld them into a team. What? You can't mix styles like that, they'll never
be able to adapt, you'll just end up with a nothing team, now what you
should do is this . . . .

And so it went on. Down in Philadelphia, John Rooney who was
putting together the Spartans, found the same thing: 'There's more
experts in this game than any other sport I've ever seen.' The majority
of the experts were no such thing. They were fans – and like all fans of all
sports they had ideas about how the game should be played. The
problem was that the owners had no means of judging the worth of their
counsel.

In the midst of this uncharted sea, there were just two signposts that
everyone recognized. One read 'Pelé', the other 'World Cup'. The idea
was to use them as much as possible in publicity releases, even if it
meant dragging them in by the scruff of their necks. Players were
described as 'Haitian World Cup stars' or 'Jamaican World Cup stars',
countries that had never got past the preliminary rounds of that competition. For others, strange-sounding names from faraway places, the
trick was to link them with Pelé, even if it was once or twice removed.
The Baltimore Bays described their new player, Hipolito Chilinque, as
formerly of 'Cruzeiro in Brazil's first division. Cruzeiro pulled the
Brazilian soccer upset of the year last season when they beat Santos in
the Brazilian Cup Final. Pelé, the greatest soccer player in the world,
stars for Santos.' The Los Angeles Toros player Lucio Calonga was

boosted as having 'held Brazil's world-famed Pelé to one goal in two games'. And when the Philadelphia Spartans signed Ruben Navarro, they said that Pelé had called him 'the greatest defensive player I have ever faced'. True or false? . . . nobody could be sure. It was all designed to create the impression that a league of top quality was on the way. After all, World Cup meant that magnificent England-Germany game, and Pelé meant the best there was. The people who knew soccer, mostly the ethnic groups, were not fooled by all this Madison Avenue trickery – they knew better. The uninitiated showed little interest in the matter. The only ones who do seem to have been taken in were the owners themselves.

Meanwhile, back in Europe, things were hotting up a bit. The U.S.A.'s agents who were going round trying to sign up top teams, found that none of the top teams was available; all had previous commitments of one sort or another, and it was proving difficult to find *any* team that could come for the full seven-week period that the U.S.A. wanted. They were forced to lower their sights, and the names of the teams they were dealing with suggested that they were going to end up with some decidedly mediocre squads.

The N.P.S.L. was beginning to chafe under the 'outlaw' label that had been pinned to them. Being an outlaw league, they were not obliged to follow any of the conventions set up over the years by organized soccer but they had been very careful to stick to the rules – particularly in signing players. The practice here was that approaches must be made to a player's club, not to the player himself, even when the player's contract had expired. By January of 1967, the N.P.S.L. evidently felt that this restraint was getting them nowhere – certainly it did not seem to be hastening recognition. They announced that in the future, they would approach directly players whose contracts had expired: 'We have agreed to sign such players without further concern about the foreign custom,' said the N.P.S.L. president Bob Hermann.* He also added a slap at the way in which soccer was run: 'We feel professional teams should be ruled by professional associations, leaving the amateurs to the amateurs.'

Hermann meant that the sport should be run by those who had invested money in it, those who were in it for profit, not 'for the good of the game' or any schmaltzy nonsense of that sort. The attitude was spelled out by Joe Peters, owner of the N.P.S.L.'s Toronto Falcons. In

---

* His reference to a foreign custom was probably designed to give the move the appeal of an America v. the Rest atmosphere. In fact, the custom is widely – and more stringently – practised in America. It is called the reserve clause.

London he announced that, if the U.S.A. went through with its plans to import foreign teams, then the N.P.S.L. would take them to court, on the grounds that they and the U.S.S.F.A. were deliberately excluding the N.P.S.L. from dealing with foreign teams: 'If they attempt to use this monopoly in this way,' he said, 'as the teams arrive, we will slap them with an injunction and do everything we can to keep them in the United States – I believe the maximum period is twenty-one days – until a court decides the matter.' The English journalists thought this was going a bit too far. 'You can bet on it, and why not?' replied Peters. 'We are in this for business.'

But how unbusinesslike they were being! Already they had brought about a situation where there were two leagues fighting each other, when it was not at all certain that one league, devoting all its energies to promoting soccer, could make a go of it. And now they were threatening lawsuits.

On top of all that there was the glaring lack of soccer expertise at the top of both leagues. The N.P.S.L., looking around for someone who could help them with their recognition problem, came up with Sir George Graham, a former secretary of the Scottish Football Association. It was an appointment that was greeted with disbelief by most English journalists, who regarded Sir George as the most conservative of all Britain's soccer administrators. At least it evened things up over the matter of titles. The N.P.S.L. could now match F.I.F.A.'s Sir Stanley Rous with their own Sir George Graham.

Before either league could be said to be complete, there was the matter of Commissioners to be settled. The U.S.A. were the first to make the appointment. They chose Dick Walsh, who until that moment had spent a lifetime in baseball administration. One of his first statements was: 'I don't even know what a soccer ball looks like.' The N.P.S.L. could hardly allow themselves to be outdone at the top, so they also came up with someone who knew nothing about soccer. Ken Macker came in fresh from a six-year stint as publisher of three newspapers in the Philippines.

The N.P.S.L. and the U.S.A. blundered towards the opening kick-offs, both leagues top-heavy with administrative know-how and with hope, both with their feet planted firmly in mid air.

By the time opening day arrived, the N.P.S.L. had accomplished the impossible. They had conceived, gestated and – not without parturition problems – given birth to ten brand-new sports teams. They had imported over one hundred players, often with wives and children, and found them places to live. They had thought up names for the teams. John Rooney's wife had recently seen the film *The Spartans*, so his team became the Philadelphia Spartans. In Baltimore they opted for some local chauvinism with the Baltimore Bays. John Pinto thought up 'fifty-or-so names' for the New York team, and liked Generals the best – one, because it was a good name, and two, because it provided an association with the parent company, General Tyre & Rubber Company. He thought the league might find it too commercial, but they OKed it without any trouble. As most of the initial soccer support in the Los Angeles area was expected to come from the large Mexican population there, the team got a Spanish name, the Toros. The Atlanta team, owned by the baseball club the Atlanta Braves, decided to continue with the Indian motif and to become the Atlanta Chiefs.

When it came to team colours, the reasons for choices ranged from a simple 'because they were bright and easy to see on the field' for the Philadelphia Spartans' maroon and gold, to the sympathetic magic of New York's green and gold, chosen because the Green Bay Packers, then the most successful American football team around, wore them. The Pittsburgh Phantoms chose purple, because the 'Phantom of the Opera' had worn purple.

Perhaps the biggest single difficulty faced by all the teams was the language barrier – or barriers. Most of them were polyglot assemblies of several nationalities, and communication presented quite a problem. The Chicago Spurs, for instance, had sixteen players on their roster – four Germans, two Poles, a Frenchman, a Peruvian, a Mexican, a Greek, an Italian, an Irishman, a Yugoslav, an Austrian, and two Americans. The story was told of how one general manager was sitting in his office one morning wondering how he could converse with one of his players who spoke only German. An assistant rushed into the office with the answer: 'I've got just the guy we need – he knows all about soccer, *and* he speaks six languages! *Six* languages!' The man was ushered in, and the manager quickly explained to him what he wanted to say to the German player. The multilingual wizard stood there with a blank look on his face – as it happened, he did speak six languages, but English was not one of them.

'I often wonder', mused John Rooney of the Philadelphia Spartans, 'what was the final translation of a coach's talk. It was given in English, then a Spanish guy would give it in Spanish, then someone else would translate from Spanish into German.' They also had, at Philadelphia, a player who claimed he could speak any language after a couple of weeks living in the country. When an airline stewardess walked down the aisle asking the players their names and he replied 'Coca Cola', his teammates knew how much truth there was in that. The Pittsburgh owners found the problem serious enough to need special English-language lessons at the Berlitz School for the players and their wives.

As opening day neared, the Pittsburgh Phantoms appeared, on paper, which was the only way to judge as yet, to have built up the strongest team. Their most likely rivals were the California Clippers, who had hired a Yugoslavian coach who, in turn, had successfully lured nine players from that country. It was rumoured that some of them had jumped their contracts, and had left Yugoslavia under false names. The Yugoslavian Football Association had issued a harsh statement that any Yugoslav who agreed to play in the N.P.S.L. would be banned from soccer in Yugoslavia – for life.

On 16 April 1967, after a variety of opening-day ceremonies with personalities kicking out the first ball – it was the Governor of Pennsylvania in Philadelphia, and the film actress Julie Christie in Oakland – all ten N.P.S.L. teams took the field. It was an apprehensive moment for the owners, who would now get some indication of whether all their money and effort was going to be rewarded. It was neither the worst of days, nor the best of days. The five games attracted a total of 45,000 spectators, or 9,000 per game. The biggest success was in Philadelphia, where the Spartans had stiff competition from major-league baseball and basketball games, both being played in the city the same afternoon. The Spartans drew 14,000 people – more than either of the other sports could manage. The smallest crowd was 4,725 in Chicago, where it was claimed that a tornado warning had kept the crowd down. But an average of 9,000 fans a game was inconclusive – it proved neither the optimists nor the pessimists to be right. One thing was agreed, though: it was a historic occasion. As the television commentator put it: 'You'll be able to tell your grandchildren, you were there when they brought major-league soccer to the United States.'

As the season progressed, two further things became clear. The crowds were not getting any bigger, and all the advance talk of top-class soccer had been just that – talk. The standard was usually around the English third-division level, with occasional flashes of something better. In the U.S.A.'s mini-league of foreign teams – all of which now dropped their real names and assumed the names of their adopted cities – there was not one that could truly be called a top team. In New York, the franchise owners, Madison Square Garden, wanted an Italian team. All they could get was the team that was at that time in last place in the Italian First Division. Bob Wolff, the president, felt it would be an insult to the New York Italians to bring in one of their worst teams. A more likely looking prospect was a Uruguayan team, Cerro, that had finished third in its league, right behind the world famous teams Penarol and Nacional, and they were signed up. Admittedly, there were not that many Uruguayans in New York, but it was hoped that a winning team would prove to be attractive. Once again, the lack of information caused a miscalculation: nobody knew that the Uruguayan league at that stage was very much of a two-team affair. Third place Cerro was not in the same class as the two teams that finished above it.

Boston, naturally enough, believed that they could find success with an Irish team. They got Dublin's Shamrock Rovers, the most famous name in Irish soccer. They remained blissfully ignorant – until the season started – that the Irish league was one of the weakest around, equivalent to the English third division.

From the end of May until half way through June, the two leagues were operating simultaneously, fighting each other for the soccer dollar which both could now sense was not as readily available as they had foreseen. In five cities – Toronto, Chicago, New York, Los Angeles and San Francisco – there were teams from both leagues, and in Toronto, New York, and Los Angeles, the rival teams actually played in the same stadium. New York, a city of ten million people, possessed only two stadiums that filled the major-league image wanted by the leagues. One of them, Shea Stadium, was definitely out, as the New York Mets baseball team would not allow soccer to be played there during the baseball season. That left only Yankee Stadium, and gave the owners of Yankee Stadium a very strong hand in naming their price – a situation that they took advantage of by demanding – and getting – $40,000 rental for each game played there.

The result was that soccer was not coming through in a clear straight-forward way to potential fans. They were confused – said the promoters – by never knowing which league was which, and what the difference between them was. No doubt some of them were left wondering whether it mattered that much anyway.

One clear difference was television. The N.P.S.L. had a contract with C.B.S., the U.S.A. had nothing. One hundred years behind the rest of the world in most soccer matters, the United States overtook everybody in a twinkling when it came to electronics. They presented for the first time anywhere, a complete season of soccer televised live and in colour.

Every Sunday afternoon, the soccer telecast competed for viewers with baseball on other channels, and it came off surprisingly well with 4·8 million viewers for each game. Here was a perfect opportunity for American know-how to make itself felt, and C.B.S. took it. It covered each game with six cameras, including one used for video-taping only goalmouth action for instant replay use. The commentators were Jack Whitaker, an American with a wide experience in sports broadcasting, and Danny Blanchflower, the former Irish international player. But it seemed that at every point that soccer came into contact with the American way, there was friction. C.B.S. was paying the N.P.S.L. some $500,000 for the rights to televise the games. The money, of course, was to be recouped by selling advertising time during the transmissions. The trouble was, *when* during the transmissions? One of the big selling points of the sport, something that it was felt would attract Americans, was its non-stop action. 'See the stars in NON-STOP Action,' said the handbills at St Louis. 'Fantastic non-stop Action!' cried the Los Angeles Toros. It was not so fantastic for C.B.S. who were faced with the task of fitting some twenty commercials into a ninety-minute game, that had very few natural breaks, and that was likely to feature only one or two goals. To interrupt the transmissions for a commercial while the game was going on meant missing some of the 'non-stop action' and quite possibly the only score of the game. There was just no moment – apart from halftime – when one could be certain of a pause long enough to accommodate a commercial. Injuries, where the trainer had to run onto the field to wave his magic sponge, would be suitable, but you could never be sure how many such injuries there were going to be during a game. There might not be any at all. During the third televised game, it was apparent that something strange was going on. One of the New York Generals' forwards was brought down in the Philadelphia Spartans penalty area. Although no foul was called, the referee came running up, shouting, 'Take your time, take your time!' The Generals' player, who was by this time getting to his feet, sank back to the ground, and the trainer was called on. There followed a minute of fussing, and at last the player stood up, whereupon the trainer commenced to rub his head and shoulders down with the towel. The trainer slowly left the field, at which point the referee took over, going up to the player, and apparently checking him over to make sure the trainer had done a good job. Only then did play get under way again. Two weeks later, during a televised game from Toronto, the cat leapt out of the bag, and the N.P.S.L. was in trouble. The 7,500 spectators at the game were soon hooting at the referee for what they regarded as too frequent and too lengthy stoppages of the game. It all came over rather well on the telecast. After the game, the referee admitted that he had an electronic device strapped to his back: 'I get three beeps on the radar thing,' he said, 'and then I hear the producer saying, "A commercial coming up", so I have to get the play stopped.' He was also quoted as saying that he visited the dressing rooms before the game to instruct the players on when they should fall down and feign injury. The cat was not only out of the bag, it was among the pigeons. N.P.S.L. Commissioner, Ken Macker, jumped in immediately to absolve C.B.S. from any blame. He accepted personal responsibility for what had happened* and revealed that the league had been experimenting for several weeks to find a way of mixing commercials and soccer. In the future, he said, the referee would wave a red flag to indicate to the television director that a suitable moment for a commercial had arrived – it would be during goal kicks, or injuries. If the action resumed before the commercial was over, and anything particularly important was missed, it would be repeated on the instant replay. It was the system that C.B.S. used for the rest of the season, and it worked remarkably well. During some 120 commercial breaks, only five goals were missed.

Halfway through this unreal season, with the N.P.S.L. still an unsanctioned league, there came a most curious development. The N.P.S.L. announced that they were now ready to meet all the terms asked by U.S.S.F.A. – the same ones that they had refused to meet in 1966. There was no response from U.S.S.F.A. At this, F.I.F.A. began to show signs of impatience and they issued a statement broadly hinting that it was time for U.S.S.F.A. to sanction the N.P.S.L. The United States representative on the F.I.F.A. Executive Committee, James McGuire, was instructed to convey the sentiment to U.S.S.F.A. McGuire, it was recorded, assured the Committee that he would do his best to bring the N.P.S.L. within authorized and recognized soccer. Apparently F.I.F.A. did not know, or did not consider it important, that McGuire was also the President of the United Soccer Association, the league that U.S.S.F.A. had sanctioned and that therefore had a considerable interest in keeping the N.P.S.L. out of organized soccer.

* There was also an investigation into the incident by the Federal Communication Commission, the government agency that grants, and has the power to rescind broadcasting licences. Their report, issued in August 1967, exonerated C.B.S. from any blame.

The situation did not 'soon find a satisfactory settlement' as F.I.F.A. had hoped – neither then nor by the end of the season. On 14 July the U.S.A. played their championship game, and this contest among the world's top teams was won by the Wolverhampton Wanderers, who had played the previous season in the English second division. Seventy-three games had been played and had drawn 568,118 people – about 7,800 per game. On the whole, the season had proceeded remarkably smoothly, considering the rush with which the whole thing was put together. A linesman had been punched in Boston; a referee chased from the field by hordes of spectators in New York; a match abandoned with seventeen minutes to play in Detroit, and in Toronto 'Italian Day' had turned sour, when the Italian team Cagliari, representing Chicago, had walked off the field in protest against a referee's decision. But all the strife was counterbalanced by a splendid final game, won 6–5 by the Wolves representing Los Angeles over Aberdeen (representing Washington). It was tailor-made for the American taste – plenty of goals, and the excitement of a sudden-death finish in the second overtime period.

The N.P.S.L.'s much longer season did not finish until September, when the Oakland Clippers beat the Baltimore Bays for the title. By this time, it was obvious to even the most obdurate millionaire that soccer was not going to provide instant riches for anybody. The league's 159 games had drawn 775,846 fans, or 4,250 per game. This was less than half what was regarded as the required minimum. The fans had not stormed the turnstiles – even when there were extra attractions like ball day, shirt day, Ladies Day, Pony Night, and Italian Night or Irish-American night. Baltimore had had some success by having The Fifth Dimension perform at one of their games, but New York's attempt to launch a new dance, the Soccerloo, had mercifully died aborning.

For the Pittsburgh owners, the season proved altogether too much. Their coach problems, which started before the season had even begun, got worse as time went on. Their second coach was not popular with the players, who regarded him as too strict; they went to the management and demanded his dismissal. So the coach was fired – with the team in first place. One of the players got the job, and discipline disintegrated. 'There had been talk at the beginning of the season,' said Dick George, 'that the Phantoms were too strong for the rest of the league, and that some of their players should be sold to other teams. It wasn't necessary – the Phantoms broke themselves up.' Yet another coach arrived, but could do little. The Phantoms finished next to last, both in the league and in attendance.* Enough was enough for the Phantoms, and they announced that they were ceasing operations. In their one season they had lost around $325,000, and their collapse was to leave quite a few unhappy creditors. Their only assets were the players, some of whom they sold to other teams in the league – without getting paid for them. Nobody saw why they should pay transfer fees to an insolvent organization.

The Philadelphia Spartans, who had lost $200,000, were next to go. The Phantoms and the Spartans were not alone in losing money, because all ten of the N.P.S.L. clubs ended the season in the red. But the ominous thing was not so much the loss of money, but the fact that there had been no discernible growth in attendances as the season progressed. The hoped-for 'swing to soccer' had not occurred.

Could these super-shrewd investors have been wrong in their basic assumption? Or could they have made mistakes during the season's operation? The answer – and it came from the investors themselves – was no. Well, admittedly, there had been cases of bad luck – like all those rainy days at the beginning of the Pittsburgh season that had kept attendance down – but those were minor matters. The main – one sometimes had the impression it was the *only* – excuse for all the woes was the existence of the two leagues. This was the root of all evil. A strange impasse had been reached, where both leagues were saying that a merger was essential, U.S.S.F.A. was nodding in approval – yet there was no merger. On 9 September 1967 – the day of its final game – the N.P.S.L. gave matters a dramatic push. They started legal action under the anti-trust laws, against U.S.S.F.A., all the member clubs of the U.S.A. and F.I.F.A. The defendants were charged with having entered into a conspiracy to drive the N.P.S.L. out of professional soccer, and the court was asked to declare that the U.S.S.F.A.-U.S.A. agreement was an illegal monopoly. The N.P.S.L. also declared that as a result of having to operate as an 'outlaw' league, they had lost $6 million during the season, and therefore they claimed triple damages of $18 million. A highly imposing gathering of expensive legal minds had barely started work on the case when they were flabbergasted by a decision that was even more incredible than anything that had gone before in that most

* They finished a clear first in marital problems. Dick George recalls: 'Out of eighteen players we had under contract, I think twelve of them were married. After the season only about four of these marriages were still intact. Well, these guys were coming in from Amsterdam, Rotterdam, Essen, and so on, and we were housing them out there by the airport in Moon Township, and of course all the airline stewardesses stay out there . . . ' Of course.

incredible of seasons. It came from, of all people, F.I.F.A. Evidently running out of patience with the apparently intractable American problems that were besmirching the good name of soccer, they handed U.S.S.F.A. an ultimatum: settle this law suit or you will be suspended. What caused the all-round gasp was that F.I.F.A. informed the N.P.S.L. – the plaintiffs in the lawsuit – of what they had done, thus neatly pulling the rug out from under U.S.S.F.A. F.I.F.A.'s thoughtfulness in giving the upper hand to the very people who were suing them may have been a nasty shock for U.S.S.F.A., but it may not, in the long run, have been all that significant. For by now the N.P.S.L. had dropped its idea of operating as a separate – but sanctioned – league. The financial facts of 1967 left no room for doubt that the only chance was for one league. A merger it had to be. It took the best part of four months for it to be worked out, and the agreement was announced at a meeting at the Waldorf Astoria Hotel in New York in January 1968. The new seventeen-team league was to be called the Professional Soccer League – but not for long. The following day, it was renamed the North American Soccer League, almost as though an attempt were being made to cancel out the 1967 season. For this was the same name that the U.S.A. had used less than a year ago, before they adopted the United Soccer Association title.*

Perhaps the most crucial announcement came from C.B.S., who decided that they were going to continue the weekly telecasts. The money that C.B.S. were paying the league was really its most important source of income, an assured subsidy that kept open the hope that C.B.S. might eventually do for soccer what N.B.C. had done for the American Football League: pump in enough money to guarantee its success.† There was a change in the telecasts, though. During the first year Danny Blanch-flower had come face to face with a sorry truth in modern American professional sport: the indecently intricate involvement of television, not just in the recording of sports events, but in their conduct and in their success. C.B.S., with a considerable amount of money being spent on soccer, was a decidedly interested partner. The N.P.S.L. was C.B.S.'s league, theirs to sink or swim with, and they were in a very strong position to influence the way in which the game was sold to the public.

* As one journalist asked: 'Is the new league trying to save money by re-using the old N.A.S.L. stationery?' The question was not taken too seriously by anyone. The thought of the league making even a slight gesture in the direction of parsimony was too much of a novelty.

† For the story of the association between television and the American Football League, see Chapter 2, page 38ff.

The telecasts were almost certainly *the* most important single factor – quite apart from monetary considerations – in promoting the spread of the game, in introducing new fans to the game, and in educating them to its finer points. They were like soccer seminars, and the professor was Danny Blanchflower. But C.B.S. and the league did not see it that way at all. To them, the broadcasts were more like commercials designed to sell a product – in this case, soccer – with Blanchflower in the role of the salesman. The difference was fundamental, the two roles could obviously not be reconciled. Blanchflower was continually breaking the Golden Rule of American TV (*Never* criticize anything), pointing out that a player was out of position, or that another had made a silly error.*

There were those who found it highly agreeable, like the television critic of the *New York Times*, who did not like the soccer, but found that Blanchflower's 'blend of running criticism, boundless compassion, and sterling cliché eased the visual ennui', and John Rooney, owner of the Philadelphia Spartans, who thought that Blanchflower 'did a great job – he was honest, and he was something new in sports in this country'. Rooney did admit to 'cringing a little' at some of Blanchflower's sallies. The majority of the owners did more than cringe; they were openly horrified. Bill Bergesch, General Manager of the New York Generals, looked back on the season and moaned that: 'Blanchflower killed us last year, pointing out all the bad things. He was so honest, he hurt us. His job was to *promote* the sport. That's what we were paying him to do.'

The owners' point was that soccer was, at this stage, a very delicate child, that should be mollycoddled and protected from the harsh winds of truth. Blanchflower was in the impossible position of knowing that much of what he was watching was second-rate soccer; he could not describe it as 'great', as C.B.S. and the owners wanted, so he chose to make constructive criticisms. When the 1968 season started, Danny Blanchflower was not re-hired.

For the 1968 season there were eight new teams to be created – the entries from the former United Soccer Association. It might have been thought that the ten N.P.S.L. teams, assembled one year earlier, had between them revealed all the errors that could be made and that the new entries could profit from that experience, but Dallas is in Texas, and down in Texas they have their own way of doing things. Lamar Hunt, son of the oil-tycoon H. L. Hunt, was co-owner of the Dallas franchise

---

* For a discussion of the role of the American sports commentator, see Chapter 2, pages 35-36.

with Bill McNutt, whose business is making fruitcakes. First they came up with a singular name – the Dallas Tornado.* 'We thought of it as representing a ferocious, devastating, whirling terror,' said Hunt. Next they hired an obscure coach who had the theory that the way to form the team was to recruit young players and have them play as many games as possible to weld them into a unit. Sixteen players, mostly nineteen and twenty-year-olds, and all of them unknowns, were assembled in Spain for preliminary training. They were all given blazers and ten-gallon hats, and apparently they were a big hit with the local girls. In September 1967 they set out on what was hailed as 'the greatest world tour ever undertaken by a soccer team'. Geographically speaking, it was certainly that. For over five months, the Dallas Tornado roamed over the earth, from Spain to Turkey to Iran to Pakistan to India to Burma, Indonesia, South Vietnam, Taiwan, Japan, the Philippines, Australia, New Zealand and Fiji. Forty-five games they played, against all sorts of mediocre teams, and they managed to win only ten. The crowds turned out – especially in Asia – to see this American soccer team. Frequently the Dallas Tornado were put up on the scoreboard as 'U.S.A.'. A game in Malaysia ended in a fracas, with the players being stoned off the field amid anti-American slogans. There was not one American on the team, the majority of whom were English and Scandinavian.

The Dallas Tornado arrived in the States – for the first sight of the city they were representing – in April 1968. Either they were a hardened experienced team as the Dallas management claimed, or they were totally exhausted, as almost everybody else believed.

With the two-league confusion gone, Danny Blanchflower banished from the land, and the errors of the opening season behind them, the owners' enthusiasm climbed back to its pre-1967 level. Asked about the defensive play of the champion Oakland Clippers, their publicity man replied without a blush, 'Yes, we have the best defence of any team in the world.' Dick Walsh said: 'With any luck with the weather, we're hoping to average 15,000 paid for our opening games. Several cities may even top the 20,000 figure.'

If this was an attempt at self-fulfilling prophecy, it was a lamentable failure. The largest crowd was 11,000 at Atlanta, and the smallest was the measly 1,400 who turned out to welcome the globetrotting Tornado in Dallas. Those who had ridiculed the Tornado's world tour were to be

---

* It was intended to be grammatically singular too. 'We've had a hard time of it stopping people use it in the plural,' Hunt admitted. Most of the press references – outside Dallas – were to the Dallas Tornadoes.

proved right. Dallas lost their opener, 6–0, and just went on losing and losing all through the season. The coach was dispatched to Europe to find some new players, quickly. While he was away, the team was coached by the co-owners, Lamar Hunt and the fruitcake-king, Bill McNutt, who were unable to work any magic. By the end of July, the record of the Dallas Tornado stood at: Games played – 21; games won – 0; games tied – 3; games lost – 18.* Even the signing of new players and the firing of the old coach made little difference. The end of the season record for the Tornado was won – 2, lost – 26, tied – 4, and there was not much talk anymore of ferocious, devastating terrors.

Lack of fans was not limited to Dallas. All over the league the crowds, far from being larger than in 1967, were smaller and a record low for the league was registered in Chicago when only 336 people showed up.

When the season was over, the flimsy nature of the professional soccer edifice was exposed. It started to crumble at once. All the clubs were awash in red ink, and it was now clear that the commitment of the majority of the owners was not to soccer, but to their wallets. The enthusiasm, the confidence, the assurances that they were 'in this thing for the long run' – all these suddenly evaporated. There was a frantic and unseemly rush for the exits. The tide of defections began to take on the air of a *sauve qui peut* and was soon climaxed by the announcement that the league Commissioner, Dick Walsh, had resigned. His departure was symbolic of the whole soccer scene. He had come to soccer direct from a long career in baseball administration, and he now revealed that he was returning to that sport – 'my first love'. His allegiance to soccer then – like that of most of the owners – had been something less than total, a piece of opportunism to be abandoned as soon as things started to go wrong. When the dust settled, where once had stood the imposing North American Soccer League, seventeen teams strong, there remained but a shell, propped up by only five clubs.† The businessmen had found soccer an unsatisfactory investment. The attitudes that operating a sports team is merely another form of business, and that a sport is simply

---

* Asked what the team's appalling record, plus the low attendances at their games, indicated for the future of soccer in Dallas, Bill McNutt replied: 'When the season ends, we'll just have to sell the heck out of fruitcakes.'

† The N.A.S.L. did not go out of business. It operated on a much less ambitious scale, while devoting more energy towards building up the sport at the junior levels. By the beginning of the 1974 season, the N.A.S.L. had expanded to fifteen teams and had moved its headquarters from Atlanta – where it had retreated during darker days – back to New York.

a commodity to be marketed, carry with them certain perfectly logical consequences. Namely, that the success of the team be measured not merely in terms of monetary profit, but of how much and how quickly. For investors, this is the crucial point. When asked why R.K.O.-General withdrew from the N.P.S.L. after only one year of operation, despite its previous assurances of long-term support, the vice-president, John Pinto, replied: 'Our management decided they'd rather put their money into other areas, as this didn't seem to be something that was going to move ahead as fast as we had hoped.'

The indecorous collapse of the Great Soccer Experiment should not be allowed to obscure the truly remarkable nature of the undertaking. It was something that had never before been attempted anywhere – and that, in all probability, will never be attempted again. Because it is unlikely that the necessary circumstances will ever arise again: a sport played the whole world over, with the exception of one country, and that country the richest in the world, the only one with the resources to launch a major-league operation. But it was not simply a question of resources. There had to be, first of all, a climate of opinion that would sustain the idea. Without a doubt, such an idea would have been quietly shelved in any other country in the world, and the man who suggested it sent to a psychiatrist. To Americans, it was not silly, it was a challenge.

Did they know what they were doing, these rich and powerful men? At the time, their enthusiasm, their conviction of their own rightness, their certainty of success gave even the most cynical onlookers pause. But in retrospect, it is clear that they did not know what they were about.

Quite extraordinary, for instance, was the slapdash approach to marketing that was adopted. This was, after all, America, the birthplace of marketing research, of consumer surveys, of careful costing estimates – yet none of these techniques was utilized. Soccer was treated as though it were another form of hula-hoop, something that would sweep America in a trice. Nobody seemed to remember that the hula-hoop had lasted all of six months.

To succeed, soccer needed a nationwide mass-following. How could this be obtained within the space of one short season by offering the public a second-rate version of a sport they knew little about, played by 'stars' whose names meant absolutely nothing, and reported by journalists who were often as much in the dark as the fans?

For, even if you can create fans overnight, you certainly cannot create knowledgeable soccer writers in that time. The result was that the games were frequently covered by newspapermen who were at best resentful at having to waste their time at a minor sport, at worst actively hostile to the game. Phrases like 'best thing for sleep since pillows' and 'clumsy basketball played with the feet' were certainly not going to help soccer on its way, but far worse were the deadly descriptions of the games themselves, where the writer would cover up his lack of soccer knowledge by expatiating on the size of the crowd, the state of the field, the weather, finishing up with a few trite quotes from the coaches. The press room at Yankee Stadium before a New York Generals game might hold some twenty journalists, grouped at five or six tables. They were talking about baseball or football or basketball – rarely soccer. How could it have been otherwise? Soccer writers do not drop from the heavens, ready made, at the summons of the N.P.S.L. or the U.S.A.

It was an area that had been overlooked, perhaps one that it had been assumed would take care of itself. This was natural enough in an atmosphere where the rush and panic to build up the business structure of a league had almost totally obliterated thoughts of what it was all to be based on: soccer.

Instead of the scientific approach, soccer got a hefty dose of the old-fashioned sales pitch, replete with exaggeration, misrepresentation, and the inevitable elements of fraud. The idea was to shout 'Major-league soccer,' as loud and long as possible, almost as if the wish would father the reality. The result was a great deal of attention to the packaging, to the external trappings of what was inescapably an inferior product.

The verdict was passed: Americans don't like soccer and will not support a professional league. An article that appeared in *Forbes Magazine* in 1969 placed the blame for what it called 'the $15 million mistake' squarely on the sport itself. Of six reasons given, four were concerned with the nature of soccer, and not one mentioned the amateurish methods that had marked the whole endeavour.

Throughout the entire *contretemps* between the N.P.S.L. and F.I.F.A., U.S.S.F.A., and U.S.A., there was one extremely relevant point about which a tactful silence was maintained by all sides. This was that the whole concept of sport as a business enterprise is totally alien to the spirit of organized soccer. Further than that, it is illegal by F.I.F.A.'s own regulations, which state unequivocally that 'a club . . . shall not be used as a source of profit to its directors or shareholders. Nevertheless in regard to the latter, the payment of a normal rate of interest is permissible'. As nobody made a profit, the application of the rule was academic. But its strict enforcement would surely deter the majority of potential investors in America, where the mixture of amateur ideals and professional promotion that F.I.F.A. represents has absolutely no parallel.

In fact there is little evidence to suggest that Americans are in some strange way immune to the charms of soccer. The sport is widely played at high-school and college level, where its growth-rate exceeds that of any other sport. One reason for that is economic – it has become increasingly prohibitive to outfit a football team, while a soccer team costs virtually nothing to equip. Another reason is that football is disliked by many parents because of its roughness and the risk of serious injury; it has also become increasingly a sport that can only be played by big boys, whereas soccer offers an opportunity to boys of all shapes and sizes.

The criticism that soccer is not violent enough is hardly worth considering – were it not for the fact that some of the promoters *did* believe it. No doubt they had hockey in mind – a sport in which fights are an integral part of the action, and which would lose much of its attraction without them. Just before the N.P.S.L. was launched in 1967, Bill Bartholomay, one of the directors of the Atlanta club, went to a game in London and was reportedly highly pleased when two of the players engaged in a fight, uttering: 'That's what this game needs. This'll make the hockey boys worry.' It is true that football and hockey rely heavily on crude violence for their appeal. Against that, basketball does not, it is like soccer, more a game of finesse and artistry.

It is difficult to believe that, ultimately, soccer will not become a major-league sport in the United States. Quite aside from its intrinsic attractions, it offers one enormous plus that no other American professional sport has: international competition. It is equally difficult to believe that success can be imposed from the top; the development of basketball and football as professional sports shows that the way lies through the colleges which are, after all, nothing more than professional minor leagues. The surest way to success for soccer is to build up college teams as a spectator attraction.

To succeed, soccer has to make room for itself alongside baseball, football and basketball. This it can do, but only with genuine first-class soccer organized by people who know something about the sport. The ersatz version of 1967 and all its attendant ballyhoo and its blatant mismanagement by the quick-money promoters was never a serious candidate.

Postscript

In the middle of the 1968 season, about the time when most of the wealthy backers who had recently appeared on the soccer scene were preparing to bow out, a new, and rather different promoter arrived. Enter Joe Martin. Hungarian born, Martin had made himself a fortune as proprietor of a tobacco company in Canada. Now he had invested some $40,000 of it in an invention he called American Soccer System, the idea of which was to speed the game up. Its chief feature was adopted from ice hockey, and consisted of a three-foot-high wall all around the field, so that the ball would not be able to run out of play. The goals were enlarged, and the offside rule was abolished. Two games were announced in New York and fans were informed that 'You can be the first to witness the world's greatest sport-history-making event'. The publicity also announced that, once the game had caught on – which, one gathered, it could hardly fail to do – there would be a World Championship, with the winning teams receiving $200,000. Journalists who might be inclined to cast a jaundiced eye over the project, were informed that 'the world's best ninety-six reporters elected each year by the registered club members receive a trophy and a prize of $10,000 each'. *Each?* That's what it said. Fans were advised to get their tickets early for THE WORLD'S MOST SPECTACULAR TWO GAMES TOURNAMENT THAT HAS NEVER BEEN SEEN.

The historic evening proved something of a letdown to those dozen or so journalists who turned up as their first step towards a $10,000 prize – and no doubt Joe Martin was not too pleased either. The 20,000 capacity stadium was sprinkled with 243 fans. The American All-Stars beat the Canadian All-Stars 14–11 in a singularly dull game. The only constructive remark heard all evening in the press box suggested that if the wall around the field were 9 ft high instead of only 3 ft, nobody would be able to see anything and what a relief that would be. The players whom Martin had engaged turned up at his Manhattan hotel the following morning for their pay. Mr Martin had been called away it seemed. The second game was never played, and the World's Most Spectacular Two Games Tournament That Has Never Been Seen remained just that.

11 Of Midgets, Mudville and the Mets

There was once a time, not all that long ago, when hunting and fishing were, quite literally, matters of life or death. The pressures to succeed could hardly have been greater. If you failed you were likely to starve. And there was also a time, not too distant, when games like soccer and baseball were enjoyable diversions played for fun and recreation.

But man has forged ahead since those times. Professionalism, with its attendant commercialism, has come to games. The pressure to win has become overwhelming, and nobody even thinks in terms of leisurely enjoyment any more. If you want *that* sort of thing, you should go fishing, or hunting maybe. This is a world-wide phenomenon. Wherever sports have become important enough for massive commercialization – English and Italian soccer every bit as much as American football – the fun has been slowly but surely draining away.

If there is to be anywhere a last stand against this lamentable trend, then surely it will be baseball that holds out. How could the National Pastime not reflect the America of Mark Twain or Damon Runyon or James Thurber or any of that long and distinguished line of American humourists?

Unthinkable. James Thurber, for instance, wrote one of his funniest stories about baseball. *You Could Look It Up* it was called, and Americans who were unaware of this found out all about it, suddenly and hilariously, on Sunday 19 August 1951. Out in St Louis the Detroit Tigers, last in the league, were playing the St Louis Browns, next to last. Not exactly the season's most fascinating contest, yet it turned out to be one of the great days in the history of baseball. The man responsible was the Browns' owner, Bill Veeck – he of Hawaiian orchid and exploding scoreboard fame.*

Bill had discovered another loophole in the baseball rules. This is what the rules require: when the pitcher delivers the ball, he must do so

* See Chapter 2, page 41.

with reasonable accuracy, he must throw it so that when it reaches the batter it arrives somewhere between his knees and his armpits – an area known as the strike-zone. If the pitcher throws four pitches that are higher or lower than that, then the batter (provided he just watches the pitches sail by and does not swing his bat at any of them) automatically goes to first base, where he becomes a potential run scorer. The average-sized baseball player would have a strike zone about 30 inches high.

It was left to Bill Veeck to find a baseball player who was clearly anything but average-sized. When it came the St Louis Browns' turn to bat, there emerged from their dugout, swinging a tiny toy bat, a fully-uniformed but decidedly under-sized batter. The loudspeaker said it was 'Number one-eighth. Eddie Gaedel'. Maybe, but the umpire knew a midget when he saw one, and he went straight to the St Louis dugout to demand what the hell was going on here. Veeck was ready for this. His manager produced a genuine player's contract for Gaedel, duly approved by the American League (who, of course, had approved it without enquiring about Gaedel's stature). Everything was in order, Gaedel was legally a St Louis Brown player, and the Detroit pitcher would have to pitch to him. Which was not going to be easy, what with Eddie Gaedel, Number one-eighth, being only 3 ft 7 ins tall even when standing upright; crouched menacingly in his batting stance he presented a strike zone that Bill Veeck had personally measured at $1\frac{1}{2}$ inches. The Detroit pitcher never even came close, and after four pitches, Eddie Gaedel set off on the long ninety-foot trek to first base. With his Lilliputian strides it took him much longer than the fans were used to, but they cheered him all the way. When he finally did arrive at first base, he was immediately replaced by a substitute. Gaedel left the field to a standing ovation of cheers and laughter, bowing and waving his little cap all the way, basking unashamedly in his brief moment of major-league baseball glory.

It was humorous fiction turned hilarious fact, for that had been the theme of Thurber's *You Could Look It Up* – a midget who always got on base because the pitchers could never get the ball anywhere near his miniature strike zone. And, naturally, it was all utterly deplorable, and vulgar, not to mention cheap and tawdry as well. The fans may have loved every minute of it, but the baseball establishment were scandalized. It was 'conduct detrimental to baseball' and once again Bill Veeck had made 'a travesty of the sport'. To treat baseball with anything less than serious devotion was bad enough, but Veeck had perpetrated a far more outrageous sacrilege. He was guilty of ridiculing the sacrosanct belief that only big tough guys could play sports; he had sent a midget up to

15 Eddie Gaedel, all 3 ft 7 ins of him 'making a travesty' of baseball.
His miniature professional career lasted precisely one time at bat.

16 Casey Stengel, still clowning at the age of eighty-one, re-enacts an
episode from his playing days and releases a live bird from under his cap.

bat, and the midget had effortlessly got on base, something that the professionals on the St Louis Browns were not too good at – a state of affairs that could not be allowed to continue for one moment. The very next day the League brought the curtain crashing down on Eddie Gaedel's baseball career when they banned him permanently from the game. 'Discrimination against the little people,' said Veeck, and he called – unsuccessfully – for further clarification: 'Should the height of a player be 3 ft 6 ins, 4 ft 6 ins, 6 ft 6 ins, or 9 ft 6 ins?' The official response was stiff-necked silence, but it was quite clear that whatever the height of a professional baseball player might be, it was *not* going to be 3 ft 7 ins.

*

It is quite a jump, in years as well as in feet and inches, from Eddie Gaedel to Mighty Casey. Yet the two – one diminutive reality, the other towering legend – have one thing in common: they both did their best to undermine the dynasty of the Big Man in American sports – Gaedel by doing what he had no business doing, and Casey by not doing what everyone was confident he would do.

The saga of the mighty Casey began on 3 June 1888 with the publication in the *San Francisco Examiner* of a poem entitled *Casey at the Bat*, an undistinguished, mildly humorous ballad about baseball:

Casey at the Bat

The outlook wasn't brilliant for the Mudville nine that day;
The score stood four to two with but one inning more to play.
And then when Cooney died at first, and Barrows did the same,
A sickly silence fell upon the patrons of the game.

A straggling few got up to go in deep despair. The rest
Clung to that hope which springs eternal in the human breast;
They thought if only Casey could but get a whack at that –
We'd put up even money now with Casey at the bat.

But Flynn preceded Casey, as did also Jimmy Blake,
And the former was a lulu, and the latter was a cake;
So upon that stricken multitude grim melancholy sat,
For there seemed but little chance of Casey's getting to the bat.

But Flynn let drive a single, to the wonderment of all,
And Blake, the much despis-ed, tore the cover off the ball;
And when the dust had lifted, and the men saw what had occurred,
There was Johnnie safe at second and Flynn a-hugging third.

Then from 5,000 throats and more there rose a lusty yell;
It rumbled through the valley, it rattled in the dell;
It knocked upon the mountain and recoiled upon the flat,
For Casey, mighty Casey, was advancing to the bat.

There was ease in Casey's manner as he stepped into his place;
There was pride in Casey's bearing and a smile on Casey's face.
And when, responding to the cheers, he lightly doffed his hat,
No stranger in the crowd could doubt 'twas Casey at the bat.

Ten thousand eyes were on him as he rubbed his hands with dirt;
Five thousand tongues applauded when he wiped them on his shirt.
Then while the writhing pitcher ground the ball into his hip,
Defiance gleamed in Casey's eye, a sneer curled Casey's lip.

And now the leather-covered sphere came hurtling through the air,
And Casey stood a-watching it in haughty grandeur there.
Close by the sturdy batsman the ball unheeded sped –
'That ain't my style,' said Casey. 'Strike one,' the umpire said.

From the benches, black with people, there went up a muffled roar,
Like the beating of the storm-waves on a stern and distant shore.
'Kill him! Kill the umpire!' shouted someone on the stand;
And it's likely they'd have killed him had not Casey raised his hand.

With a smile of Christian charity great Casey's visage shone;
He stilled the rising tumult; he bade the game go on;
He signalled to the pitcher, and once more the spheroid flew;
But Casey still ignored it, and the umpire said, 'Strike two.'

'Fraud!' cried the maddened thousands, and echo answered fraud;
But one scornful look from Casey and the audience was awed.
They saw his face grow stern and cold, they saw his muscles strain,
And they knew that Casey wouldn't let that ball go by again.

The sneer is gone from Casey's lip, his teeth are clenched in hate;
He pounds with cruel violence his bat upon the plate.
And now the pitcher holds the ball, and now he lets it go,
And now the air is shattered by the force of Casey's blow.

Oh, somewhere in this favored land the sun is shining bright;
The band is playing somewhere, and somewhere hearts are light,
And somewhere men are laughing, and somewhere children shout;
But there is no joy in Mudville – mighty Casey has struck out.

Casey at the Bat was saved from oblivion by a young comedian, De Wolf Hopper, who took to reciting it on stage. It soon became the most popular part of his act, demanded by audiences wherever he went. Almost single-handedly Hopper turned it into a lasting piece of American folklore – 'the only truly great comic poem written by an American' he called it.

The author, a quiet, scholarly Harvard graduate named Ernest Thayer, did not agree: 'Its persistent vogue is simply unaccountable, and it would be hard to say, all things considered, if it has given me more pleasure than annoyance.' To a publisher, he wrote, 'All I ask is never to be reminded of it again.'

Which made Thayer a minority of one. The great American public could not get enough of Casey. It was set to music, it was filmed (twice), it was made into a cartoon, it even became an opera. It achieved respectability. Professor Phelps of Yale (the same Professor Phelps who had invited Gene Tunney to address his students) found it 'a centrifugal tragedy, by which our minds are turned from the fate of Casey to the universal. For this is the curse that hangs over humanity – our ability to accomplish any feat is in inverse ratio to the intensity of our desire'.

Centrifugal tragedy, comic monologue, or just plain corny verse, whatever it may be, there can be no dispute about the popularity of *Casey at the Bat*. Most Americans, even today, know why there is no joy in Mudville. Casey has been striking out for over eighty years, all the while carving himself a unique niche in American folklore. As the slugger who failed to slug when it mattered most, Casey has made his name as a most unlikely figure: an anti-hero from the success-worshipping world of sports.

Unlike Thurber's midget, the fictional Casey never did turn into fact. Or perhaps he did, a thousand times in a thousand different places, a thousand mute Caseys for whose inglorious exploits one legendary figure, the mighty Casey of Mudville, would forever shoulder the blame.

But a real live Casey did come upon the baseball scene. Not an incarnation of mighty Casey, but a character in his own right. Charles Dillon Stengel was born in 1890 (just two years after *Casey at the Bat*), and his first nickname was 'Dutch': but when he entered professional baseball in 1910 he was called by the initials of his home town, Kansas City. And K.C. soon became Casey.

Right from his first game Stengel was a livewire, always in the news, always doing the unusual, and often coming into conflict with authority. Arguing with umpires was one of his specialities, but his fielding position

– way out in the outfield – meant that he had a long way to run before he could get into the fray. The umpires could see him coming, and would wave him off before he got anywhere near them. In a game in 1918 he solved this one by running all the way in – backwards. The umpire was waving wildly to shoo him away, but Stengel kept backing in and started arguing as soon as he was within earshot. The umpire had the answer – he threw Stengel out of the game. Ejected from another game, Stengel took off his shirt as he headed for the locker room. The next day he got a telegram from the president of the league telling him he was fined $50 for his 'shocking conduct in disrobing on the ballfield'. He came up to bat that day with the telegram pinned around his sleeve, which caused more trouble which Stengel escaped by enlisting in the Navy.

Earlier that same season Stengel had pulled his most celebrated caper. He was playing for Pittsburgh against the Brooklyn Dodgers, his former team, and the Dodger fans were giving him the bird. Stengel gave it right back. Somehow he got hold of a live sparrow during the game, and when he went up to bat he hid it under his cap ('I could feel it moving, you know, inside there on my scalp'). With the crowd booing for all they were worth, Stengel made a grand, low bow, and lifted his hat. Out flew the much relieved sparrow, and the booing changed to an astonished collective gasp.

There was a famous incident that Stengel swore he had nothing to do with, but as he was there when it happened and the whole thing had a very Stengelian style to it, no one really knows whether to believe him. It happened during Stengel's days with the Brooklyn Dodgers, when the manager was one Wilbert Robinson, Uncle Willie. This was 1915, the early days of manned flight, and the players were wondering what it would be like to try and catch a ball dropped from an airplane. So one of them went up in one of those early machines and flew it over the training field, and out dropped the ball. Everyone ran to get underneath it, but it drifted over to where Uncle Willie was standing. He waved everyone away and waited for the ball as it got bigger and bigger. And bigger and much bigger – much bigger than it should have been, until at the last moment, as Willie put up his glove to catch it, everyone could see that it was a grapefruit. *Splat!* Robinson spun round and round and collapsed with grapefruit all over his face and front.

Stengel's tongue was always quick and lively. When he was criticized by a manager for not sliding into third base, he shot back: 'With the salary I'm getting here I'm so hollow and starving that I'm liable to explode like a light bulb if I ever hit the ground too hard.' In fact Stengel talked in a way that was always a bit of puzzle to all who heard him. The words flowed endlessly and somehow, despite them, the sense emerged, but only just. They called it Stengelese, and it was characterized by non-sequiturs, tautology, pronouns without antecedents, mangled metaphors and a syntax hitherto unknown to the Western World.

In 1924 Stengel married, and he spent his honeymoon playing baseball, which was natural enough, only he did it in England, which was totally Stengelian. He was a member of the New York Giants team that toured Europe along with the Chicago White Sox. They performed at Stamford Bridge, where the crowd included King George V, and Casey loved to boast in later years that he 'hit a triple in Wimbledon Stadium in the presence of the King'. Well, Stengelese never paid much attention to getting names right.

Casey's new wife, Edna, did not think too much of English food, and was not greatly impressed by royalty either: 'I wound up having tea with Queen Mary, but if there'd been any better place to go that day, I'd probably have gone there instead.'

Stengel moved on to managing, though his early efforts were not always regarded as an unmixed blessing. When he was running the Boston Braves in 1943 he got himself knocked down by a taxi, and a local sportswriter nominated the cab driver for Boston's Man of the Year award. Stengel's antics during his playing career and his early managing days (when, if he disagreed with an umpire's decision, 'I'd fall over like I'd fainted dead away from the shock') led people to write him off as a clown. Some clown. Stengel was appointed manager of the New York Yankees in 1949 and for the next twelve years he presided over the most successful club in the history of baseball. Ten times they won the American League, and seven times they won the World Series. The Yankees of the Stengel era were the lords of baseball, the other clubs just so many serfs to be dealt with as the occasion arose. Of course, when you are that good, you tend not to be too popular, and the Yankees were not much liked. Their image was one of impersonal, almost mechanical efficiency, hardly the sort of thing a fan could *feel* deeply about. Said one sportswriter: to be a fan of the Yankees is like rooting for General Motors. Tallulah Bankhead was a New York Giants fan who did not like the Yankees (just one of many) because 'they're bleak perfectionists, insolent in their confidence, the snobs of the diamond. The Yankees are all technique, no colour or juice'.

That was not quite true because there was always Casey, and no one was more colourful than Casey. With his system of platooning, in which he changed his team line-up and switched player-positions about for almost every game, he gained the reputation of master manipulator. He did confess, though, after yet another of those Yankee triumphs, that 'I couldn't have done it without the players'. This was good news for all the other managers, who were beginning to suspect witchcraft.

The Yankees fired Stengel in 1960. Too old, they said, which was ridiculous, he was barely seventy. Casey retired to live with Edna in California. The Dodgers were gone, the Giants too,* and now old Casey had joined them out West. In 1960 New York was almost unrecognizable to baseball fans. But a bigger change than any of these was on the way.

From the moment the Giants and Dodgers had departed in 1958, there had been a small group of men determined to bring National League baseball back to New York City. By 1960 they had come to the very verge of success. The National League was going to expand by adding two new teams for the 1962 season, one of them in Houston, the other in New York. All that was needed now was . . . well, just about everything. Somewhere to play, a name, an administrative staff, fans, and players. Houston and New York were called 'expansion teams', they were to be conjured up out of nothing. The idea was that all the other clubs in the National League would be required to put a certain number of their players into a pool from which Houston and New York would take their pick. But not for nothing. For each player selected they had to pay $125,000. This was on top of the $1·8 million they had already paid into the League for the privilege of operating the franchises.

Once the question of a name for the New York club had been settled – they were to be known as the New York Mets – the owners set to work finding a manager. Phone calls and visits to the West Coast finally convinced a doubtful Casey Stengel that he should come back to baseball and New York. In accepting, he announced that he was very happy to be running the New York Knickerbockers (which happens to be the name of New York's basketball team).

The players that Houston and New York were being offered were, to put it mildly, tarnished. Said Stengel: 'I want to thank all those generous owners for giving us those great players they didn't want.'

Where to play? The city was going to build a brand new stadium out in Queens (which was going to cost the taxpayers over $19 million) but they had only just started on that and were still arguing about such things as

* See Chapter 2, page 29.

how many toilets to put in. The only thing to do was to take a large feather duster and some paint and spruce up the old Polo Grounds, where the New York Giants used to play, and which had one thing in their favour – they were *there*.

Early in 1962 the players who were to make up the Mets assembled for spring training in St Petersburg, Florida. The seventy-one-year-old Stengel was there to greet them. He had decided to go after the Youth of America, and tried to get young players interested in joining the Mets: 'They'll be better off with the Mets than they will be with any club they was previously with before they're gonna join us.' To the cynical newsmen who had come along for the laughs, he said the Mets would be 'amazin''. In addition to the twenty-two players that the Mets had paid for as the nucleus of their team, there were all sorts of other hopefuls, young and old, hanging around the training camp. There was Butterball Botz, pitcher who couldn't pitch, Bruce Fitzpatrick, hitter who couldn't hit, and Dawes Hamilt, who couldn't do much of anything. Admittedly, these were the ones who did not make it. The trouble was that the ones who did were not always noticeably better.

The Mets played a batch of friendly games down in Florida. The very first, against the St Louis Cardinals, they lost 8–0. But the pre-season games did not turn out too badly, as the Mets won thirteen and lost fifteen, and the record included a win over the New York Yankees, particularly pleasing to Stengel as a rebuttal to those who had said he was too old.

Then it was time to head north for the beginning of the season proper. The Mets were to play their first game in St Louis. The day before the great event, sixteen newly-minted Mets jammed themselves into the hotel elevator, which promptly got stuck between floors. Among the players was Roger Craig, who had been chosen as the Mets' first starting pitcher, a history-making role if ever there was one. Craig, who already sensed that there was something special about the Mets, became fatalistic, convinced that the elevator would be stuck for twenty-four hours, and he would miss his date with destiny. It took only twenty minutes to get them out, and Craig needn't have worried because the weather took a hand and the opening day game was rained out. The Amazin' Mets took the field a day late, and went down to an inglorious 11–4 defeat. It was felt that after that things could not get worse. The feeling was quite wrong.

The Mets lost their first nine games in a row. Not too disastrous in a season of 162 games, maybe, but coming right at the start, it set Stengel pondering that the Mets might lose all 162, which he thought would probably be a new record. It never got that bad, not quite that bad. The Mets did set a new record for losses that season, but it was only 120. They were, officially, the worst team in the history of baseball. Yet they were also one of the most popular. Not just with opposing fans, that was to be expected, but in their home town of New York, where they regularly put on display their stunning lack of talent. The fans came in increasing numbers, noisy, irreverent, good-humoured (they had to be that), knowledgeable. A journalist called them 'the new breed' and the name stuck;* no doubt many of them were old Giant and Dodger fans, but there were also many too young to remember those days. They knew the Mets were losers, but they loved them anyway, they cheered their futility almost louder than their few moments of glory.

The Mets, however strange all this must have seemed to them, reacted perfectly. They not only lost games, they lost them with great style, by doing things that nobody had ever thought to see on a professional baseball field, they lost them by monumental scores and by close scores, they lost them tragically and they lost them hopelessly. Above all, they lost them.

Opposing batters would hit lazy fly balls to the Mets outfield, easy catches for any half-competent player. Two or three Mets would converge underneath the ball, then all stand back for someone else to catch it, and the ball would plop to earth between them. On one such play, things very nearly did go right. As centre-fielder Richie Ashburn ran in for the ball he saw an infielder running out for it. Ashburn did the right thing. He shouted. He not only shouted, but – because he knew the infielder was from Venezuela and did not speak English too well – he shouted in Spanish. *Yo le tengo!* he screamed as he raced in, *Yo le tengo!* It was all beautifully done, except that Ashburn had not seen the left fielder Frank Thomas also racing for the ball. Thomas, alas, had no idea what *Yo le tengo!* meant, so he just kept running, eyes on the ball, until he crashed into Ashburn and knocked him out cold. The ball fell to the ground, untouched by human hand.

When the Mets were batting, and actually succeeded in getting men on base, they even managed to commit the most juvenile of baseball errors, the runners getting so confused that two of them ended up on the same base. This was embarrassing, to say the least, but not to the fans,

---

* The term had been used by Bernard Malamud in his 1952 novel *The Natural*, a story ostensibly about baseball, but mainly about America.

who loved and cheered every silly minute of it. And things of that sort just kept on happening. Stengel told his pitchers not to be afraid of allowing opposing batters to hit the ball hard out to centre-field in the Polo Grounds; there was an awful lot of room out there, and the chances were that even one of the Met outfielders would be able to make the catch. Soon after that one of the Chicago Cubs players *did* slam the ball out to centre field, just as Stengel had said. The Met centre-fielder ran back to catch it, but had to watch it sail way over his head into the seats for a colossal home run. It was the first time in the fifty-year history of the Polo Grounds that a ball had been hit that far. 'I was shocked,' said Casey.

Following the Mets was fun, and it was eventful. The new breed who turned out to watch – and apparently enjoyed watching – a team lose were thought to be those who were life's losers, those who saw and recognized some familiar spark in the Mets' increasingly futile efforts to cope with a situation that was always on the verge of getting out of hand. 'Caught in the treadmill of their own maladies and eccentricities, their futile endeavours to escape serve only to actuate its mechanism, to keep in motion the clockwork of their strange, ineluctable, fatal daily round.' Proust had written those words fifty years before the Mets dropped their first catch, and it does not seem too likely that many Met fans were aware of them, but they said it all.

For the fans to identify with a team was not quite enough, however. An individual was needed to put the whole thing on a more personal, a more intimate level. And, as we all know, great moments call forth great men. To the centre of the stage stepped twenty-nine-year-old Marvin Throneberry, sport's first truly modern figure, the anti-star.

Marvellous Marv was a compact, balding, husky man with a Mona Lisa sort of a grin; his style of play was pretty inscrutable, too, a compound of animal enthusiasm and occasional competence. With a bat he was unpredictable: he might strike out, or he might hit the ball hard, it was a tossup. His fielding play was totally predictable – it was disastrous. The fans soon recognized that Marvellous Marv was the one they'd been waiting for, so they naturally started to boo him for his errors, which they secretly loved.

There was a celebrated occasion when Marv hit a triple, and head down, roared around the bases to end up, all smiles, standing on third base. The crowd's astonished roar turned to the usual boos when the umpire called Marv OUT! because, quite humanly after all, in his hurry to get to third base, he had forgotten to step on first base on his way round. Marv trotted off the field, bemused at the sheer wonder of it all, while manager Casey Stengel galloped on to the field to protest to the umpire that Marv had indeed touched first. The umpire told him not to waste his breath – Marv had not touched second base either.

But the incident that most highlights Marv's folklore role as the human loser was the one of the sailboat. One of the publicity gimmicks arranged by the Mets involved a huge painted sign, installed in left field in the Polo Grounds by a firm that manufactured clothes. The idea was that, at the end of the season, the Met hitter who had hit the sign most frequently would be awarded a brand new sailboat, worth some $6,000. It was Marvellous Marv who did the trick. The same clothing company also awarded another, identical, sailboat to Frank Thomas, the Met who had been voted the most valuable player on the team in a poll of sports-writers. The difference was that Marv's boat had been earned in a competition of skill, so he had to pay taxes on it. Thomas's had been a gift, therefore no taxes. As Marv said: 'Things just sort of keep on happening to me.'

One of the things was the fans. Now they chanted 'Cranberry, strawberry, we love Throneberry!' and they wore T-shirts with VRAM! stencilled on them. They still booed, but it was all good-hearted, and mostly they cheered as Marvellous Marv responded by fluffing plays regularly, usually at highly dramatic moments, and occasionally doing something right that had everyone weeping with hysteria. When another Met misfielded and was jeered by the crowd, Marv growled 'Whaddya tryin' to do – steal my fans?'

And while Stengel's Mets were looking up at the baseball world from the bottom of the National League, the Yankees as usual were looking down from the top of the American League. The thought that fans might prefer Marvellous Marv to the Yankees' gallery of superstars was too absurd to contemplate, yet the fact remained that the Yankee paid attendance in 1962 had slipped by 250,000. It was just a straw in the wind, and it sailed by without anyone paying too much notice. Rightly so, too; obviously you could not take seriously a last-place team playing in a ramshackle old stadium, a team that let all sorts of riff-raff in to watch, and allowed them to parade all around the stadium with bed-sheet banners that said silly things like 'We Love Marvellous Marv', and 'Let's Go Stengel Lancers' and 'Our Mom Loves the Mets' and 'Bring Back Butterball Botz' and one that said, starkly, 'Help'.

Throughout the Mets' wall-to-wall ineptitude Casey Stengel had done what he could, trying desperately to make a silk purse out of a sow's ear, but ending up with something that looked depressingly like a battered sow's ear. The descent from the smooth efficiency of the Yankees to the total incompetence of the Mets worried Stengel not a bit, and it provided the perfect subject matter for Stengelese. In his first speech to his new players he told them 'Spend carefully, take your shoes off when you come into the clubhouse,' and added, almost as an afterthought, 'and play good.' They played lousy, and Stengel got dizzy sitting in the dugout watching opposing players whizz round the bases, scoring runs in unpredecented amounts. At one point, with the Mets deep into one of their by now traditional losing streaks, he thought a return to fundamentals might help. He held up a ball. 'This here is a baseball,' he announced. 'Wait a minute,' said catcher Choo Choo Coleman, 'you're going too fast.'* Stengel's optimism did wear a bit thin now and then, on one occasion he is said to have uttered the immortal *cri de coeur*: 'Can't anybody here play this game?' But he kept trying. All his old tricks and wiles – and none of them worked. After one of his ploys had backfired, he justified his move with 'Well, they tell me it can't be done, but sometimes it doesn't always work.'

In their second season, in 1963, the Mets were marginally better. They opened with an exhibition game against a Mexican team in Mexico City. They lost it. When Stengel was asked if the altitude had affected his players, he replied (according to which newspaper you happened to read) either 'No, my players can lose at any altitude' or 'The altitude always bothers my players, even in the Polo Grounds, which is below sea level.' During the season they managed to win one of their games by the colossal score of 19–1. When told that the Mets had scored nineteen runs that day a fan exclaimed 'Great! Did they win?' They lost only 111 games this time, but they still finished a most convincing last. The fans continued to pour in, just over 1 million of them, which was only some 200,000 less than the Yankees (who, ho hum, again won the American League) had drawn. This was the Mets last year in the old Polo Grounds; in 1964 they at last were able to open the season at the shining new Shea Stadium in Queens. And this was the year that the Yankees sensed that something was up. For years they had lorded it as the perpetual winners, but now these upstart Mets were the talk of the town, they were getting all the publicity and far too many of the fans. The Yankees made a move to steal some of the limelight that Stengel and his antics were

* It was Choo Choo Coleman who provided the all-time classic empty answer during a TV interview. 'How did you get the nickname Choo Choo?' asked the interviewer. 'I don't know,' said Choo Choo.

monopolizing. They appointed a new manager – Yogi Berra, a former star player, and one who had a reputation for saying droll things. Things like how an older player had 'learned me his experience', and the one about the restaurant that nobody went to any more because it was always too crowded. Ha ha, that would show the Mets.

What happened in 1964 was this. The Mets finished last in the National League. The Yankees finished first in the American League. The first-place Yankees drew 1,300,000. The last-place Mets drew 1,700,000. And in August, the Yankee owners sold their baseball club to C.B.S., best known for their television network, but in the process of diversifying their holdings. The first thing the Yankees did for C.B.S. was to lose the World Series. It was also the last thing. For the impossible had happened. Suddenly the Emperor Yankees were seen to be wearing no clothes at all. They had lost all their stars, and no one was available to replace them. For the first time in forty years, the Yankees were just another team. In 1965 they finished tenth in the American League, which meant that New York now had two last-place teams. 1965 was also the year when the incredible Stengel did finally retire. It took a broken hip to make him do it, but he went. Back to California and Edna. He was seventy-five-years old and it was pretty obvious that his chances of living to see the Mets actually win anything were remote indeed.* The Mets did take a step in the right direction in 1966 when they rose all the way to ninth place, but the effort was evidently too much for them, and they dropped back to tenth in 1967. In 1968 they got back up to ninth again. In seven years of existence the Mets had finished last five times, and next to last twice.

If you went around asking people what was the epoch-making event of 1969, the one that broadened man's vision, heightened his dignity, and so on, most would probably answer, 'Getting to the moon'. Around New York they thought that was pretty good, too, but the answer to the question would simply be 'The Mets'. If you did not know what they meant, they would not want to talk to you anymore. 1969 was the year of the Mets, the year they *won*, not only the National League champion-ship, but the World Series too. It was ridiculous, it was impossible, it

---

* There were those who thought that a broken hip at seventy-five would finish Casey. They were wrong, so wrong. In 1968 word filtered through that Stengel was in hospital after a car accident. The police were not sure if he'd been drinking, or if he always spoke like that. As it happened, he had been drinking, and they fined him $300. Then at the beginning of 1969 he had an operation for an ulcer, and he got over that too.

was fantastic, a fairy-tale in the flesh. To judge just how impossible it was you can look at the odds they gave the Mets at the start of the season – 100-1 shots to win the World Series. All through the season the Mets hovered near the top of the table without actually occupying top place, while nobody took them seriously and waited for them to collapse. But when the season ended the Mets were on top, and Stengel acknowledged from California that 'several of them look fairly alert'.

For the first time since 1964 the World Series was coming back to New York, and it was the Mets, not the Yankees, who had done it. (The Yankees, in fact, were well-nigh forgotten, a nothing team that on one occasion during the season had seen just 413 people turn up for a game in their 60,000-seat stadium.) There was no stopping the Mets now. It was, said everyone, a matter of destiny. This was the year when the gods rewarded them for all those years when everything had gone wrong. Poor Baltimore Orioles, they never had a chance. The Mets let them win the first game, then took the next four, and it was all over. At 3.17 P.M., 16 October 1969, the Mets were World Champions. It had been quite an afternoon in New York. Schoolteachers had simply given up trying to teach against the insistent buzz of transistors, bars were jammed with non-drinking TV watchers, offices were hives of inactivity. When the Moment arrived a deluge of tickertape and heaven knows what else started to pour out of the skyscraper windows in midtown Manhattan. It was one of New York's most convincing celebrations, for this was spontaneous, this was no ceremonial welcoming with a carefully planned parade. There was not anyone important down there under all that paper, just other New Yorkers. For once, people were really dancing in the streets. Traffic jams built up, but for once no one got too annoyed. On Madison Avenue a bus driver was so far carried away that he refused to charge his passengers – 'Everyone free!' he shouted, and that's not the sort of thing that happens every day in New York.

The next day the Mets' win was the main front page story in the *New York Times* while inside their editorial writers came up with this:

In man's climb from the primordial bogs, history records a handful of inspiring achievements. The invention of the wheel. Grapes pressed into wine. Homer's *Odyssey* and Plato's *Dialogues*. The light in a painting by Rembrandt, the *David* of Michelangelo. The glass slipper fitting Cinderella. Aspirin and penicillin. The frankfurter with mustard and sauerkraut. Men walking on the moon. The New York Mets winning the World Series.

It is never all that easy to tell with the *New York Times* editorials, but it was assumed by most that this was written tongue-in-cheek.

The Mets had touched the heights while the Yankees were plumbing the depths. That is the way it is with baseball clubs, they come and they go. But old Casey Stengel just seemed to go on forever. In 1973 both the Mets and the Yankees held 'Old Timer' days, when they trotted out all their famous players of yesteryear, and played an embarrassing game for a minute or two while all the fans wondered how on earth those guys could ever have been stars. In fact the indisputable star at both events was Casey Stengel, eighty-three years old, trotting out and clowning all the while to acknowledge the cheers of the fans. New York mayor, John Lindsay, proclaimed a 'Casey Stengel Day' and presented Casey with an award honouring his many years as manager of the Yankees and the Mets, and 'his contributions to the evolution of the English language'. Casey gave a little speech, in which he admitted that 'most people my age are now dead at the present time'. But Casey was still the most alive person in the gathering, still doing what he had been doing for years, and what his illustrious namesake had so conspicuously failed to do: bringing joy to Mudville.

Appendices

This book has, I hope, been written in such a way that it can be understood without any detailed knowledge of the way in which the three most frequently mentioned sports – baseball, basketball and football – are actually played. There will, nonetheless, be those who will want to know something of the intricacies of these sports, and for them I append some details, necessarily simplified, of what goes on down on the field and the court. Before getting into the individual sports there are several themes common to all three that should be mentioned:

Number of players
The professional leagues place a limit on the number of active players (i.e., players who attend a game in uniform, ready to play) that a team can have. This limited list of active players is called the roster.

Substitution
American sports are very big on substitution. Basketball and football allow 'free' substitution, which means that any player on the roster can be taken out of and put back into the game any number of times. Baseball is more restricted in that once a player has been removed from the game he cannot be re-inserted. Substitution means that the coach (or manager as he is called in baseball) becomes an important figure during the actual playing of the game, continually making tactical decisions of who to send in and who to take out.

Time-outs
All three sports allow for the players or the coaches to stop play by calling time-out. Generally speaking time-outs can be called only when the ball is not in play, or if it is in play only by the team that has possession. In football and basketball the number of time-outs is limited; in football, for instance, each team is permitted 3 time-outs in each half. Time-outs are usually called either to stop the clock and thus conserve time, or to allow the coach to have a discussion with his players.

Tied scores

As mentioned on page 51, Americans do not like games that end without a winner. In basketball, if the scores are level at the end of regulation time, an overtime period of five minutes is played; if the scores are still level after that another five minutes are played, and so on until a result is obtained. In baseball, if the score is tied after nine innings, extra innings are played until the winning run is scored. Tied games are theoretically possible in football, but not very common; during the 1972 season, out of 182 games, only five were tied.

Scorelines

The convention in American newspapers is to print the scoreline with the name of the winning team first – unlike the world-wide soccer convention that always prints the home team first.

League tables

Instead of awarding points for each game won, all three sports use a curious and unnecessarily complicated system of percentages to decide league positions. A three-digit figure is worked out giving the percentage of games won, so that a league table looks like this:

	W	L	T	Pct
Pittsburgh	11	3	0	.786
Cleveland	10	4	0	.714
Cincinnati	8	6	0	.571
Houston	1	13	0	.071

Promotion and relegation

There are no such things in American sports. A major-league club is always a major-league club – it does not run the risk of being demoted to the minor leagues if it finishes last in the league table.

Timing of games

In football and basketball there is an official timekeeper and, prominently displayed where players and fans alike can see it, at least one large digital clock ticking off minutes and seconds. This is controlled by the timekeeper and gives the official time of the game.

College sports

College baseball, basketball and football are similar, but not identical, to the professional versions of these sports described below.

BASEBALL
Organization
League structure
Nominally, baseball has two leagues – the American League (AL) and the National League (NL). In practice the two work closely together and are, for all practical purposes, one league. Each league is divided into two divisions:

National League

Eastern Division

Chicago Cubs
Montreal Expos
New York Mets
Philadelphia Phillies
Pittsburgh Pirates
St Louis Cardinals

Western Division

Atlanta Braves
Cincinnati Reds
Houston Astros
Los Angeles Dodgers
San Diego Padres
San Francisco Giants

American League

Eastern Division

Baltimore Orioles
Boston Red Sox
Cleveland Indians
Detroit Tigers
Milwaukee Brewers
New York Yankees

Western Division

California Angels
Chicago White Sox
Kansas City Royals
Minnesota Twins
Oakland Athletics
Texas Rangers

Season
Baseball activity begins in March with the spring-training period. The clubs assemble in the warm climate of the south – most of them in Florida. Here they get ready for the coming season by playing a series of exhibition games. At the beginning of April the clubs head north to their home cities and the season proper begins. It goes on until the end of September, with each team playing 162 games – around six games a week, half of them night games under the floodlights. During the season a team plays only the teams (from both divisions) of its own league. A typical week's schedule for a baseball club would be: night games on Tuesday, Wednesday and Friday, an afternoon game Saturday, and a double-header (two games, one immediately following the other, against the same opponent) on Sunday afternoon-evening.

Play-offs
When the regular season is over, each league has two divisional winners.

The A.L. East winner then plays the A.L. West winner, while the N.L. East and West winners play each other, both in best-of-5-games series.

Championship

The winners of these two series – the champions of the American and National Leagues – then meet, starting in the second week of October, in the best-of-7-games World Series to decide the 'World Championship' of baseball.

World Series Winners Since 1965

1965 Los Angeles Dodgers (NL)
1966 Baltimore Orioles (AL)
1967 St Louis Cardinals (NL)
1968 Detroit Tigers (AL)
1969 New York Mets (NL)
1970 Baltimore Orioles (AL)
1971 Pittsburgh Pirates (NL)
1972 Oakland Athletics (AL)
1973 Oakland Athletics (AL)

The Game

Roster size: twenty-five players

Team size: nine players

Substitution

Any and all of the twenty-five players can be used during a game, though once a player has been removed from the game he cannot be put back in.

Time of game

A regular 9-innings game averages two and a half hours.

Equipment

A baseball bat is a smooth, rounded stick, not more than 42 inches long and not more than $2\frac{3}{4}$ inches in diameter at its thickest, tapering to a thinner handle. It is usually made of white ash, though other materials, including aluminium, are being experimented with. The ball consists of a cork or rubber core around which are wound some 350 yards of yarn, encased in a stitched horsehide cover. It has a circumference of between 9 and $9\frac{1}{4}$ inches and weighs between 5 and $5\frac{1}{4}$ ounces. (The vital statistics of a cricket ball are: circumference $8\frac{3}{16}$ to 9 inches, weight $5\frac{1}{2}$ to $5\frac{3}{4}$ ounces.)

All the players wear spiked shoes and, up until a few years ago, all wore what appeared to be baggy flannel pyjamas, but more elegant

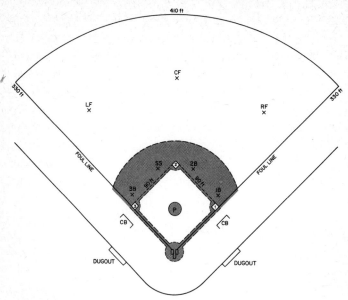

1. The baseball field

The playing surface is grass (either natural or artificial), except for the shaded area, which is composed of a loose, sandy earth. The term *diamond* originally referred to the infield area, but is now frequently used to mean the whole baseball field.

The approximate positions taken up by the fielding side are marked x:

Outfielders	Infielders		
LF – left fielder	1B – first baseman	P	– pitcher
CF – centre fielder	2B – second baseman	CB	– Coach's box
RF – right fielder	3B – third baseman	1 2	– 1st base, 2nd base,
	SS – short stop	3	3rd base

2. Enlargement of home plate area

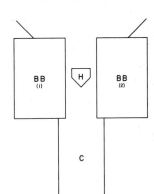

BB – batter's box:
 (1) for right handed,
 (2) for left-handed batter
H – home plate
C – position of the catcher

tighter-fitting uniforms are now the rule. All members of the fielding side wear leather gloves; the catcher, who is the equivalent of the wicket keeper, wears the largest glove, plus shin guards, a face mask, and a chest protector. The batters wear protective plastic helmets.

Officials

Four umpires, stationed at 1st, 2nd, and 3rd base, and behind the catcher at home plate. The home-plate umpire wears a chest protector and face mask.

The Field

The overall dimensions of baseball fields vary from stadium to stadium, and those given in the diagram are averages. But the infield distances are fixed: it is always 60 ft 6 ins from the pitcher's mound to home plate, always 90 ft between the bases. *Home plate* is a slab of white rubber fixed to and flush with the ground. The other bases, 1st, 2nd and 3rd, are white canvas bags, 15 ins square and between 3 and 5 inches high, filled with soft material and securely anchored to the ground. Built into the stands opposite the 1st and 3rd baselines are the *dugouts*, one for each team, where the manager and the players not actively involved in the game sit. The playing surface is grass (either natural or artificial) except for the area which is shaded in the diagram. This is composed of a loose sandy earth. The term *diamond* originally referred to the infield area, but is now frequently used to mean the whole baseball field.

How It's Played

Runs are what count in baseball, and the side that has scored more of them after 9 innings wins the game. One run is scored every time a player is able to make a complete circle of the bases, from home plate, via 1st, 2nd and 3rd bases, back to home plate. Each inning (the word takes an 's' only in the plural) has a top half, in which the visiting team bats, and a bottom half in which the home team bats. An inning closes when three of the batting side are out – it is not necessary to dismiss the whole side.

At the heart of baseball is the battle between the pitcher and the batter. The pitcher stands on the 10-inch-high *pitching mound* and throws the ball. He uses a genuine throwing action, not a stiff-armed action as in cricket, and the ball reaches the batter without bouncing. The batter stands in one of the batter's boxes (which one depends on whether he's a right- or left-handed hitter) and tries to hit the ball into fair territory (anywhere in the quadrant between the two foul lines) and where the fielders cannot get to it. When he does hit the ball fair, even if it goes straight to a fielder, he *must* start running towards 1st base. He does not take his bat with him, but drops it as soon as he starts running.

The pitcher has three ways of getting the batter out:

a) by making him hit the ball into the air so that it can be caught by a fielder.

b) by making him hit the ball on the ground so that it can be fielded by one of the infielders who can then throw it to the 1st baseman before the batter can run to first base.

c) by striking him out. This hinges around a magical little couplet called *the count* and requires some explanation. When the pitcher throws the ball he does not just throw it any old where. He is aiming it at an imaginary area called the *strike zone*. This is a rectangle the width of home plate (17 ins) and stretching from the batter's arm-pits down to the top of his knees. Any pitch thrown into this zone is a *strike*. Any pitch outside it is a *ball* – unless the batter swings at it, in which case, even though it may have been well out of the strike zone, it is deemed a strike. It is the job of the home-plate umpire, crouching immediately behind the catcher, to rule on whether a pitch is a ball or a strike. Strikes work in favour of the pitcher (three of them and the batter is out – *struck out*), while balls are in the batter's favour (four of them and he is allowed to go to first base – he is said to have been *walked* by the pitcher). The count is thus a record of the balance between balls and strikes. For example: the batter swings and misses at the first pitch: count is 0 and 1 (no balls, one strike). On the second pitch the batter *takes* – he does not swing, judging the pitch to be outside the strike zone, and the umpire agrees: 1 and 1. On the third pitch he takes again, but this time his judgement is wrong, the umpire calls a strike: 1 and 2. On the next pitch he swings and misses – that is the third strike and he is out, struck out by the pitcher.

The batter's task is to get on base. This he does by hitting a fair ball that is not caught by a fielder, and that cannot be fielded and thrown to 1st base before he runs there. (He can also get on base if he is walked by the pitcher, or if he is hit by the pitched ball.) A typical hit is one that gets the ball over the heads of the infielders but drops short of the out-fielders, enabling the batter to reach first base – this is a one-base hit called a *single*. If the ball is hit more powerfully and finds a gap between the outfielders, the batter, running at full speed, may have time to get to second base (a *double*) or even to third (a *triple*). If he hits a fair ball out of the playing area and into the stands, that is baseball's ultimate weapon

– the *home run*. Like a six in cricket, there is nothing the fielding side can do except wave the ball goodbye as the batter trots ceremonially around the bases. A home run automatically scores one run – at least. Because if there are any other players on base they also score, swept home ahead of the home run. Should there be runners on all three bases (the *bases loaded*) then a home run scores four runs with one swing of the bat.

Most runs, though, do not come from home runs, but from groups of lesser hits such as singles and doubles. A typical three-run inning might be constructed as follows:

Batter	Runners on base	Total outs	Total runs
Batter A singles	A on 1st	0	0
Batter B strikes out	A on 1st	1	0
Batter C singles (A goes to 3rd base on the hit)	A on 3rd C on 1st	1	0
Batter D doubles (A scores, C goes to 3rd)	C on 3rd D on 2nd	1	1
Batter E pops ball into the air and is caught out (C and D do not advance)	C on 3rd D on 2nd	2	1
Batter F singles (C and D both score on the hit)	F on 1st	2	3
Batter G strikes out	F on 1st	3	3

The third out closes the inning; the team has scored three runs on four hits (three singles and a double) and left one runner stranded on base. The inning by inning score of a baseball game looks like this:

	1st	2nd	3rd	4th	5th	6th	7th	8th	9th	
Chicago Cubs	0	1	0	1	0	0	2	1	0	5
New York Mets	0	0	2	0	4	0	0	0	–	6

When the Cubs failed to score in the top of the ninth inning, the Mets became the winners 6–5 and did not need to bat in the bottom half of the inning.

Baseball Glossary
Batting Average: a hitter's average is calculated by dividing his total number of hits by the number of times he has been at bat and expressing the figure as a percentage. Thus a hitter who gets a hit every third time at bat is hitting ·333 (three-thirty-three). This is a good average – anyone hitting over three hundred (·300) for the season is doing well. The top batting average for a season is usually around the ·350 mark. The last time a batter hit over four hundred (·400) for a full season was 1941.

Bullpen: a special area of the ballpark, often built into the outfield stands, where relief pitchers (see *Pitcher*) warm up during a game. Each team has its own bullpen which is in contact by telephone with the dugout.

Bunt: a soft type of hit in which the bat is pushed at the ball with only a short swing.

Diamond: a name originally given to the baseball infield (which is actually a square set on a corner) but now often used to mean the whole field.

Double-play: a fielding play in which two base-runners are put out by one pitch. The usual double-play occurs when, with a runner on first base, the batter hits a ground ball towards second base. At this point the runner on first base *must* run towards second, and the batter *must* run to first. If the fielding side can get the ball to second base and then on to first before either runner arrives, they are both out. Double-plays occur regularly in every game. It is possible, if there are two or three runners on base, for the fielding side to make a *triple-play* but this is extremely rare.

Foul ball: if the batter swings and makes contact with the ball, but hits it behind the foul lines, it is a foul ball. The batter cannot run on a foul ball. If the ball is in the air, and if a fielder can catch it, the batter is out. If the ball is on the ground, or if it drops into the stands, a foul ball counts as a strike against the batter, unless he already has a count of two strikes on him, in which case the count remains the same.

Full count: a count of three and two (three balls and two strikes) is called a full count because, theoretically, something must happen on the next pitch. If it is a ball the batter goes to first base; if it is a strike, he is struck out. The other possibilities are a hit by the batsman; or a foul ball, in which case the count remains the same.

Grapefruit league: a name used for the spring-training exhibition games played in Florida.

No-hitter: if a pitcher pitches a complete game and does not allow any opposing batter to get a hit, he has pitched a no-hitter. This does not mean that no one reached base, as he may have allowed opponents to reach 1st base by walking them. A pitcher who allows no hits and gives up no walks has pitched a *perfect game* – he will have faced the minimum number of opposing batters, twenty-seven (three in each of the nine innings).

Pinch hitter: this is a batter sent up to hit for another player, usually at a crucial stage in the game. Similarly, also at a crucial stage, if a slow runner gets on base, the manager may send out a faster *pinch runner* to replace him.

Pitcher: for each game the manager announces a *starting pitcher*. Usually a club will have four or five starting pitchers on its roster, using them in rotation so that each gets a three- or four-day rest between starts. If he is pitching strongly the starting pitcher will last the whole game. But if he weakens, if he starts to give up too many hits, he will be replaced by a *relief pitcher* from the bullpen (*q.v.*). The manager will have six or seven relief pitchers to choose from, and he may change pitchers five or six times in a game if things are not going well. Pitchers may be left- or right-handed, and may specialize in different types of pitch – fast balls, curve balls, sinker balls and so on.

Seventh-inning stretch: for apparently unknown reasons the pause between the top and the bottom of the seventh inning is traditionally a time when fans stand up and stretch their limbs.

Signals: the team that is batting stations a coach in each of the coach's boxes outside 1st and 3rd bases. One of their tasks is to relay signals from the manager in the dugout to the hitter and any base-runners. Each team has its own system of 'secret' signals; they consist of things like the coach touching his cap then his breast, clapping his hands twice and so on. Interpreted properly, these tell the hitter things like whether he should swing at the next pitch or whether he should take it. The fielding side also uses signals, particularly between the catcher and the pitcher. As pitchers continually mix up the types of pitches they throw, it is vital for the catcher to know what is coming. For the pitcher to do the signalling, in full view of the batter, would invite detection. It is therefore the catcher, crouched behind the hitter, who makes the signals for the type of pitch. If the pitcher does not agree he shakes his head until the catcher signals the pitch that he wants to throw.

Switch-hitter: a batter who can hit either left- or right-handed. It is considered easier to hit left-handed pitching when batting right-handed, and right-handed pitching when batting left-handed.

Tag: a means of putting out a base runner by touching him with the ball, or with the glove or hand holding the ball. Base runners slide feet first into base to make tagging more difficult for the fielder.

BASKETBALL

Organization

League Structure

Since 1967 basketball has operated with two competing leagues: the National Basketball Association (N.B.A.) and the newer American Basketball Association (A.B.A.). The teams from the two leagues meet each other only in pre-season exhibition games. Attempts to merge the leagues have been going on for several years (see pages 131–2) but the 1973–74 season was played with the two still operating independently.

The National Basketball Association

Western Conference

Pacific Division

Golden State Warriors
Los Angeles Lakers
Phoenix Suns
Portland Trail Blazers
Seattle Sonics

Midwest Division

Chicago Bulls
Detroit Pistons
Kansas City-Omaha Kings
Milwaukee Bucks

Eastern Conference

Central Division

Atlanta Hawks
Capital Bullets
Cleveland Cavaliers
Houston Rockets

Atlantic Division

Boston Celtics
Buffalo Braves
New York Knicks
Philadelphia 76ers

Season

Pre-season exhibition games begin in mid-September, with the regular season starting in the second week of October. It is an eighty-two-game season, with teams playing every other team in the league, though they meet those in their own division more frequently than those from the other divisions.

Play-offs

Play-offs begin in the first week of April. Within each Conference the divisional winners, plus the two teams with the next best records (it could be the 2nd place teams from each division, or it could be the 2nd and 3rd team from one division), play-off in best-of-7-games series to decide the Conference Champions.

Championship
The two Conference Champions meet in a best-of-7-games series starting the first week in May.

National Basketball Association Champions since 1965
1965 Boston Celtics
1966 Boston Celtics
1967 Philadelphia 76ers
1968 Boston Celtics
1969 Boston Celtics
1970 New York Knicks
1971 Milwaukee Bucks
1972 Los Angeles Lakers
1973 New York Knicks

The American Basketball Association

West Division	*East Division*
Denver Rockets	Carolina Cougars
Indiana Pacers	Kentucky Colonels
San Antonio Spurs	Memphis Tams
San Diego Conquistadors	New York Nets
Utah Stars	Virginia Squires

Season
Pre-season exhibition games begin in mid-September, with the eighty-four-game regular season starting in the second week of October. Teams play those in their own division eleven times, those from the other division eight times each.

Play-offs
Play-offs begin the first week of April. Within each division the top four clubs play-off in best-of-7-games series to decide the Divisional Champions.

Championship
The two Divisional Champions meet in a best-of-7-games series starting the first week in May.

American Basketball Association Champions since 1968
1968 Pittsburgh Pipers (no longer operating)
1969 Oakland Oaks (no longer operating)
1970 Indiana Pacers

1971 Utah Stars
1972 Indiana Pacers
1973 Indiana Pacers

The Game

Roster size: N.B.A. – twelve players, A.B.A. – eleven players.

Team size: five players

Substitution

Free substitution – any player can be sent into the game and taken out as many times as the coach wishes.

Time of game

Playing time is forty-eight minutes, divided into four twelve-minute quarters. Allowing for intervals and periods when the game clock is stopped, a basketball game takes about two hours to complete.

Equipment

The basketball (circumference 30 inches) is slightly larger than a soccer ball (28 inches). The N.B.A. uses the standard orange-coloured ball, but the A.B.A. plays with a gaily-coloured red, white and blue ball. The players wear shorts, sleeveless shirts, and gym shoes. Some choose to wear pads on their knees and elbows.

Officials

Two referees with equal jurisdiction.

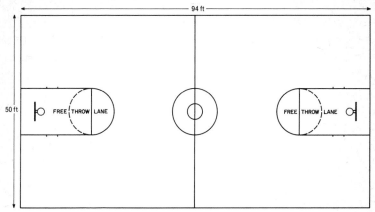

3. The basketball court.
The area marked 'Free Throw Lane' is also known as the Foul Lane, the Lane, and the Key.

The Court

The court is a rectangle 94 feet long by 50 feet wide, divided into two halves by a centre-line. At each end are the baskets, suspended 10 feet above the floor and attached to *backboards* 6 feet long by 4 feet high. The *baskets* consist of a hoop with an inside diameter of 18 inches, and with an 18-inch open-ended net dangling from it.

How It's Played

Scoring in basketball is accomplished by throwing the ball through the hoop. Each time this is done as a result of a shot during game action it is called a *field goal* and counts as 2 points. When it is done as the result of a *free throw* (see below) it counts 1 point. (In the A.B.A. a field goal scored from more than 25 feet out counts 3 points.) The ball is moved about the court either by dribbling, with the player continually bouncing it as he runs, or by passing it – throwing it from one player to another. Players are not permitted to run while holding the ball.

Pushing, holding, elbowing, obstructing are all fouls. When these are committed, play is stopped and the player fouled goes to the free-throw line where he takes an unopposed shot at the basket (if he was fouled while in the act of shooting, he gets two free throws.) The player who committed the foul is charged with a personal foul, and a record is kept of the number of fouls committed by each player during a game. When a player is charged with his sixth personal foul, he has *fouled out* and can take no further part in the game.

A team is not allowed to maintain indefinite possession of the ball without attempting to score. It must attempt a shot within twenty-four seconds of gaining possession (thirty seconds in the A.B.A.). At vantage points around the court, usually at ground level in each corner, there are digital clocks on which the seconds click off from twenty-four downwards. The twenty-four-second clock is reset each time a shot is taken, whether successful or not. If Team A scores a field goal, Team B takes over possession and puts the ball back into play with twenty-four seconds in which to score. If Team A's shot is unsuccessful – if it hits the hoop or the backboard and bounces out – the ball belongs to whichever team can control the rebound. If Team A fails to get off a shot within twenty-four seconds a buzzer sounds, play is stopped, and the ball is turned over to Team B.

To discourage bunching underneath the baskets, players are not allowed to remain in the area known as *the free throw lane* (also known as *the foul lane, the lane* and *the key*) for more than three seconds at a time. This means that both attackers and defenders must be continually moving in this area, weaving in and out of the key.

Basketball is a high-scoring game, and points totals of over 100 are common. The scores of the 1973 N.B.A. championship games, for instance, were 115–112, 99–95, 87–83, 103–98 and 102–93.

Basketball Glossary

Defence: defensive play is based on man-to-man marking. The zone defence, which gives the game a heavily defensive flavour, is banned in professional basketball.

Double dribble: a player who is dribbling is not allowed to stop running then start dribbling again. If he stops he must pass the ball to a team-mate. (See *Turnover.*)

Dunking: a method of scoring in which a player stretches his arms directly above the hoop and jams the ball forcefully downwards through it. Also known as *stuffing*.

Goaltending: if a shot is dropping towards the basket it must not be interfered with. A defensive player who knocks such a ball away is guilty of goaltending, and the offensive team is awarded a field goal (2 points).

Jump-ball: the method of starting each period of the game. The referee throws the ball into the air at the centre circle and one player from each team leaps for it, trying to tap it away to a team-mate. Also called the *tap-off*.

Palming: an offence in which the player momentarily holds the ball while dribbling. (See *Turnover.*)

Positions: the five players are the *centre*, two *forwards*, and two *guards*. The centre is usually the tallest player on the team, while the guards are the playmakers – but the functions of the players overlap to a considerable extent.

Technical foul: a non-body-contact foul, such as verbal abuse of the referee. It can be called on players and coaches, and results in a single free-throw for the non-offending team.

Travelling: a dribbling offence in which the player takes too many paces without bouncing the ball. The limit is two and a half paces. (See *Turnover.*)

Turnover: on certain non-body-contact offences, e.g., double dribble, palming, travelling, the game is stopped and the ball is turned over to the other team.

FOOTBALL

Organization
League Structure
There is one league, the National Football League (N.F.L.), divided into two Conferences, the American Football Conference (A.F.C.) and the National Football Conference (N.F.C.). Each Conference has three divisions:

American Football Conference	National Football Conference
Eastern Division	*Eastern Division*
Baltimore Colts	Dallas Cowboys
Buffalo Bills	New York Giants
Miami Dolphins	Philadelphia Eagles
New England Patriots	St Louis Cardinals
New York Jets	Washington Redskins
Central Division	*Central Division*
Cincinnati Bengals	Chicago Bears
Cleveland Browns	Detroit Lions
Houston Oilers	Green Bay Packers
Pittsburgh Steelers	Minnesota Vikings
Western Division	*Western Division*
Denver Broncos	Atlanta Falcons
Kansas City Chiefs	Los Angeles Rams
Oakland Raiders	New Orleans Saints
San Diego Chargers	San Francisco 49ers

Season
Football begins with pre-season exhibition games in August, leading into the fourteen-game season which starts in the third week of September. Each team plays the other teams in its division twice, plus games against certain teams from the other divisions of both Conferences. The bulk of

the games are played on Sunday afternoons but each week, for the benefit of television, there is one Monday night game. The season lasts fourteen weeks, finishing just before Christmas.

Play-offs
The six divisional winners go into the play-offs, joined by the two teams, one from each Conference, with the best 2nd-place records. Three games (two semi-finals, one final) within each Conference decide the Conference Champions.

Championship
The two Conference Champions meet in the final game, called the Super Bowl, in the second week in January.

Super Bowl Winners (first played 1966)
1966 Green Bay Packers
1967 Green Bay Packers
1968 New York Jets
1969 Kansas City Chiefs
1970 Baltimore Colts
1971 Dallas Cowboys
1972 Miami Dolphins
1973 Miami Dolphins

The Game

Roster size: forty players

Team size: eleven players

Substitution
Free substitution – any player can be sent into the game and taken out as many times as the coach wishes.

Time of game
Playing time is one hour, in four fifteen-minute quarters, with a fifteen-minute interval at half-time. However, since the clock is frequently stopped when the ball is not in play, football games take considerably longer than seventy-five minutes to complete: the average is close to three hours per game.

Equipment
The football is officially described as having 'the shape of a prolate spheroid', which makes it look like a slim rugby ball with pointed ends.

It is 11 to 11¼ inches long, and weighs 14 to 15 ounces. The size of the players, already formidable, is increased by the staggering amount of equipment they wear: helmet, with face mask, plus various forms of padding for the shoulders, ribs, hips, hands, forearms, upper arms, elbows, thighs, knees and shins.

Officials

There are six officials on the field, each with his own area of responsibilities: they are the referee, umpire, head linesman, line judge, back judge, and field judge. The referee is the senior official and the final authority on rule interpretations.

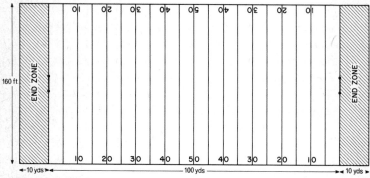

4. The football field

The field

All football fields are the same size: 100 yards long (plus a 10-yard *end-zone* at each end) and 160 feet wide. Lines are marked across the field at 5-yard intervals. The goalposts consist of a crossbar 18 ft 6 inches wide, 10 feet above the ground and supported by a single central post; at each end of the crossbar there is an upright post at least 20 feet high.

How It's Played

American football has little to do with the feet. It is a handling game, a direct but much modified descendant of rugby. It retains that sport's scoring method: the ball must be moved over the opponent's goal line. This is a *touchdown*, worth 6 points which can then be converted, by a place kick that sends the ball through the uprights, worth another 1 point. A *field goal* is a place kick through the uprights, worth 3 points. It can be taken at any time, from any distance – it does not have to be preceded by a touchdown.

The key to football is the concept of *possession*, introduced into the sport in 1882. This is essentially an application of the innings concept of cricket and baseball where first one team, then the other, gets an opportunity to score. In football the team in possession of the ball (the *offensive* team) is allowed four plays, or *downs*, in which to advance the ball 10 yards. If it does gain the required 10 (or more) yards in four (or fewer) downs it retains possession of the ball and starts another series of four downs. If it fails to gain 10 yards, it has to turn the ball over to its opponents, who then start their own series of downs.

The ball is advanced in one of two ways: *on the ground* when it is carried by a runner, or *in the air* when it is passed (in football, unlike rugby, the forward pass is legal). Players on the offensive team are permitted to *block* opponents to prevent them from getting to the ball-carrier. The blocker may use his body and his forearms, but never his hands. Defensive players are allowed to push blockers away.

The system of downs means that the play is broken up into a series of isolated plays, which, on average, last no more than five seconds each. After a down, the offensive team must start the next down within thirty seconds.

After each play the ball is placed on the ground at a spot that marks the limit of forward progress on that play. An imaginary line drawn across the field through this spot marks the *scrimmage line*, from which the next play starts. All plays, except kick-offs, begin from a scrimmage line, in which the two lines of players, about one yard apart, face each other in crouching positions. The offensive team must have at least seven players on the line, as follows:

left	left	left		right	right	right
end	tackle	guard	centre	guard	tackle	end

These are the *linemen*. The other four players behind them are the *backs*, including the *quarterback*. The middle five players of the offensive line are positioned about a foot apart, but the ends are often split wider. The formation of the backs depends on the team's style of play. Most modern formations are modifications of the basic T, in which the quarterback stands immediately behind the centre, with the other three backs in a line about four yards behind him.

The defensive team can adopt whatever formation it likes; it will usually have from four to six men on the line, two or three a short distance behind them (the *linebackers*), plus three or four deeper men to guard against long passes.

The game starts with a kick-off. Team B places the ball on its own 40-yard line and kicks it as far as possible into Team A's half of the field. If it carries over the end zone, Team A will recommence play, as the offensive team, from its own 20-yard line. If the ball falls short of the end zone, a player of Team A can catch it and attempt to run it back to Team B's goal-line. If he makes it all the way, he scores a touchdown. Far more often, he will be stopped while still in his own half, and his team then has four downs in which to gain 10 yards.

All teams have a large number of pre-arranged plays, within which every player has an assigned role. Before each play, the offensive team gathers into a circle – called the *huddle* – to decide which play to use. Usually it is the quarterback who calls the plays. The team then goes to the scrimmage line, with the centre crouched over the ball. At a shouted signal from the quarterback, the centre *snaps* the ball back through his legs directly into the quarterback's hands. As soon as the ball is snapped, the two opposing lines make contact as the defensive team tries to get to the ball-carrier and the offensive team tries to keep them away by blocking.

On a *running play* the quarterback hands the ball to one of his backs who will try either to run it around one end of his line, or to run into the line and through a gap which, hopefully, his linemen have opened by blocking defenders out of the way. On a *passing play*, the quarterback drops back with the ball, while his linemen form a defensive semi-circle around him to prevent him from being tackled before he gets off the pass.

An offensive play may gain yardage, or it may be stopped at the line of scrimmage for no gain, or – particularly if the defensive team gets to the quarterback before he can pass – it may lose yardage. A team that has not gained 10 yards after three downs will usually use the fourth down in one of two ways. If they are within about 40 yards of their opponent's goal line, they will attempt to kick a field goal. If they are further away than this, they will punt the ball downfield so that their opponents, who will take over possession on the next play, will have to start their drive from as far downfield as possible. The defensive team can gain early possession of the ball by intercepting a pass, or by recovering a fumble (i.e., a loose ball that the ball-carrier has dropped or had knocked out of his hands).

A team that infringes the rules is penalized by having the ball moved back closer to its own goal-line. *Minor fouls* – offside, deliberate delay of the game, for example – cost 5 yards; for *major offences* such as rough play the offending team loses 15 yards. For example: on a first down play (i.e., with 10 yards to gain) Team A gains only one yard and one of its players is detected holding an opponent's jersey. This is illegal use of the hands, and brings a 15-yard penalty. The official who spots the infraction allows play to continue, but signals the foul by dropping a coloured marker (it is like a large handkerchief). At the end of the play Team B has two options: (1) to accept the penalty in which case the down is replayed, but with Team A pushed back 15 yards nearer their goal-line; Team A still has four downs, but must now gain 25 yards. (2) to reject the penalty, allowing the previous play (which gained 1 yard) to stand, so that Team A now has 9 yards to gain, but only three downs left in which to gain them.

Because of free substitution and the large number of players – forty – that can be used in a game, football has become a sport for specialists. Each side does, in fact, consist of two basic teams: an offensive eleven that is on the field when the side has possession of the ball, and that is replaced *en masse* by eleven defensive players when the side loses possession. The most specialized player of all is probably the field-goal kicker, who enters the field only to make the kick, and leaves it immediately he has done so.

It is also one of the oddities of football that the majority of the players handle the ball only rarely. The defensive team get hold of it only by interception or recovering a fumble, while on the offensive team the job of the centre, guards and tackles is to block and wrestle opponents – the ball virtually never comes their way.

Football Glossary

Chain-gang: a crew of three men, stationed on the sideline, who carry between them a chain exactly 10 yards in length. They are called onto the field whenever the officials need a measurement to be certain that a team has advanced the ball 10 yards.

Clipping: bringing down an opponent, other than the ball-carrier, by throwing the body across the back of his legs. It is illegal and brings a 15-yard penalty.

Down: football action is broken up into individual plays called *downs*. A down starts with the snap of the ball through the centre's legs, and continues until the ball next becomes dead – e.g., because the ball-carrier has been tackled and his forward movement halted, or because a forward pass has been dropped, or because a touchdown has been scored. The average down lasts only about five seconds.

First-and-ten: the beginning of a series of downs – indicating first down and 10 yards to gain. A gain of 4 yards on the first down will bring up a second-and-six situation.

Forward pass: one forward pass is allowed during each down. It is usually thrown by the quarterback, using a regular one-handed throwing motion. In a well-thrown pass the ball travels pointed end forward, spinning in flight. Accurate passes of up to 60 yards can be thrown.

Gridiron: another name for the football field, because of the appearance that the transverse lines give it. (The term 'pitch' is not used by Americans.)

Necktie tackle: a high tackle around the neck. Its opposite is the *shoe-string* tackle.

Lateral: a rugby-type sideways pass.

Offside: a player who advances beyond the scrimmage line before the ball is snapped is offside. The penalty is 5 yards.

Playbook: each player has a book containing detailed instructions for his role within the team's set plays.

Red dog: a play by the defensive team which is an all-out attack on the opposing quarterback. The linebackers rush through their opponents' line in an attempt to tackle the quarterback. Also called a *blitz*.

Spotter: a coach or team member placed high up in the stadium where he has a bird's eye view of the game and can sometimes see developments not apparent from ground level. He is in telephone contact with his head coach on the sideline.

Index

admission prices to professional sports, 22

advertising endorsements by athletes, 30; by black athletes, 152

Alcindor, Lew (Kareem Abdul-Jabbar), 130

Alger, Horatio, 48ff.

association football, *see* soccer

Astrodome, Houston, 21

athletic scholarships, 171-2, 179

Austen, Jane: baseball mentioned in *Northanger Abbey*, 68

BASEBALL, 64-95, 261-8;
diagram of field, 263; glossary of terms, 266; professional leagues: organization and teams, 261; champions since 1965, list of, 262; rules and description of game, 262-6;
admission prices, 22; American League, 78; ball, changes in composition of, 91; black players, 91, 134ff., Black Sox gambling scandal, 84, 189ff.; Cartwright, Alexander, 70; Chadwick Henry, 14, 66; club owners, 23; Doubleday, Abner, 66; early history, 5; Federal League, 82; floodlit, 90; franchises, cost of, 40; gambling and, 72, 84, 189ff., 200-2; Landis, Judge, 84, 193-5, 198; minor leagues,

effects of television on, 33; National League, 73; origins of, 66ff., 117; pensions for ex-players, 28; professionalization of, 71; Robinson, Jackie, 144-7; rounders and, 66; Ruth, Babe, 85ff.; Stengel, Casey, 246ff.; teams moved to new cities, 28; television and, 33-4; Twain, Mark, 65; umpiring problems, 78; wages, 29; Whitman, Walt, 76; Wolfe, Thomas, 64; World Series, 80, 255

BASKETBALL, 125-33, 269-74;
diagram of court, 271; glossary of terms, 273; professional leagues: organization and teams, 269-70; champions since 1965, list of, 270; rules and description of game, 271-3;
admission prices, 22; Alcindor, Lew, 130; American Basketball Association, 130; black players, 128, 149, 154ff., 161; Chamberlain, Wilt, 130; college game, 127; gambling and, 174ff., 203-4; Harlem Globetrotters, 128n, 160; high-school game, 18; ideal city sport, 132; international sport, 133; Naismith, Dr James, 126;

imp of spt in a violent Soc

Am searched for its own identity
— & found it in Baseball